Oliver Optic

Vine And Olive Oil

Young America in Spain and Portugal - A Story of Travel and Adventure

Oliver Optic

Vine And Olive Oil

Young America in Spain and Portugal - A Story of Travel and Adventure

ISBN/EAN: 9783744758956

Printed in Europe, USA, Canada, Australia, Japan

Cover: Foto ©Andreas Hilbeck / pixelio.de

More available books at **www.hansebooks.com**

YOUNG AMERICA ABROAD — SECOND SERIES.

VINE AND OLIVE;

OR,

YOUNG AMERICA IN SPAIN AND PORTUGAL.

A STORY OF TRAVEL AND ADVENTURE.

BY

WILLIAM T. ADAMS
(*OLIVER OPTIC*),

AUTHOR OF "OUTWARD BOUND," "SHAMROCK AND THISTLE," "RED CROSS," "DIKES AND DITCHES," "PALACE AND COTTAGE," "DOWN THE RHINE," "UP THE BALTIC," "NORTHERN LANDS," "CROSS AND CRESCENT," "SUNNY SHORES," ETC.

BOSTON:
LEE AND SHEPARD, PUBLISHERS.
NEW YORK:
CHARLES T. DILLINGHAM.

TO MY FRIEND,

HENRY RUGGLES, Esq.,

"CONSULADO DE LOS ESTADOS UNIDOS, EN BARCELONA, EN TIEMPOS PASADOS,"

WHEN WE "ASSISTED" TOGETHER AT A BULL-FIGHT IN MADRID, VISITED EL ESCORIAL AND TOLEDO, AND WITH WHOM THE AUTHOR RELUCTANTLY PARTED AT CASTILLEJO,

THIS VOLUME

IS RESPECTFULLY DEDICATED.

PREFACE.

VINE AND OLIVE, the fifth volume of the second series of "YOUNG AMERICA ABROAD," contains the history of the Academy Squadron during the cruise along the shores of Spain and Portugal, and the travels of the students in the peninsula. As in the preceding volumes, the professor of geography and history discourses on these subjects to the pupils, conveying to them a great deal of useful information concerning the countries they visit. The surgeon of the ship is a sort of encyclopædia of travel; and, while he is on shore with a couple of the juvenile officers, he enlightens them by his talk on a great variety of topics; and the description of "sights" is given in these conversations, or in the "waits" between the speeches. In addition to the cities of the peninsula on the Atlantic and the Mediterranean, the young travellers cross the country from Barcelona to Lisbon, visiting on the way Sáragossa, Burgos, the Escurial, Madrid, Toledo, Aranjuez, Badajos, and Elvas. In another excursion by land, they start from Malaga, and take in Granada and the Alhambra, Cordova, Seville, and Cadiz. Besides the ports mentioned, the party vessels visit Valencia, Alicante, — from which they make an excursion to Elche to see its palms — Carthagena, and Gibraltar.

The author has visited every country included in the titles of the eleven volumes of the two series of which the present volume is the last published. He has been abroad twice for the sole purpose of obtaining the materials for these books; his object being to produce books that would instruct as well as amuse.

The story of the incendiaries and of the young Spanish officer of the Tritonia, interwoven with the incidents of travel, is in accordance with the plan adopted in the first, and followed out in every subsequent volume of the two series. Doubtless the book will have some readers who will skip the lectures of the professor and the travel-talk of the surgeon, and others who will turn unread the pages on which the story is related; but we fancy the former will be larger than the latter class. If both are suited, the author need not complain; though he especially advises his young friends to read the historical portions of the volume, because he thinks that the maritime history of Portugal, for instance, ought to interest them more than any story he can invent.

The titles of all the books of this series were published ten years ago. The boys and girls who read the first volume are men and women now; and the task the author undertook then will be finished in one more volume.

With the hope that he will live to complete the work begun so many years ago, the author once more returns his grateful acknowledgments to his friends, old and young, for the favor they have extended to this series.

TOWERHOUSE, BOSTON, Oct. 19, 1876.

CONTENTS.

		PAGE.
I.	Something about the Marines	11
II.	At the Quarantine Station	26
III.	A Grandee of Spain	41
IV.	The Professor's Talk about Spain	53
V.	A Sudden Disappearance	79
VI.	A Look at Barcelona	87
VII.	Fire and Water	102
VIII.	Saragossa and Burgos	116
IX.	The Hold of the Tritonia	133
X.	The Escurial and Philip II.	145
XI.	The Cruise in the Felucca	159
XII.	Sights in Madrid	173
XIII.	After the Battle in the Felucca	187
XIV.	Toledo, and Talks about Spain	202
XV.	Trouble in the Runaway Camp	221
XVI.	Bill Stout as a Tourist	233
XVII.	Through the Heart of Spain	245

CONTENTS.

		PAGE
XVIII.	AFRICA AND REPENTANCE	261
XIX.	WHAT PORTUGAL HAS DONE IN THE WORLD	274
XX.	LISBON AND ITS SURROUNDINGS	292
XXI.	A SAFE HARBOR	305
XXII.	THE FRUITS OF REPENTANCE	319
XXIII.	GRANADA AND THE ALHAMBRA	333
XXIV.	AN ADVENTURE ON THE ROAD	349
XXV.	CORDOVA, SEVILLE, AND CADIZ	358
XXVI.	THE CAPTURE OF THE BEGGARS	373
XXVII.	THE BULL-FIGHT AT SEVILLE	390

VINE AND OLIVE.

VINE AND OLIVE;

OR,

YOUNG AMERICA IN SPAIN AND PORTUGAL.

CHAPTER I.

SOMETHING ABOUT THE MARINES.

"LAND, ho!" shouted the lookout in the foretop of the Tritonia.

"Where away?" demanded the officer of the deck, as he glanced in the direction the land was expected to be found.

"Broad on the weather bow," returned the seaman in the foretop.

"Mr. Raimundo," said the officer of the deck, who was the third lieutenant, calling to the second master.

"Mr. Scott," replied the officer addressed, touching his cap to his superior.

"You will inform the captain, if you please, that the lookout reports land on the weather bow."

The second master touched his cap again, and hastened to the cabin to obey the order. The academy squadron, consisting of the steamer American Prince and the topsail schooners Josephine and Tritonia, were bound from Genoa to Barcelona. They had a short and very pleasant passage, and the students on board of all the vessels were in excellent spirits. Though they had been seeing sights through all the preceding year, they were keenly alive to the pleasure of visiting a country so different as Spain from any other they had seen. The weather was warm and pleasant for the season, and the young men were anxiously looking forward to the arrival at Barcelona. On the voyage and while waiting in Genoa, they had studied up all the books in the library that contained any thing about the interesting land they were next to visit.

The Tritonia sailed on the starboard, and the Josephine on the port quarter, of the American Prince. The two consorts had all sail set, and were making about eight knots an hour, which was only half speed for the steamer, to which she had been reduced in order to keep company with the sailing vessels. Though the breeze was tolerably fresh, the sea was smooth, and the vessels had very little motion. The skies were as blue and as clear as skies can ever be; and nothing could be more delicious than the climate.

In the saloon of the steamer and the steerage of the schooners, which were the schoolrooms of the academy squadron, one-half of the students of the fleet were engaged in their studies and recitations. A quarter watch was on duty in each vessel, and the same portion were off duty. But the latter were not idle: they were, for the most part, occupied in reading about the new land they were to visit; and the more ambitious were preparing for the next recitation. Their positions on board for the next month would depend upon their merit-roll; and it was a matter of no little consequence to them whether they were officers or seamen, whether they lived in the cabin or steerage. Some were struggling to retain the places they now held, and others were eager to win what they had not yet attained.

There were from two to half a dozen in each vessel who did only what they were obliged to do, either in scholarship or seamanship. At first, ship's duty had been novel and pleasant to them; and they had done well for a time, — had even struggled hard with their lessons for the sake of attaining creditable places as officers and seamen. They had been kindly and generously encouraged as long as they deserved it; but, when the novelty had worn away, they dropped back to what they had been before they became students of the academy squadron. Mr. Lowington labored hard over the cases of these fellows; and, next to getting the fleet safely into port, his desire was to reform them.

In the Tritonia were four of them, who had also challenged the attention and interest of Mr. Augustus Pelham, the vice-principal in charge of the vessel, who had formerly been a student in the academy ship, and who had been a wild boy in his time. The interest which Mr. Lowington manifested in these wayward fellows had inspired the vice-principal to follow his example. Possibly the pleasant weather had some influence on the laggards; for they seemed to be very restive and uneasy under restraint as the squadron approached the coast of Spain. All four of them were in the starboard watch, and in the second part thereof, where they had been put so that the vice-principal could know where to find them when he desired to watch them at unusual hours.

The third lieutenant was the officer of the deck, assisted by the second master. The former was planking the weather side of the quarter deck, and the latter was moving about in the waist. The captain came on deck, and looked at the distant coast through his glass; but it was an old story, and he remained on deck but a few minutes. Raimundo, the officer in the waist, was a Spaniard, and the shore on the starboard was that of "his own, his native land." But this fact did not seem to excite any enthusiasm in his mind: in fact, he really wished it had been somebody else's native land, and he did not wish to go there. He bestowed more attention upon the four idlers, who had coiled themselves away in the lee side of the waist, than upon the shadowy shore of the home of his ancestors. He was a sharp officer; and this was his reputation on board. He could snuff mischief afar off; and more than one conspiracy had been blighted by his vigilance. He seemed to be gazing at the clear blue sky, and to be enjoying its azure transparency; but he had an eye to the laggards all the time.

"I wonder what those marines are driving at," said he to himself, after he had studied the familiar phenomenon for a while, and, as it appeared, without any satisfactory result. "I never see those four fellows talking together as long as they have been at it, without an earthquake or some sort of a smash following pretty soon after. I suppose they are going to run away, for that is really the most fashionable sport on board of all the vessels of the fleet."

Perhaps the second master was right, and perhaps he was wrong. Certainly running away had been the greatest evil that had tried the patience of the principal; but there had been hardly a case of it since the squadron came into the waters of the Mediterranean, and he hoped the practice had gone out of fashion. It had been so unsuccessful, that most of the students regarded it as a played-out expedient.

Raimundo was one of those whom this nautical institution had saved to be a blessing, instead of a curse, to the community; but he was truly reformed, and, over and above his duty as an officer, he was sincerely desirous to save the "marines" from the error of their ways. He did not expect them to uncover their plans all at once, and he was willing to watch and wait.

Having viewed the marines from the officer's side of the question, we will enter into the counsels of those who were the subjects of this official scrutiny. After the first few months of life in the squadron, these four fellows had been discontented and dissatisfied. They had been transferred from one vessel to another, in the hope that they might find their appropriate sphere; but there seemed to be no sphere below — at least, as far as they had gone — where they could revolve and shine. They had been "sticks," wherever they were. One country seemed to be about the same as any other to them. They did not like to study; they did not like to "knot and splice;" they did not like to stand watch; they did not like to read even stories, fond as they were of yarns of the coarser sort; they did not like to do any thing but eat, sleep, and loaf about the deck, or, on shore, but to dissipate and indulge in rowdyism.

Two of them had been transferred to the Tritonia from the Prince at Genoa, and the other two had been in the schooner but two months.

"I'm as tired as death of this sort of thing," said Bill Stout, the oldest and biggest fellow of the four.

"I had enough of it in a month after I came on board," added Ben Pardee, who was lying flat on his back, and gazing listlessly up into the clear blue sky; "but what can a fellow do?"

"Nothing at all," replied Lon Gibbs. "It's the same thing from morning to night, from one week's end to the other."

"Can't we get up some sort of an excitement?" asked Bark Lingall, whose first name was Barclay.

"We have tried it on too many times," answered Ben Pardee, who was perhaps the most prudent of the four. "We never make out any thing. The fellows in the Tritonia are a lot of spoonies, and are afraid to say their souls are their own."

"They are good little boys, lambs of the chaplain's fold," sneered Lon Gibbs. "There is nothing like fun in them."

"We are almost at the end of the cruise, at any rate," said Bark Lingall, who seemed to derive great comfort from the fact. "This slavery is almost at an end."

"I don't know about that," added Bill Stout.

"Spain and Portugal are the last countries in Europe we are to visit; and we shall finish them up in three or four weeks more."

"And what then? we are not to go home and be discharged, as you seem to think," continued Bill Stout. "We are to go to the West Indies, taking in a lot of islands on the way — I forget what they are."

"I can stand it better when we are at sea," said Ben Pardee. "There is more life in it as we are tumbling along in a big sea. Besides, there will be something to see in those islands. These cities of Europe are about the same thing; and, when you have seen one, you have seen the whole of them."

"I don't know about that," suggested Lon Gibbs, who, from the chaplain's point of view, was the most hopeful of the four; for his education was better than the others, and he had some taste for the wonders of nature and art. "Spain ought to be worth seeing to fellows from the United States of America. I suppose you know that Columbus sailed from this country."

"Is that so?" laughed Bark Lingall. "I thought he was an Italian; at any rate, we saw the place where he was born, or else it was a fraud."

"I think you had better read up your history again, and you will find that Columbus was born in Italy, but sailed in the service of Spain," replied Lon Gibbs.

"That will do!" interposed Bill Stout, turning up his nose. "We don't want any of that sort of thing in our crowd. If you wish to show off your learning, Lon, you had better go and join the lambs."

"That's so. It's treason to talk that kind of bosh in our company. We have too much of it in the steerage to tolerate any of it when we are by ourselves," said Ben Pardee.

"I thought you were going to do something about it," added Bill Stout. "We are utterly disgusted, and we agreed that we could not stand it any longer. We shall go into the next place — I forget the name of it"—

"Barcelona," added Lon Gibbs, who was rather annoyed at the dense ignorance of his friend.

"Barcelona, then. I suppose it is some one-horse seaport, where we are expected to go into ecstasies over tumble-down old buildings, or pretend that we like to look at a lot of musty pictures. I have had enough of this sort of thing, as I said before. I should like to have a right down good time, such as we had in New York when we went round among the theatres and the beer-shops. That was fun for me. I'm no book-worm, and I don't pretend to be. I won't make believe that I enjoy looking at ruins and pictures when it is a bore to me. I will not be a hypocrite, whatever else I am."

Bill Stout evidently believed that he had some virtue left; and, as he delivered himself of his sentiments, he looked like a much abused and wronged young man.

"Here we are; and in six or eight hours we shall be in Barcelona," continued Ben Pardee.

"And it is no such one-horse place as you seem to think it is," added Lon Gibbs. "It is a large city; in fact, the second in size in Spain, and with about the same population as Boston. It is a great commercial place."

"You have learned the geography by heart," sneered Bill Stout, who had a hearty contempt for those who knew any thing contained in the books, or at least for those who made any display of their knowledge.

"I like, when I am going to any place, to know something about it," pleaded Lon, in excuse for his wisdom in regard to Barcelona.

"Are there any beer-shops there, Lon?" asked Bill.

"I don't know."

"Then your education has been neglected."

"Spain is not a beer-drinking country; and I should say you would find no beer-shops there," continued Lon. "Spain is a wine country; and I have no doubt you will find plenty of wine-shops in Barcelona, and in the other cities of the country."

"Wine-shops! that will do just as well, and perhaps a little better," chuckled Bill. "There is no fun where there are no wine or beer shops."

"What's the use of talking?" demanded Bark Lingall. "What are the wine or the beer shops to do with us? If we entered one of them, we should be deprived of our liberty, or be put into the brig for twenty-four hours; and that don't pay."

"But I want to break away from this thing altogether," added Bill Stout. "I have been a slave from the first moment I came into the squadron. I never was used to being tied up to every hour and minute in the day. A fellow can't move without being watched. What they call recreation is as solemn as a prayer-meeting."

"Well, what do you want to do, Bill?" asked Ben Pardee, as he glanced at the second master, who had halted in his walk in the waist, to overhear, if he could, any word that might be dropped by the party.

"That's more than I am able to say just at this minute," replied Bill, pausing till the officer of the watch had moved on. "I want to end this dog's life, and be my own master once more. I want to get out of this vessel, and out of the fleet."

"Would you like to get into the steamer?" asked Lon Gibbs.

"I should like that for a short time; but I don't think I should be satisfied in her for more than a week or two. It was just my luck, when I got out of the Young America, after she went to the bottom, to have the American Prince come to take her place, and leave me out in the cold. No, I don't want to stay in the steamer; but I should like to be in her a few days, just to see how things are done. All the fellows have to keep strained up in her, even more than in the Tritonia; and that is just the thing I don't like. In fact, it is just the thing I won't stand much longer."

"What are you going to do about it? How are you going to help yourself?" inquired Lon Gibbs. "Here we are, and here we must stay. It is all nonsense to think of such a thing as running away."

"I want some sort of an excitement, and I'm going to have it too, if I am sent home in some ship-of-war in irons."

"You are getting desperate, Bill," laughed Ben Pardee.

"That's just it, Ben; I am getting desperate. I cannot endure the life I am leading on board of this vessel. It is worse than slavery to me. If you can stand it, you are welcome to do so."

"We all hate it as bad as you do," added Bark Lingall, who had the reputation of being the boldest and pluckiest of the bad boys on board of the Tritonia.

"I don't think you do. If you did, you would be as ready as I am to break the chains that bind us."

"We are ready to do any thing that will end this dog's life," replied Bark. "We will stand by you, if you will only tell us what to do."

"I think you are ready for business, Bark; but I am not so sure of the others," he added, glancing into the faces of Lon Gibbs and Ben Pardee.

"I don't believe in running away," said the prudent Ben.

"Nor I," added Lon.

"I knew you were afraid of your own shadows," sneered Bill.

"We are not afraid of any thing; but so many fellows have tried to run away, and made fools of themselves, that I am not anxious to try it on. The principal always gets the best of it. There were the two fellows, De Forrest and Beckwith, who had been cabin officers, that tried it on. Lowington didn't seem to care what became of them. But in the end they came back on board, like a couple of sick monkeys, went into the brig like white lambs, and to this day they have to stay on board when the rest of the crew go ashore, in charge of the big boatswain of the ship."

"Well, what of it? I had as lief stay on board as march in solemn procession with the professors through the old churches of the place we are coming to — what did you say the name of it was?"

"Barcelona," answered Lon.

"But that's not the thing, Bill," protested Ben. "It is not so much the brig and the loss of all shore liberty as it is the being whipped out at your own game."

"That's the idea," added Lon. "When those fellows came on board, though they had been absent for weeks, the principal only laughed at them as he ordered them into the brig. There was not a fellow in the ship who did not feel that they had made fools of themselves. I would rather stay in the brig six months than feel as I know those fellows felt at that moment."

"I don't think of running away," continued Bill. "I have a bigger idea than that in my mind."

"What is it?" demanded the others, in the same breath.

"I won't tell you now, and not at all till I know that you can bear it. Desperate cases require desperate remedies; and I'm not sure that any of you are up to it yet."

No amount of teasing could induce Bill Stout to expose the dark secret that was concealed in his mind; and at noon the watch was relieved, so that they had no other opportunity to talk till the first dog-watch; but the secret came out in due time, and it was nothing less than to burn the Tritonia. Bill believed that her ship's company could not be accommodated on board of the other vessels, which were all full, and therefore the students would be sent home. At first Bark Lingall was horrified at the proposition; but having talked it over for hours with Bill Stout alone, for the conspirator would not yet trust the secret with Ben Pardee and Lon Gibbs, he came to like the plan, and fully assented to it. He would not consent to do any thing that would expose the life of any person on board. It was not till the following day that Bark came to the conclusion to join in the conspiracy. Towards night, as it was too late to go into port, the order had been signalled from the Prince to stand off and on; and this was done till the next morning.

The plan was discussed in all its details. It was believed that the vessels would be quarantined at Barcelona, and this would afford the best chance to carry out the wicked plot. One of their number was to conceal himself in the hold; and, when all hands had left the vessel, he was to light the fire, and escape the best way he could. If the fleet was not quarantined, the job was to be done when the ship's company landed to see the city.

At eight bells in the morning, the signal was set on the Prince to stand in for Barcelona. The conspirators found no opportunity to broach the wicked scheme to Ben and Lon. For the next three hours the starboard watch were engaged in their duties. As may be supposed, Bill Stout and Bark Lingall, with their heads full of conspiracy and incendiarism, were in no condition to recite their lessons, even if they had learned them, which they had not done. They were both wofully deficient, and Bill Stout did not pretend to know the first thing about the subject on which he was called upon to recite. The professor was very indignant, and reported them to the vice-principal. Mr. Pelham found them obstinate as well as deficient; and he ordered them to be committed to the brig, and their books to be committed with them. They were to stand their watches on deck, and spend all the rest of the time in the cage, till they were ready to recite the lessons in which they had failed. The "brig" was the ship's prison.

Mr. Marline, the adult boatswain, took charge of them, and locked them up. The position of the brig had been recently changed, and it was now under the ladder leading from the deck to the steerage. The partitions were hard wood slats, two inches thick and three inches apart. Two stools were the only furniture it contained, though a berth-sack was supplied for each occupant at night. Their food, which was always much plainer than that furnished for the cabin and steerage tables, was passed in to them through an aperture in one side, beneath which was a shelf that served for a table.

Bark looked at Bill, and Bill looked at Bark, when the door had been secured, and the boatswain had left them to their own reflections. Neither of them seemed to be appalled by the situation. They sat down upon the stools facing each other. Bark smiled upon Bill, and Bill smiled in return. This was not the first time they had been occupants of the brig.

"Here we are," said Bill Stout, in a low tone, after he had made a hasty survey of the prison. "I think this is better than the old brig, and I believe we can be happy here for a few days."

"What will become of our big plan now, Bill?" asked Bark.

"Hush!" added Bill in his hoarsest whisper, as he looked through the slats of the prison to see if any one was observing them.

"What's the matter now?" demanded Bark, rather startled by the impressive manner of his companion.

"Not a word," replied Bill, as he pointed and gesticulated in the direction of the flooring under the ladder.

"Well, what is it?" demanded Bark.

"Don't you see?" and again he pointed as before.

"I don't see any thing."

"Then you are blind! Don't you see that the new brig has been built over one of the scuttles that lead down into the hold?"

"I see it now. I didn't know what you meant when you pointed so like Hamlet's ghost."

"Don't say a word, or look at it," whispered Bill, as he placed his stool over the trap, and looked out into the steerage.

The vice-principal passed the brig at this moment, and nothing more was said.

CHAPTER II.

AT THE QUARANTINE STATION.

WHILE these events were transpiring below, the signal had come from the Prince to shorten sail on the schooners, for the squadron was within half a mile of the long mole extending to the southward of the tongue of land that forms the easterly side of the harbor of Barcelona. A signal for a pilot was exhibited on each vessel of the fleet, but no pilot boat seemed to be in sight. As the bar could not be far distant, it was not deemed prudent to advance any farther; and the steamer had stopped her engine.

"Signal on the steamer to heave to, Mr. Greenwood," said Rolk, the fourth master, as he touched his cap to the first lieutenant, who was the officer of the deck.

"I see it," replied Greenwood. "Haul down the jib, and back the fore-topsail!"

The necessary orders were given in detail, and in a few moments the three vessels of the fleet were lying almost motionless on the sea. Greenwood took a glass from the beckets at the companion-way, and proceeded to a make a survey of the situation ahead. But there was nothing to be seen except the mole, and the high fortified hill of Monjuich on the mainland, across the harbor.

"Where are your pilots, Raimundo?" asked Scott of the second master; and both of them were off duty at this time.

"You won't see any pilots yet awhile," replied the young Spaniard.

"Are they all asleep?"

"Do you think they will be weak enough to come on board before the health officers have given their permission for the vessels to enter the harbor?" added Raimundo. "If they did so they would be sent into quarantine themselves."

"They are prudent, as they ought to be," added Scott. "I suppose you begin to feel at home about this time; don't you, Don Raimundo?"

"Not half so much at home as I do when I am farther away from Spain," replied the second master, with a smile that seemed to be of a very doubtful character.

"Why, how is that?" asked Scott. "This is Spain, the home of your parents, and the land that gave you birth."

"That's true; but, for all that, I would rather go anywhere than into Spain. In fact, I don't think I shall go on shore at all," added Raimundo, and there was a very sad look on his handsome face.

"Why, what's the matter, my Don?"

"I thought very seriously of asking Mr. Lowington to grant me leave of absence till the squadron reaches Lisbon," replied the second master. "I should have done so if it had not been for losing my rank, and taking the lowest place in the Tritonia."

"I don't understand you," answered Scott, puzzled by the sudden change that had come over his friend;

for, being in the same quarter watch, they had become very intimate and very much attached to each other.

"Of course you do not understand it; but when I have the chance I will tell you all about it, for I may want you to help me before we get out of the waters of Spain. But I wish you to know, above all things, that I never did any thing wrong in Spain, whatever I may have done in New York."

"Of course not, for I think you said you left your native land when you were only ten years old."

"That's so. I was born in this very city of Barcelona; and I suppose I have an uncle there now; but I would not meet him for all the money in Spain," said Raimundo, looking very sad, and even terrified. "But we will not say any thing more about it now. When I have a chance, I will tell you the whole story. I am certain of one thing, and that is, I shall not go on shore in Barcelona if I can help it. There is a boat coming out from behind the mole."

"An eight-oar barge; and the men in her pull as though she were part of a funeral procession," said the first lieutenant, examining the boat with the glass. "She has a yellow flag in her stern."

"Then it is the health officers," added Raimundo.

All hands in the squadron watched the approaching boat; for by this time the quarantine question had excited no little interest, and it was now to be decided. The oarsmen pulled the man-of-war stroke; but the pause after they recovered their blades was so fearfully long that the rowers seemed to be lying on their oars about half of the time. Certainly the progress of the barge was very slow, and it was a long time before it reached the American Prince. Then it was careful not to come too near, lest any pestilence that might be lurking in the ship should be communicated to the funereal oarsmen or their officers. The boat took up its position abreast of the steamer's gangway, and about thirty feet distant from her.

A well-dressed gentleman then stood up in the stern-sheets of the barge, and hailed the ship. Mr. Lowington, in full uniform, which he seldom wore, replied to the hail in Spanish; and a long conference ensued. When the principal said that the squadron came from Genoa, the health officer shook his head. Then he wanted to know all about the three vessels, and it appeared to be very difficult for him to comprehend the character of the school. At last he was satisfied on all these points, and understood that the academy was a private enterprise, and not an institution connected with the United States Navy.

"Have you any sickness on board?" asked the health officer, when the nature of the craft was satisfactorily explained.

"We have two cases of measles in the steamer, but all are well in the other vessels," replied Mr. Lowington.

"*Sarampion!*" exclaimed the Spanish officer, using the Spanish word for the measles.

At the same time he shrugged his shoulders like a Frenchman, and vented his incredulity in a laugh.

"*Viruelas!*" added the officer; and the word in English meant smallpox, which was just the disease the Spaniards feared as coming from Genoa.

Mr. Lowington then called Dr. Winstock, the surgeon,

who spoke Spanish fluently, and presented him to the incredulous health officer. A lengthy palaver between the two medical men ensued. There appeared to be some sort of freemasonry, or at least a professional sympathy, between them, for they seemed to get on very well together. The cases of measles were very light ones, the two students having probably contracted the disease in some interior town of Italy where they passed the night at a hotel. They had been kept apart from the other students, and no others had taken the malady.

The health officer declared that he was satisfied for the present with the explanation of the surgeon, and politely asked to see the ship's papers, which the principal held in his hand. The barge pulled up a little nearer to the steamer; a long pole with a pair of spring tongs affixed to the end of it was elevated to the gangway, between the jaws of which Mr. Lowington placed the documents. They were carefully examined, and then all hands were required to show themselves in the rigging. This order included every person on board, not excepting the cooks, waiters, and coal-heavers. In a few moments they were standing on the rail or perched in the rigging, and the health officer and his assistants proceeded to count them. The number was two short of that indicated in the ship's papers, for those who were sick with the measles were not allowed to leave their room.

The health officer then intimated that he would pay the vessel a visit; and all hands were ordered to muster at their stations where they could be most conveniently inspected. Every part of the vessel was then carefully examined, and the Spanish doctors minutely overhauled the two cases of measles. They declared themselves fully satisfied that there was neither yellow fever nor smallpox on board of the steamer. The other vessels of the squadron were subjected to the same inspection. Mr. Lowington and Dr. Winstock attended the health officer in his visit to the Josephine and the Tritonia.

"You find our vessels in excellent health," said Dr. Winstock, when the examination was completed.

"Very good; but we cannot get over the fact that you come from Genoa, where the smallpox is prevailing badly. Vessels from that port are quarantined at Marseilles for from three days to a fortnight; but I shall not be hard with you, as you have a skilful surgeon on board," replied the health officer, touching his hat to Dr. Winstock; "but my orders from the authorities are imperative that all vessels from infected or doubtful ports shall be fumigated before any person from them is allowed to land in the city. We have had the yellow fever so severely all summer that we are very cautious."

"Is it necessary to fumigate?" asked Dr. Winstock, with a smile.

"The authorities require it, and I am not at liberty to dispense with it," answered the official. "But it will detain you only a few hours. You will land the ship's company of each vessel, and they will be fumigated on shore. While they are absent our people will purify the vessels."

"Is there any yellow fever in the city now?" asked the surgeon of the fleet.

"None at all. The frost has entirely killed it; but we have many patients who are recovering from the disease. The people who went away have all returned, and we call the city healthy."

The quarantine grounds were pointed out to the principal; and the fleet was soon at anchor within a cable's length of the shore. Study and recitation were suspended for the rest of the day. All the boats of the American Prince were manned; her fires were banked; the entire ship's company were transferred to the shore; and the vessel was given up to the quarantine officers, who boarded her and proceeded with their work. In a couple of hours the steamer and her crew were disposed of; and then came the turn of the Josephine, for only one vessel could be treated at a time.

When all hands were mustered on board of the Tritonia, the two delinquents in the brig were let out to undergo the inspection with the others. The decision of the health officer requiring the vessels to be fumigated, and the fact that the process would require but a few hours, were passed through each of the schooners as well as the steamer, and in a short time were known to every student in the fleet. As usual they were disposed to make fun of the situation, though it was quite a sensation for the time. During the excitement Bark Lingall improved the opportunity to confer with Lon Gibbs and Ben Pardee. Lon was willing to undertake any thing that Bark suggested. Ben was rather a prudent fellow, but soon consented to take part in the enterprise. Certainly neither of these worthies would have assented if the proposition to join had been made by Bill Stout, in whom they had as little confidence as Bark had manifested. The alliance had hardly been agreed upon before the vice-principal happened to see the four marines talking together, and ordered Marline to recommit two of them to the brig. The boatswain locked them into their prison, and left them to their own reflections. The excitement on deck was still unabated, and the cabins and steerage were deserted even by the stewards.

"I think our time has come," said Bill Stout, after he had satisfied himself that no one but the occupants of the brig was in the steerage. "If we don't strike at once we shall lose our chance, for they say we are going up to the city to-night."

"They will have to let us out to be fumigated with the rest of the crew," answered Bark Lingall. "We haven't drawn lots yet, either."

"Never mind the lot now: I will do the job myself," replied Bill magnanimously. "I should rather like the fun of it."

"All right, though I am willing to take my chances. I won't back out of any thing."

"You are true blue, Bark, when you get started; but I would rather do the thing than not."

"Very well, I am willing; and when the scratch comes I will back you up. But I do not see how you are going to manage it, Bill," added Bark, looking about him in the brig.

"The vice has made an easy thing of it for us. While the fellows were all on deck, I went to my berth and got a little box of matches I bought in Genoa when we were there. I have it in my pocket now. All I have to do is to take off this scuttle, and go down into the hold. As we don't know how soon the fellows will be sent ashore, I think I had better be about it now."

Bill Stout put his fingers into the ring on the trap-door, and lifted it a little way.

"Hold on, Bill," interposed Bark. "You are altogether too fast. When Marline comes down to let us out, where shall I say you are?"

"That's so: I didn't think of that," added Bill, looking rather foolish. "He will see the scuttle, and know just where I am."

"And, when the blaze comes off, he will see just who started it," continued Bark. "That won't do anyhow."

"But I don't mean to give it up," said Bill, scratching his head as he labored to devise a better plan.

The difficulty was discussed for some time, but there seemed to be no way of meeting it. Bill was one of the crew of the second cutter, and he was sure to be missed when the ship's company were piped away. If Bark, who did not belong to any boat, took his oar, the boatswain, whose place was in the second cutter when all hands left the vessel, would notice the change. Bill was almost in despair, and insisted that no amount of brains could overcome the difficulty. The conspirator who was to "do the job" was certain to be missed when the ship's company took to the boats. To be missed was to proclaim who the incendiary was when the fire was investigated.

"We may as well give it up for the present, and wait for a better time," suggested Bark, who was as unable as his companion to solve the problem.

"No, I won't," replied Bill, taking a newspaper from his breast-pocket. "We may never have another chance; and I believe in striking while the iron is hot."

"Don't get us into a scrape for nothing. We can't do any thing now," protested Bark.

"Now's the day, and now's the hour!" exclaimed Bill, scowling like the villain of a melodrama.

"What are you going to do?" demanded Bark, a little startled by the sudden energy of his fellow-conspirator.

"Hold on, and you shall see," answered Bill, as he raised the trap-door over the scuttle.

"But stop, Bill! you were not to do any thing without my consent."

"All hands on deck! man the boats in fire order," yelled the boatswain on deck, after he had blown the proper pipe.

Bill Stout paid no attention to the call or to the remonstrance of his companion. Raising the trap, he descended to the hold by the ladder under the scuttle. Striking a match, he set fire to the newspaper in his hand, and then cast it into the heap of hay and sawdust that lay near the foot of the ladder. Hastily throwing the box-covers and cases on the pile, he rushed up the steps into the brig, and closed the scuttle. He was intensely excited, and Bark was really terrified at what he considered the insane rashness of his associate in crime. But there was no time for further talk; for Marline appeared at this moment, and unlocked the door of the brig.

"Come, my hearties, you must go on shore for an hour to have the smallpox smoked out of you; and I wish they could smoke out some of the mischief that's in you at the same time," said the adult boatswain. "Come, and bear a hand lively, for all hands are in boats by this time."

Bill Stout led the way; and on this occasion he needed no hurrying, for he was in haste to get away from the vessel before the blaze revealed itself. In a moment more he was on the thwart in the second cutter where he belonged. Bark's place was in another boat, and they separated when they reached the deck. The fire-bill assigned every person on board of the vessel to a place in one of the boats, so that every professor and steward as well as every officer and seaman knew where to go without any orders. It was the arrangement for leaving the ship in case of fire; and it had worked with perfect success in the Young America when she was sunk by the collision with the Italian steamer. As the boats pulled away from the Tritonia, the quarantine people boarded her to perform the duty belonging to them.

Bill Stout endeavored to compose himself, but with little success, though the general excitement prevented his appearance from being noticed. He was not so hardened in crime that he could see the vessel on fire without being greatly disturbed by the act; and it was more than probable that, by this time, he was sorry he had done it. He did not expect the fire to break out for some little time; and it had not occurred to him that the quarantine people would extend their operation to the hold of the vessel.

The boats landed on the beach; and all hands were marched up to a kind of tent, a short distance from the water. There were fifty-five of them, and they were divided into two squads for the fumigating process.

"How is this thing to be done?" asked Scott, as he halted by the side of Raimundo, at the tent.

"I have not the least idea what it is all about," replied the young Spaniard.

"I suppose we are to take up our quarters in this tent."

"Not for very long; for all the rest of the squadron have been operated upon in a couple of hours."

The health officer now beckoned them to enter the tent. It was of the shape of a one-story house. The canvas on the sides and end was tacked down to heavy planks on the ground, so as to make it as tight as possible. There was only a small door; and, when the first squad had entered, it was carefully closed, so that the interior seemed to be almost air-tight. In the centre of the tent was a large tin pan, which contained some chemical ingredient. The health officer then poured another ingredient into the pan; and the union of the two created quite a tempest, a dense smoke or vapor rising from the vessel, which immediately filled the tent.

"Whew!" whistled Scott, as he inhaled the vapor. "These Spaniards ought to have a patent for getting up a bad smell. This can't be beat, even by the city of Chicago."

"I am glad you think my countrymen are good for something," laughed Raimundo.

The students coughed, sneezed, and made all the fuss that was necessary, and a good deal more. The health officer laughed at the antics of the party, and dismissed them in five minutes, cleansed from all taint of small-pox or yellow fever.

"Where's your blaze?" asked Bark Lingall, as they withdrew from the others who had just left the tent.

"Hush up! don't say a word about it," whispered Bill; "it hasn't got a-going yet."

"But those quarantine folks are on board; and if there were any fire there they would have seen it before this time," continued Bark nervously.

"Dry up! not another word! If we are seen talking together the vice will know that we are at the bottom of the matter."

Bill Stout shook off his companion, and walked about with as much indifference as he could assume. Every minute or two he glanced at the Tritonia, expecting to see the flames, or at least the smoke, rising above her decks. But no flame or smoke appeared, not even the vapor of the disinfectants.

The second squad of the ship's company were sent into the tent after the preparations were completed; and in the course of an hour the health officer gave the vice-principal permission to return to his vessel. The boats were manned; the professors and others took their places, and the bowmen shoved off. Bill began to wonder where his blaze was, for ample time had elapsed for the flames to envelop the schooner, if she was to burn at all. Still there was no sign of fire or smoke about the beautiful craft. She rested on the water as lightly and as trimly as ever. Bill could not understand it; but he came to the conclusion that the quarantine men had extinguished the flames. The burning of the vessel did not rest upon his conscience, it is true; but he was not satisfied, as he probably would not have been if the Tritonia had been destroyed. He felt as though he had attempted to do a big thing, and had failed. He was not quite the hero he intended to be in the estimation of his fellow-conspirators.

The four boats of the Tritonia came alongside the

schooner; and, when the usual order of things had been fully restored, the signal for sailing appeared on the steamer. The odor of the chemicals remained in the cabin and steerage for a time; but the circulation of the air soon removed it. It was four o'clock in the afternoon; and, in order to enable the students to see what they might of the city as the fleet went up to the port, the lessons were not resumed. The fore-topsail, jib, and mainsail were set, the anchor weighed, and the Tritonia followed the Prince in charge of a pilot who had presented himself as soon as the fumigation was completed.

"You belong in the cage," said Marline, walking up to the two conspirators, as soon as the schooner began to gather headway.

Bill and Bark followed the boatswain to the steerage, and were locked into the brig.

"Here we are again," said Bark, when Marline had returned to the deck. "I did not expect when we left, to come back again."

"Neither did I; and I don't understand it," replied Bill, with a sheepish look. "I certainly fixed things right for something different. I lighted the newspaper, and put it under the hay, sawdust, and boxes. I was sure there would be a blaze in fifteen minutes. I can't explain it; and I am going down to see how it was."

"Not now: some one will see you," added Bark.

"No; everybody is looking at the sights. Besides, as the thing has failed, I want to fix things so that no one will suspect any thing if the pile of hay and stuff should be overhauled."

Bark made no further objection, and his companion

hastened down the ladder. Pulling over the pile of rubbish, he found the newspaper he had ignited. Only a small portion of it was burned, and it was evident that the flame had been smothered when the boxes and covers had been thrown on the heap. Nothing but the newspaper bore the marks of the fire ; and, putting this into his pocket, he returned to the brig.

"I shall do better than that next time," said he, when he had explained to Bark the cause of the failure.

Bill Stout was as full of plans and expedients as ever ; and, before the anchor went down, he was willing to believe that "the job" could be better done at another time.

CHAPTER III.

A GRANDEE OF SPAIN.

THE port, or harbor, of Barcelona is formed by an inlet of the sea. A triangular tongue of land, with a long jetty projecting from its southern point, shelters it from the violence of the sea, except on the south-east. On the widest part of the tongue of land is the suburb of Barceloneta, or Little Barcelona, inhabited by sailors and other lower orders of people.

"I can just remember the city as it was when I left it in a steamer to go to Marseilles, about ten years ago," said Raimundo, as he and Scott stood on the lee side of the quarter-deck, looking at the objects of interest that were presented to them. "It does not seem to have changed much."

"It don't look any more like Spain than the rest of the world," added the lieutenant.

"This hill on the left is Monjuich, seven hundred and fifty-five feet high. It has a big fort on the top of it, which commands the town as well as the harbor. The city is a walled town, with redoubts all the way around it. The walls take in the citadel, which you see above the head of the harbor. The city was founded by Hamilcar more than two hundred years before Christ, and afterwards became a Roman colony. There is lots of history connected with the city, but I will not bore you with it."

"Thank you for your good intentions," laughed Scott. "But how is it that you don't care to see the people of your native city after an absence of ten years?"

"I don't care about having this story told all through the ship, Scott," replied the young Spaniard, glancing at the students on deck.

"Of course I will not mention it, if you say so."

"I have always kept it to myself, though I have no strong reason for doing so; and I would not say any thing about it now if I did not feel the need of a friend. I am sure I can rely on you, Scott."

"When I can do any thing for you, Don, you may depend upon me; and not a word shall ever pass my lips till you request it."

"I don't know but you will think I am laying out the plot of a novel, like the story of Giulia Fabiano, whom O'Hara assisted to a happy conclusion," replied Raimundo, with a smile. "I couldn't help thinking of my own case when her history was related to me; for, so far, the situations are very much the same."

"I have seen all I want to of the outside of Barcelona; and if you like, we will go down into the cabin where we shall be alone for the present," suggested Scott.

"That will suit me better," answered Raimundo, as he followed his companion.

"We shall be out of hearing of everybody here, I think," said Scott, as he seated himself in the after-part of the cabin.

"There is not much romance in the story yet; and I

don't know that there ever will be," continued the Spaniard. "It is a family difficulty; and such things are never pleasant to me, however romantic they may be."

"Well, Don, I don't want you to tell the story for my sake; and don't harrow up your feelings to gratify my curiosity," protested Scott.

"I shall want your advice, and perhaps your assistance; and for this reason only I shall tell you all about it. Here goes. My grandfather was a Spanish merchant of the city of Barcelona; and when he was fifty years old he had made a fortune of two hundred and fifty thousand dollars, which is a big pile of money in Spain. He had three sons, and a strong weakness, as our friend O'Hara would express it. I suppose you know something about the grandees of Spain, Scott?"

"Not a thing," replied the third lieutenant candidly. "I have heard the word, and I know they are the nobles of Spain; and that's all I know."

"That's about all any ordinary outsider would be expected to know about them. There is altogether too much nobility and too little money in Spain. Some of the grandees are still very rich and powerful; but physically and financially the majority of them are played out. I am sorry to say it, but laziness is a national peculiarity: I am a Spaniard, and I will not call it by any hard names. Pride and vanity go with it. There are plenty of poor men who are too proud to work, or to engage in business of any kind. Of course such men do not get on very well; and, the longer they live, the poorer they grow. This is especially the case with the played-out nobility.

"My grandfather was the son of a grandee who had

lost all his property. He was a Castilian, with pride and dignity enough to fit out half a dozen Americans. He would rather have starved than do any sort of business. My grandfather, though it appears that he gloried in the title of the grandee, was not quite willing to be starved on his patrimonial acres. His stomach conquered his pride. He was the elder son; and while he was a young man his father died, leaving him the empty title, with nothing to support its dignity. I have been told that he actually suffered from hunger. He had no brothers; and his sisters were all married to one-horse nobles like himself. He was alone in his ruined castle.

"Without telling any of his people where he was going, he journeyed to Barcelona, where, being a young man of good parts, he obtained a situation as a clerk. In time he became a merchant, and a very prosperous one. As soon as his circumstances would admit, he married, and had three sons. As he grew older, the Castilian pride of birth came back to him, and he began to think about the title he had dropped when he became a merchant. He desired to found a family with wealth as well as a name. He was still the Count de Escarabajosa."

"Of what?" asked Scott.

"The Count de Escarabajosa," repeated Raimundo.

"Well, I don't blame him for dropping his title if he had to carry as long a name as that around with him. It was a heavy load for him, poor man!"

"The title was not of much account, according to my Uncle Manuel, who told me the story; for my grandfather was only a second or third class grandee — not one of the first, who were allowed to speak to the king with their hats on. At any rate, I think my grandfather did wisely not to think much of his title till his fortune was made. His oldest son, Enrique, was my father; and that's my name also."

"Yours? Are you not entered in the ship's books as Henry;" interposed Scott.

"No; but Enrique is the Spanish for Henry. When my grandfather died, he bequeathed his fortune to my father, who also inherited his title, though he gave the other two sons enough to enable them to make a start in business. If my father should die without any male heir, the fortune, consisting largely of houses, lands, and farms, in and near Barcelona, was to go to the second son, whose name was Alejandro. In like manner the fortune was to pass to the third son, if the second died without a male heir. This was Spanish law, as well as the will of my grandfather. Two years after the death of my grandfather, and when I was about six years old, my father died. I was his only child. You will see, Scott, that under the will of my grandfather I was the heir of the fortune, and the title too for that matter, though it is of no account."

"Then, Don, you are the Count de What-ye-call-it?" said Scott, taking off his cap, and bowing low to the young grandee.

"The Count de Escarabajosa," laughed Raimundo; "but I would not have the fellows on board know this for the world; and this is one reason why I wanted to have my story kept a secret."

"Not a word from me. But I shall hardly dare to speak to you without taking off my cap. The Count de

Scaribagiosa! My eyes! what a long tail our cat has got!"

"That's it! I can see just what would happen if you should spin this yarn to the crowd," added the grandee, shaking his head.

"But I won't open my mouth till you command me to do so. What would Captain Wainwright say if he only knew that he had a Spanish grandee under his orders? He might faint."

"Don't give him an opportunity."

"I won't. But spin out the yarn: I am interested."

"My father died when I was only six; and my Uncle Alejandro was appointed my guardian by due process of law. Now, I don't want to say a word against Don Alejandro, and I would not if the truth did not compel me to do so. My Uncle Manuel, who lives in New York, is my authority; and I give you the facts just as he gave them to me only a year before I left home to join the ship. Don Alejandro took me to his own house as soon as he was appointed my guardian. To make a long story short, he was a bad man, and he did not treat me well. I was rather a weakly child at six, and I stood between my uncle and my grandfather's large fortune. If I died, Don Alejandro would inherit the estate. My Uncle Manuel insists that he did all he could, short of murdering me in cold blood, to help me out of the world. I remember how ill he treated me, but I was too young to understand the meaning of his conduct.

"My Uncle Manuel was not so fortunate in business as his father had been, though he saved the capital my grandfather had bequeathed to him. The agency of a large mercantile house in Barcelona was offered to him if he would go to America ; and he promptly decided to seek his fortune in New York. Manuel had quarrelled with Alejandro on account of the latter's treatment of me ; and a great many hard words passed between them. But Manuel was so well satisfied in regard to Alejandro's intentions, that he dared not leave me in the keeping of his brother when he went to the New World. Though it was a matter of no small difficulty, he decided to take me with him to New York.

"I did not like my Uncle Alejandro, and I did like my Uncle Manuel. I was willing to go anywhere with the latter ; and when he called to bid farewell to my guardian, on the eve of his departure, he beckoned to me as he went out of the house. I followed him, and he managed to conceal his object from the servants ; for my Uncle Alejandro did not attend him to the front door. He had arranged a more elaborate plan to obtain possession of me ; but when he saw me in the hall, he was willing to adopt the simpler method that was then suggested to him. His baggage was on board of the steamer for Marseilles, and he had no difficulty in conveying me to the vessel. I was kept out of sight in the state-room till the steamer was well on her way. I will not trouble you with what I remember of the journey; but in less than three weeks we were in New York, which has been my home ever since."

"But what did your guardian say to all this ? " asked Scott. "Did he discover what had become of you ? "

"I don't know what he said ; but he has been at work for seven years to obtain possession of me. As I disappeared at the same time my Uncle Manuel left, no doubt Alejandro suspected what had become of me. At any rate, he sent an agent to New York to bring me back to Spain; but Manuel kept me out of the way. As soon as I could speak English well enough, he sent me to a boarding-school. I 'cut up' so that he was obliged to take me away, and send me to another. I am sorry to say that I did no better, and was sent to half a dozen different schools in the course of three years. I was active, and full of mischief; but I grew into a strong and healthy boy from a very puny and sickly one.

"At last my uncle sent me on board of the academy ship; but he told me before I went, that if I did not learn my lessons, and behave myself like a gentleman, he would send me back to my Uncle Alejandro in Spain. He would no longer attempt to keep me out of the way of my legal guardian. Partly on account of this threat, and partly because I like the institution, I have done as well as I could."

"And no one has done any better," added Scott.

"No doubt my Uncle Manuel has received good accounts of me from the principal, for he has been very kind to me. He wrote to me, after I had informed him that the squadron was going to Spain, that I must not go there; but he added that I was almost man grown, and ought to be able to take care of myself. I thought so too: at any rate, I have taken the chances in coming here."

"But you are a minor; and I suppose Don Alejandro, if he can get hold of you, will have the right to take possession of your *corpus*."

"No doubt of that."

"But does your guardian know that you are a student in the academy squadron?" asked Scott.

"I don't know: it is not impossible, or even improbable. Alejandro has had agents out seeking me, and they may have ascertained where I am. For aught I know, my guardian may have made his arrangements to capture me as soon as the fleet comes to anchor. But I don't mean to be captured; for I should have no chance in a Spanish court, backed by the principal, the American minister, and the counsel. By law I belong to my guardian; and that is the whole of it. Now, Scott, you are the best friend I have on this side of the Atlantic; and I want you to help me."

"That I will do with all my might and main, Don," protested Scott.

"I don't ask you to tell any lies, or to do any thing wrong," said Raimundo.

"What can I do for you? that's the question."

"I shall keep out of sight while the vessels are at this port; and I want you to be on the lookout for any Spaniards in search of a young man named Raimundo, and let me know. When you go on shore, I want you to find out all you can about my Uncle Alejandro. If I should happen to run away at any time, *you* will know, if no one else does, why I did so."

"Don't you think it would be a good thing to tell the vice-principal your story, and ask him to help you out in case of any trouble?" suggested Scott.

"No: that would not do. If Mr. Pelham should do any thing to help me keep out of the way, he would be charged with breaking or evading the Spanish laws; and that would get him into trouble. I ought not to have come here; but now I must take the responsibility, and not shove it off on the vice-principal."

"Who pays your bills, Don?"

"My Uncle Manuel, of course. He has a half interest in the house for which he went out as an agent; and I suppose he is worth more money to-day than his father ever was. He is as liberal as he is rich. He sent me a second letter of credit for a hundred pounds when we were at Leghorn; and I drew half of it in Genoa in gold, so as to be ready for any thing that might happen in Spain."

"Do you really expect that your uncle will make a snap at you?" asked Scott, with no little anxiety in his expression.

"I have no knowledge whatever in regard to his movements. I know that he has sent agents to the United States to look me up, and that my Uncle Manuel has had sharp work to keep me out of their way. I have been bundled out of New York in the middle of the night to keep me from being kidnapped by his emissaries; for my uncle has never believed that he had any case in law, even in the States."

"It is really quite a serious matter to you, Don."

"Serious? You know that my countrymen have the reputation of using knives when occasion requires; and I also know that Don Alejandro has not a good character in Barcelona."

"But suppose you went back to him: do you believe he would ill-treat you now?"

"No, I don't. I have grown to be too big a fellow to be abused like a child. I think I could take care of myself, so far as that is concerned. But my uncle has been nursing his wrath for years on account of my absence. He has sons of his own, who are living on my property; for I learn that Alejandro has done nothing to increase the small sum his father left him. He and his sons want my fortune. I might be treated with the utmost kindness and consideration, if I returned; but that would not convince me that I was not in constant peril. Spain is not England or the United States, and I have read a great deal about my native land," said Raimundo, shaking his head. "I agree with my uncle Manuel, that I must not risk myself in the keeping of my guardian."

"Suppose Don Alejandro should come on board as soon as we anchor, Don: what could you do? You would not be in condition to run away. Where could you go?" inquired Scott.

"I know just what I should do; but I will not put you in condition to be tempted to tell any lies," replied Raimundo, smiling. "One thing more: I shall not be safe anywhere in Spain. My uncle does not want me for any love he bears me; and it would answer his purpose just as well if I should be drowned in crossing a river, fall off any high place, or be knifed in some lonely corner. There are still men enough in Spain who use the knife, though the country is safe under ordinary circumstances."

"Upon my word, I shall be hardly willing to let you go out of my sight," added Scott. "I shall have to take you under my protection."

"I am afraid your protection will not do me much good, except in the way I have indicated."

"Well, you may be sure I will do all I can to serve

and save you," continued Scott, taking the hand of his friend, as the movements on deck indicated that the schooner was ready to anchor.

"Thank you, Scott; thank you. With your help, I shall feel that I am almost out of danger."

Raimundo decided to remain in the cabin, as his watch was not called; but Scott went on deck, as much to look out for any suspicious Spaniards, as for the purpose of seeing what was to be seen. The American Prince had already anchored; and her two consorts immediately followed her example. The sails were hardly furled, and every thing made snug, before the signal, "All hands attend lecture," appeared on the flag-ship.

All the vessels of the fleet were surrounded by boats from the shore, most of them to take passengers to the city. The adult forward officers were stationed at the gangways, to prevent any persons from coming on board; and the boatmen were informed that no one would go on shore that night. Scott hastened below, to tell his friend that all hands were ordered on board of the steamer to attend the lecture. Raimundo declared, that, as no one could possibly recognize him after so many years of absence, he should go on board of the Prince, with the rest of the ship's company.

The boats were lowered; and in a short time all the students were assembled in the grand saloon, where Professor Mapps was ready to discourse upon the geography and history of Spain.

CHAPTER IV.

THE PROFESSOR'S TALK ABOUT SPAIN.

AS usual, the professor had a large map posted where all could see it. It was a map of Spain and Portugal in this instance, in which the physical as well as the political features of the peninsula were exhibited. The instructor pointed at the map, and commenced his lecture.

"The ancient name of Spain was *Iberia;* the Latin, *Hispania.* The Spaniards call their country *España.* Notice the mark over the *n* in this word, which gives it the value of *ny,* the same as the French *gn.* You will find it in many Spanish words.

"With Portugal, Spain forms a peninsula whose greatest length, from east to west, is six hundred and twenty miles; and, from north to south, five hundred and forty miles. It is separated from the rest of Europe by the Pyrenees Mountains: they extend quite across the isthmus, which is two hundred and forty miles wide. It contains two hundred and fourteen thousand square miles, of which one hundred and seventy-eight thousand belong to Spain, and thirty-six thousand to Portugal. Spain is not quite four times as large as the State of New York; and Portugal is a little larger than the State of Maine.

"Spain has nearly fourteen hundred miles of sea-coast, four-sevenths of which is on the Mediterranean. Spain is a mountainous country. About one-half of its area is on the great central plateau, from two to three thousand feet above the level of the sea. The mountain ranges, you observe, extend mostly east and west, which gives the rivers, of course, the same general direction. The Cantabrian and the Pyrenees are the same range, the former extending along the northern coast to the Atlantic. Between this range and the Sierra Guadarrama are the valleys of the Duero and the Ebro. This range reaches nearly from the mouth of the Tagus to the mouth of the Ebro, and takes several names in different parts of the peninsula. The mountains of Toledo are about in the centre of Spain. South of these are the Sierra Morena, with the basin of the Guadiana on the north and that of the Guadalquiver on the south. Near the southern coast is the Sierra Nevada, which contains the Cerro de Mulahacen, 11,678 feet, the highest peak in the peninsula. *Sierra* means a saw, which a chain of mountains may resemble; though some say it comes from the Arabic word *Sehrah*, meaning wild land.

"There are two hundred and thirty rivers in Spain; but only six of them need be mentioned. The Minho is in the north-west, and separates Spain and Portugal for about forty miles. It is one hundred and thirty miles long, and navigable for thirty. The Duero, called the Douro in Portugal, has a course of four hundred miles, about two-thirds of which is in Spain. It is navigable through Portugal, and a little way into Spain, though only for boats. The Tagus is the longest river of the peninsula, five hundred and forty miles. It is navigable only to Abrantes in Portugal, about eighty miles; though Philip II. built several boats at Toledo, loaded them with grain, and sent them down to Lisbon. The Guadiana is in the south-west, three hundred and eighty miles long, and navigable only thirty-five. Near its source this river, like the Rhone and some others, indulges in the odd freak of disappearing, and flowing through an underground channel for twenty miles. The river loses itself gradually in an expanse of marshes, and re-appears in the form of several small lakes, which are called 'los ojos de la Guadiana,' — the eyes of the Guadiana.

"The Guadalquiver is two hundred and eighty miles long, and, like all the rivers I have mentioned, flows into the Atlantic. It is navigable to Cordova, and large vessels go up to Seville. The Ebro is the only large river that flows into the Mediterranean. It is three hundred and forty miles long, and is navigable for boats about half this distance. Great efforts have been made to improve the navigation of some of these rivers, especially the largest of them. There are no lakes of any consequence in Spain, the largest being a mere lagoon on the seashore near Valencia.

"Spain has a population of sixteen millions, which places it as the tenth in rank among the nations of Europe. In territorial extent it is the seventh. It is said that Spain, as a Roman province, had a population of forty millions.

"Spain, including the Balearic and Canary Islands, contains forty-nine provinces, each of which has its local government, and its representation in the national legislature, or *Cortes*. But you should know something of the old divisions, since these are often mentioned in the history of the country. There are fourteen of them, each of which was formerly a kingdom, principality, or province. Castile was the largest, including Old and New Castile, and was in the north-central part of the peninsula. This was the realm of Isabella; and, by her marriage with Ferdinand, it was united with Aragon, lying next east of it. East of Aragon, forming the north-east corner of Spain, is Catalonia, of which Barcelona is the chief city. North of Castile, on or near the Bay of Biscay, are the three Basque provinces. Bordering the Pyrenees, nearest to France, is the little kingdom of Navarre, with Aragon on the east. Forming the north-western corner of the peninsula is the kingdom of Galicia. East of it, on the Bay of Biscay, is the principality of the Asturias. South of this, and between Castile and Portugal, is the kingdom of Leon, which was attached to Castile in the eleventh century. Estremadura is between Portugal and New Castile. La Mancha, the country of Don Quixote, is south of New Castile. Valencia and Murcia are on the east, bordering on the Mediterranean. Andalusia is on both sides of the Guadalquiver, including the three modern provinces of Seville, Cordova, and Jaen. Granada is in the south, on the Mediterranean. You will hear the different parts of Spain spoken of under these names more than any other.

"The principal vegetable productions of Spain are those of the vine and olive. The export of wine is ten million dollars; and of olive-oil, four millions. Raisins, flour, cork, wool, and brandy are other important exports, to say nothing of the fruits of the South, such as grapes and oranges. Silver, quicksilver, lead, and iron are the most valuable minerals. Silk is produced in Valencia, Murcia, and Granada.

"The climate of Spain, as you would suppose from its mountainous character, is very various. The north, which is in the latitude of New England, is very different from this region of our own country. On the table-lands of the centre, it is hot in summer and cold in winter. In the south, the weather is hot in summer, but very mild in winter. Even here in Barcelona, the mercury seldom goes down to the freezing point. The average winter temperature of Malaga is about fifty-five degrees Fahrenheit.

"Three thousand miles of railroad have been built, and two thousand miles more have been projected. One can go to all the principal cities in Spain now by rail from Madrid; and those on the seacoast are connected by several lines of steamers.

"The army consists of one hundred and fifty thousand men, and may be increased in time of war by calling out the reserves; for every man over twenty is liable to do military duty. The navy consists of one hundred and ten vessels, seventy-three of which are screw steamers, twenty-four paddle steamers, and thirteen sailing vessels. Seven of the screws are iron-clad frigates. They are manned by thirteen thousand sailors and marines; and this navy is therefore quite formidable.

"The government is a constitutional monarchy. The king executes the laws through his ministers, but is not held responsible for any thing. If things do not work well, the ministers are to bear the blame, and his Majesty may dismiss them at pleasure. The laws are made by the *Cortes*, which consists of two bodies, the Senate and the Congress. Any Spaniard who is of age, and not deprived of his civil rights, may be a member of the *Congreso*, or lower house. Four senators are elected for each province. They must be forty years old, be in possession of their civil rights, and must have held some high office under the government in the army or navy, in the church, or in certain educational institutions.

"The present king is Amedeo I., second son of Vittorio Emanuele, king of Italy. He was elected king of Spain Nov. 16, 1870.[1]

"All but sixty thousand of the population of Spain are Roman Catholics; and of this faith is the national church, though all other forms of worship are tolerated. In 1835 and in 1836 the *Cortes* suppressed all conventual institutions, and confiscated their property for the benefit of the nation. In 1833 there were in Spain one hundred and seventy-five thousand ecclesiastics of all descriptions, including monks and nuns. In 1862 this number had been reduced to about forty thousand, which exhibits the effect of the legislation of the *Cortes*. The archbishop of Toledo is the head of the Church, primate of Spain.

"Though there are ten universities in Spain some of them very ancient and very celebrated, the population

---

[1] King Amedeo abdicated Feb. 11, 1874; and Alfonso XII., son of Isabella II., was proclaimed king of Spain Dec. 31, 1874, thus restoring the Bourbons to the throne. Alfonso was about seventeen when he became king.

of Spain have been in a state of extreme ignorance till quite a recent period. At the beginning of the present century, it was rare to find a peasant or an ordinary workman who could read. Efforts have been put forth since 1812 to promote popular education; but with no great success, till within the last forty years. In 1868 there were a million and a quarter of pupils in the public and private schools; and not more than one in ten of the population are unable to read. But the sum expended for public education in Spain is less per annum than the city of Boston devotes to this object.

"Money values in Spain are generally reckoned in *reales*, a *real* being five cents of our money. This is the unit of the system. The *Isabelino*, or Isabel as it is generally called, is a gold coin worth one hundred *reales*, or five dollars. A *peso*, or *duro*, is the same as our dollar: it is a silver coin. The *escudo* is half a dollar. The *peseta* is twenty cents; the half *peseta* is ten. The *real* is the smallest silver coin. Of the copper coins, the *medio real* means half a real. You will see a small copper coin stamped '1 *centimo de escudo*,' which means one hundredth of an *escudo*, or half dollar. It is the tenth of a *real*, or half a cent. Then there is the *doble decima*, worth one cent; and the *medio decima*, worth a quarter of a cent. But probably you will not hear any of these copper coins mentioned. Instead of them the small money will be counted in *cuartos*, eight and a half of them making a real. An American cent, an English halfpenny, a French sou, or any other copper coin of any nation, and about the same size, will go for a *cuarto*. A *maravedis* is an imaginary value, four of which were equal to a *cuarto*.

It is used in poetry and plays; and, though there is no such coin, any piece of base metal, even a button, will pass for a *maravedis*. There is a vast quantity of bad money in circulation in Spain, especially of the gold coins; and the traveller should be on the lookout for it. There are also a great many counterfeit *escudos*, or half-dollars. Travellers should have nothing to do with paper money, as it is not good away from the locality where it is issued.

"Having said all that occurs to me on these general topics, I shall now ask your attention to the history of Spain, which is very interesting to the student, though I am obliged to make it quite brief. I hope you have read the historical writings of our own Prescott, which are more attractive than the novels of the day. If you have not read these works, do so before you are a year older; and here in Spain is the time for you to begin.

"Recent events have called an unusual amount of attention to the Spanish peninsula; and this unhappy country has long been in so uneasy a state that a revolution surprises very few. Spain has had its full share, both of the smiles and the frowns of fortune. It was as widely known in early ages for its wealth, as it has been in modern times for its beggars.

"Nearly three thousand years ago, the Phœnicians began to plant colonies in the South of Spain. They found the country abounding with silver. So plenty, indeed, was the silver ore, that, according to one account, they not only loaded their fleet with it, but they returned home with their anchors and the commonest implements made of the same precious metal.

"This is doubtless an exaggeration; but we have

reason to believe that silver was more abundant in Spain than in any other quarter of the ancient world. Few silver-mines were known in Asia in those days: yet an immense quantity of silver was in circulation there during the flourishing period of the Persian empire. Herodotus tells us that in the reign of Darius, son of Hystaspes, all the nations under the yoke of the Persians, except the Indians and the Ethiopians, paid their tribute in silver. A large portion of this was obtained from the Phœnicians, and was distributed through Asia by the traders who came to Tyre. The Carthaginians also drew uncounted treasures in silver from Spain. When Carthagina was taken from them by Scipio, the portion of the precious metals that went into the Roman treasury was eighteen thousand three hundred pounds in weight of silver, two hundred and seventy-six golden cups each weighing a pound, and silver vessels without number. Near this city is a silver-mine which is said to have employed forty thousand workmen, and which paid the Romans nearly two million dollars annually. Another mine in the Pyrenees furnished to the Carthaginians in Hannibal's time three hundred pounds every day. The quantities of gold and silver brought into the public treasury by the Roman consuls who subjugated the different parts of the Spanish peninsula were enormous. Still the country was not exhausted; for it was almost as highly favored in soil and climate as in its mineral treasures. 'Next to Italy, if I except the fabulous regions of India, I would rank Spain,' wrote Pliny in the first century of our era. At that time the country contained four hundred and nine cities; and there was not within the

Roman empire a province where the people were more industrious or more prosperous. How strongly this account contrasts with the history of modern Spain! When the Spanish monarchs were aspiring to rule the world, in the sixteenth century, the streets of their cities were overrun with beggars. Only a century ago, the number of people in Spain who were without shirts, because they were too poor to buy such a luxury, was estimated at three millions, or one-third of the population of the kingdom. Within a hundred years, however, in spite of numerous drawbacks, the wealth of the country has vastly increased, and the population has nearly doubled.

"The Spaniards are the descendants of various races, tribes, and nations. At the dawn of history, we find the country in possession of the Iberians and Celts. Of the Iberians we know but little. From them Spain received its ancient name, Iberia; and the Iberus River, now the Ebro, took the name by which, with slight changes, it is still known. The language of the Iberians is supposed to survive in that of the Basque provinces of Biscaya, Guipuzcoa, and Alava, which I located a few moments since.

"The Celts, who a little more than two thousand years ago had not lost possession of Northern Italy and the countries now known as England, Scotland, and Ireland, drove the Iberians from the South of France and from the north-western part of Spain, in very early times. In the centre of the latter country these people united, and were afterwards known as Celt-Iberians.

"About a thousand years before Christ, the Phœnicians began to build towns on the southern coast of Spain; and, a century or two later, colonies were established on the eastern coast by the Rhodians and by other Greeks. Cadiz, Malaga, and Cordova were Phœnician towns; and Rhodos and Saguntum — now Rosas and Murviedro — were among those founded by the Greeks.

"Carthage was founded by the Tyrians; but the Carthaginians did not allow relationship to stand in the way of gain or conquest. Nearly six hundred years before our era, they found an opportunity to supplant the Phœnicians in Spain; and in the course of two centuries and a half they had brought under their sway a large portion of the country. At length the Greek colonies on the coast of Catalonia and Valencia, and several independent nations of the interior, seeing no other way to avoid submitting to Carthage, called upon the Romans for help. Rome sent commissioners to Carthage in the year B.C. 227, who obtained a promise that the Carthaginians would not push their conquests beyond the Ebro, and that they would not disturb the Saguntines and other Greek colonies. But, in spite of this agreement, Saguntum was besieged eight years later, by a Carthaginian army under Hannibal. The siege and destruction of this city caused the second Punic war, lasting from B.C. 218 to 201, during which Carthage lost her last foot-hold in Spain.

"But the Romans did not obtain quiet possession of the country their great enemy had lost. Nearly all the territory had to be won again from the natives; and in some parts of the peninsula the contest was doubtful for years. As if this were not enough, many of the battles of the civil wars, during the decline of the Roman republic, were fought on the soil of Spain, which, for two centuries after the fall of Saguntum, hardly knew the blessing of peace for a single year. To say nothing of lesser celebrities, we find the names of Hasdrubal, Hanno, Mago, and Hannibal, among the Carthaginians; of Viriathus, the Lusitanian; and, of the Romans, the Scipios, Sertorius, Metellus, Pompey the Great, and Julius Cæsar, — in the military annals of Spain during this period.

"Shortly after the Roman republic became an empire, under Augustus, — B. C. 30 to A. D. 14, — war was suspended throughout the Roman empire; and the Spaniards enjoyed a large share of tranquillity from that time till the barbarians poured across the Pyrenees, at the beginning of the fifth century. As a province of the empire, Spain held a high rank. The stupendous Bridge of Alcantara, the well-preserved Theatre of Murviedro, and the celebrated Aqueducts of Segovia and Tarragona, still attest the magnificence of that period. Nor was the peninsula wanting in illustrious men during these times. The most learned and practical writer on agriculture among the ancients, — Columella, — the poets Martial and Lucan, the philosopher Seneca, the historian Florus, the geographer Pomponius Mela, and the rhetorician Quintilian, were Spaniards. Three of the Roman emperors — Trajan, one of the greatest princes that ever swayed a sceptre; Hadrian, the enlightened protector of arts and literature; and Marcus Aurelius, whose name was long held in grateful remembrance by his subjects — were also natives of the Spanish peninsula.

"After the death of Constantine, A. D. 337, the prosperity of Spain began to decline. The taxes became heavier, and were increased till they were more than the people could bear. In a short time towns were deserted, fields ran to waste, and fruit-trees were uprooted, so as to reduce the value of property in order to avoid taxation. At the close of the century nothing was to be seen but desolation, poverty, and misery. But there was still a lower deep: the barbarians crossed the Pyrenees, and the country was turned into a desert.

"The great irruption of the northern nations into the Roman empire began in 375. A century later, the western empire fell. The most important division of the barbarians, who occupy so large a place in the history of the fourth and fifth centuries, were the Germans. The Vandals and Suevi, two of the nations that entered Spain in 409, were Germans. It is not certain that the third nation coming to Spain, the Alani, were of the same race. The ravages of these barbarians were terrible. Towns were burned, the country laid waste, and the inhabitants were massacred without distinction of age or sex. Famine and pestilence made fearful havoc, and the wild beasts left their hiding-places to make war on the wretched people. Even the corpses were devoured by the starving population.

"At length the conquerors themselves saw that converting a land in which they intended to live into a desert was not the wisest policy. They divided by lot, among themselves, those parts of the peninsula which they occupied. The southern part fell to the Vandals, whence it received the name of Vandalicia, which has easily become Andalusia. Lusitania, which was very nearly the modern Portugal, went to the Alani; and the Suevi had the north-western part of the peninsula, which is now Galicia. The Romans still held the rest of the country.

"But this division was soon destroyed by the Visigoths, or West Goths, another Germanic tribe. All these Germans were only a little less savage than our North American Indians. They neglected agriculture, and no man tilled the same field more than one year. War was really their only occupation. One of them boasted to Julius Cæsar that his soldiers had been fourteen years without entering a house; another declared that the only country he knew as his home was the territory occupied by his troops; and we are told by Tacitus that war was the only work they liked.

"The Visigoths, under their King Alaric, had ravaged Greece and Italy, and had taken Rome, before they established themselves in Southern Gaul, in 411. They commenced the conquest of Spain almost immediately after the foundation of their new kingdom; but they were the nominal rather than the real masters of the kingdom for more than half a century.

"Euric (466 to 484) was the founder of the Gothic kingdom of Spain; and Amalaric (522 to 531) was the first sovereign to hold his court in the country. Before long, Spain became the most flourishing of the governments established by the Germans on the ruins of the western empire. The conquerors, as they were the few while the civilized Roman inhabitants were the many, adopted the manners, the religion, the laws, and the language, of the subject people. They mingled a little Gothic with the Latin; and from this mixture arose, in the course of time, the noble and beautiful Castilian, or Spanish language.

"By degrees the Visigoths became less warlike, and finally ceased to be a nation of soldiers. Their kings were elective, and seem to have possessed more power than those of other German tribes. Still they were controlled to a great extent by the clergy. The councils of Toledo figured largely in the history of that period; and in these the bishops were a power. 'Let no one in his pride seize upon the throne,' says one of the Visigothic laws; 'let no pretender excite civil war among the people; let no one conspire the death of the prince. But, when the king is dead in peace, let the principal men of the whole kingdom, together with the bishops — who have received power to bind and to loose, and whose blessing and unction confirm princes in their authority — appoint his successor by common consent, and with the approval of God.' But the kings were not always allowed to die in peace. From Euric to Roderick, the greater number of them were assassinated or deposed. Roderick, the last of the Gothic kings of Spain, drove his predecessor from the throne. The relations of the dethroned monarch invited the Arabs, or Moors, of Africa to their aid; and the famous battle fought on the plains of the modern *Xeres de la Frontera*, near Cadiz, a battle that lasted three days, put an end to the life of Roderick, and to the Gothic kingdom of Spain, in the year 711.

"In the days of the patriarch Jacob, the people of Arabia were far enough advanced in civilization to maintain an active overland trade with Egypt. The Midianite merchantmen to whom Joseph was sold for

twenty pieces of silver — about a dozen dollars — were
from Arabia. Yet, for more than two thousand years
from that time, the Arabs continued to be so divided
into hostile clans, that they were almost unknown to
history. The religion of Mohammed first united them;
and the history of the Arabs really begins with the
Hegira, or flight of the Prophet from Mecca, in the
year 622. For ten years Mohammed had proclaimed
his new creed in Mecca; his followers had been few,
and had suffered incessant persecution; and now he
was promised, by men from Medina, that, if he would
flee to their city, his faith should be adopted and maintained. He made his escape from Mecca, though not
without great risk, and reached Medina in safety,
accompanied by a single friend. In Mecca he had
preached patience and resignation under the wrongs
inflicted by man. At Medina, where he had followers,
his doctrine was, that one drop of blood shed in the
cause of God — meaning the new faith, of course —
was to be of more avail in working out the salvation of
his hearers than two months of fasting and prayer. At
first he made war on the caravan trade of his native
city; and Mecca sent out an army to meet him.
Mohammed had but three hundred and twenty-four
men, while the Meccans were a thousand. But the
prophet assured his followers that three thousand angels
were fighting on his side; and with these unseen allies
he utterly routed his enemy. After this first victory,
conquest followed conquest in rapid succession. In
less than a century from the Hegira, Arabia was but a
small province of the empire which had been founded
by Mohammed's successors; an empire that extended

from India to the Atlantic, and included Syria, Phœnicia, Mesopotamia, Persia, Bactriana, Egypt, Libya, Numidia, Spain, and many important islands of the Mediterranean.

"After King Roderick's defeat and death at Xeres, the Moors almost immediately took possession of the whole country, except Biscaya, Navarre, a part of Aragon, and the mountains of the Asturias. Here a few resolute Goths made a stand, under Pelayo, and established a kingdom; a stronghold which enabled the Christians step by step to recover their lost territory, till after eight centuries the last foot of Spanish soil was retaken from the Moslems.

" During a part of the Moors' dominion in Spain the country was very prosperous. For more than forty years after the conquest, however, it was ruled by viceroys dependent upon the caliphs who reigned in Damascus. This was a time of discord and civil war; and, towards the close of this period, many a city and village was laid in ruins never again to rise.

"The eighth, ninth, and tenth centuries were the most prosperous in the history of Mohammedan Spain; and the last was its golden age. The Moors, though warlike, were also industrious, and agriculture flourished during this period as it has never flourished since. Roads and bridges were built, and canals for fertilizing the land were made in all parts of the country. Learning was encouraged by the kings of Cordova; and, at the end of the eleventh century, Moorish Spain could boast of seventy large libraries; while her poets, historians, philosophers, and mathematicians were second to none of that age. Cordova, the capital, was equal to

many cities like the Cordova of to-day. At one time
there were in that city six hundred mosques, and nearly
four thousand chapels, or mosques of smaller dimensions; four hundred and thirty minarets, or towers
from which the people were called to prayers, such as
you saw in Constantinople; nine hundred baths; more
than eighty thousand shops; sixty thousand palaces
and mansions; and two hundred and thirteen thousand
common dwelling-houses. The city extended eight
leagues along the Guadalquiver. If these statistics
are correct, the city must have contained not less than
a million inhabitants. We can form some idea of its
splendors when we are told that a palace built near the
city, by Abderrahman III., had its roof supported by
more than four thousand pillars of variegated marble;
that the floors and walls were of the same costly material; that the chief apartments were adorned with
exquisite fountains and baths; and that the whole was
surrounded by most magnificent grounds.

"In 1031 the kingdom, or caliphate, of Cordova
came to an end; and several petty kingdoms took its
place. But all of them soon became dependent upon
the Moorish monarch of Northern Africa. The Christian kings of Spain were prompt in taking advantage
of this division among the infidels, as the Moors were
called; and the power of the Moslems began to decline.
The Christians gained rapidly on the Moors; and in
1238, when the kingdom of Granada was founded, the
Moors held only a part of Southern Spain. Granada
was the last realm of the Moors in Spain; and its population was largely composed of the Moslems who fled
there from the kingdoms which had been overthrown
by the victorious arms of the Christian monarchs.

The little kingdom of Granada, though it had an area of only nine thousand square miles, contained thirty-two large cities and ninety-seven smaller ones, and a population of three million souls. The city of Granada had seventy thousand houses. This kingdom held out against the Christians till the beginning of the year 1492. This was the year in which America was discovered; and Columbus followed Ferdinand and Isabella, in their campaign against the Moors, to this city.

"With the fall of Granada, came the close of the Moorish rule in the peninsula. A few years later many of the Moors were expelled from the country. In many parts of Spain the traveller still sees numerous traces of their dominion. He finds these traces in the Oriental style of the older buildings; in the *alcazars*, or palaces, they built; in the mósques now converted into Christian churches; and in the canals which still fertilize the soil from which the Moslems were driven more than three centuries ago.

"The old Gothic monarchy founded by Pelayo survived in the kingdom of the Asturias. As the Christians began to recover their lost territory from the Moors, these conquests, instead of being joined to the Asturian kingdom, were erected into independent states; but, by the middle of the fifteenth century, the number of them had been reduced to five, — Navarre, Aragon, Castile, Granada, and Portugal. We shall say something of Portugal at another time, for it has a history of its own. In 1479 Ferdinand of Aragon and Isabella of Castile united these two monarchies into one. The kingdom of the Asturias had been merged into that of Leon, which was united to Castile in 1067. Granada was added in 1492, and Navarre twenty years later.

"At the death of Ferdinand in 1516, Charles I. became king of Spain. He was the son of 'Crazy Jane,' daughter of Ferdinand and Isabella. He was elected emperor of Germany three years after his accession to the throne, as Charles V. His reign and that of his son and successor covered the most splendid period in the history of modern Spain, ending with the death of Philip in 1588. Their dominions were the most extensive among the monarchs of Europe; their armies were the best of that age; and their treasuries were supplied by the exhaustless mines of the new world which Columbus had given to Spain. But, after the death of Philip II., the monarchy rapidly declined; so rapidly indeed that a century later, when Charles II. died, in 1700, it was without money, without credit, and without troops.

"I must again call your attention to the magnificent works of our own Prescott. I hope you will all read them, for I have not time to mention a score of topics which are treated in these volumes, such as the Inquisition, the Spanish Rule in Naples, the Conquest of Granada, the Great Captain, the Cardinal Ximines, and the Spanish Rule in the Netherlands. I commend to you also the works of Motley and Washington Irving; of the latter, especially 'The Life of Columbus,' 'The Alhambra,' and 'The Conquest of Granada.'"

"Charles II., as he had no children, and there was no heir to the throne, signed an instrument, before his death, declaring Philip, Duke of Anjou, grandson of the grand monarch Louis XIV., his successor. This king was Philip V., the first of the Spanish branch of the Bourbon family, to which Isabella II., the late queen of Spain, belonged. England, Holland, and Germany objected to this arrangement, because it placed both France and Spain under the rule of the same family; and for twelve years resisted the claim of Philip to the throne. This was 'the war of the Spanish succession,' in which Prince Eugene and the Duke of Marlborough won several great victories. But Philip retained the throne, though he lost the Spanish possessions in Italy and the Netherlands, and was obliged to cede Gibraltar and Minorca to England. Under Philip V. and his successors, the prosperity of Spain revived; and the kingdom flourished till the French Revolution.

"Philip was followed by his son Ferdinand VI. in 1748; but he was mentally unfit to take an active part in the government, and was succeeded by his stepbrother Charles III. in 1759. He was a wise prince, and greatly promoted the prosperity of his country. Charles IV., who came to the throne in 1788, began his reign by following the wise policy of his father; but he soon placed himself under the influence of Godoy, his prime minister, who led him into several fruitless wars and expensive alliances, which reduced the country to a miserable condition. In 1808 an insurrection compelled him to abdicate in favor of his son, who ascended the throne as Ferdinand VII. A few days later the ex-king wrote a letter to Napoleon, declaring that he had abdicated under compulsion; and he revoked the act. Napoleon offered to arbitrate between the father and son, and he met them at Bayonne for this purpose.

He induced both of them to resign their claims to the throne, and then made his brother Joseph king of Spain. The new king started for his dominion; but the Spaniards were not satisfied with this little arrangement, and insurrections broke out all over the country. England decided to take a hand in the game, made peace with Spain, acknowledged Ferdinand VII. as king of Spain, and formed an alliance with the government. Thus began the peninsular war, in which the Duke of Wellington prepared the way for the destruction of Napoleon's power. As you travel, you will visit the battle-fields of this great conflict, and your guide-book will contain full accounts of the struggle in various places.

"In 1812, while Ferdinand was a prisoner in France, and the war was still raging, the *Cortes*, driven from Madrid to Seville, and then to Cadiz, drew up a written constitution, the first of the kind known in the peninsula. The regency acting for the absent monarch, recognized by England and Russia, took an oath to support it. In 1814 Ferdinand was released, and came back to Spain. He declared the constitution null and void, and the *Cortes* that adopted it illegal. He ruled the nation in an arbitrary manner, and even attempted to restore the inquisition, which had been abolished, and to annul the reforms which had been for years in progress. But in 1820 the patience of the people was exhausted, and a revolution was undertaken. The king was deserted by his troops; and the royal palace was surrounded by a multitude of the people, who demanded his acceptance of the constitution of 1812. The humbled monarch appeared at a balcony, holding a copy of the instrument in his hand, as an indication that he was ready to accept it, and take the oath to support it. In a few months the *Cortes* met; and the king formally swore to obey the constitution, and accept the new order of things. But this did not suit France, Austria, Russia, and Prussia: they had no stomach for liberal constitutions; and these powers sent a French army into Spain, which soon overpowered the resistance offered; and Ferdinand was again in condition to rule as absolutely as ever. It was during this period that the Spanish-American colonies, which had begun to revolt in 1808, secured their independence.

"Even those who favored the king's views were not wholly satisfied with the king, and believed he was not energetic enough for the situation. Many of the people wished to dethrone Ferdinand, and elevate his brother Carlos, or Charles, to his place. Several insurrections broke out, but they were failures. Of course this state of things did not create the best of feeling between Ferdinand and Carlos. The Bourbon family were governed by the Salic law, which excludes females from the throne. In 1830, the year in which Isabella the late queen, who was the daughter of Ferdinand VII., was born, Maria Christina induced her husband, the king, to abolish the Salic law. Two years later, when the king was very sick, the Church party compelled him to revoke the act; but he got better; and, as the *Cortes* had sanctioned the annulling of the Salic law, he destroyed the documents which had been extorted from him on his sick-bed. His queen had been made regent during his illness. When Ferdinand died, his daughter was proclaimed queen, in accordance with the programme, as Isabella II. Don Carlos had protested against his exclusion from the throne, and now he took up arms to enforce his right. In the Basque provinces he was proclaimed king, as Charles V. His arms were successful at first; but, though the war lasted seven years, it was a failure in the end.

"While the Carlist war was still raging, in 1836, a revolution in favor of a constitution broke out; and the next year that of 1812, with important amendments, was adopted by the *Cortes*, and ratified by the queen regent, for Isabella was a child of only six years. In 1841, Maria Christina having resigned, Espartero was appointed regent, by the *Cortes*, for the rest of the queen's minority. He was a progressive man, and his administration very largely promoted the prosperity of the country. The government had abolished convents, and confiscated the revenues of the Church; and this awakened the hostility of the clergy, who, for a time, prevented the sale of the property thus acquired. This question finally produced a rupture between Espartero and the clergy, resulting in a general insurrection. The regent fled to England, and the *Cortes* declared the queen to be of age when she was only thirteen years old. Espartero was recalled a few years later, and has since held many high offices. The pope eventually permitted the Church property to be sold; but the contest between the progressive and the conservative parties was continued for a long period. Narvaez, Serrano, General Prim, Castelar, and Espartero are the most prominent statesmen; and doubtless the last-named is the most able.

"The frequent insurrections gave the government

some excuse for ruling with little regard to the fundamental law of the land; and this led to another revolution in 1854, in favor of a little more constitution. The evil was corrected for the time; and the instrument adopted, or rather restored, is sometimes called the constitution of 1854. But the queen was a Bourbon, and seemed to be always in favor of tyrannical measures and of the party that advocated them; and the country has continued to be in a disorganized state largely on this account. She has been noted for the frequent changes of her ministers. A few years ago General Prim raised the standard of revolt; but the time for a change had not yet come, and the general was glad to escape into Portugal.

"The revolution of 1868 commenced with the fleet off Cadiz; but, the cry, 'Down with the Bourbons!' soon reached the army and the people, and the revolution was accomplished almost without opposition. The queen fled to France. A provisional government was organized, and an election of members of the *Cortes* was ordered to decide on the form of the new government. The *Cortes* met, and in May, 1869, decreed that the new government should be a monarchy. About the same time the crown was offered to King Louis of Portugal, who, however, declined it. Last June, Queen Isabella abdicated in favor of her son Alfonso, prince of the Asturias, who will be Alfonso XII. if he ever becomes king of Spain. Later in the year Prince Leopold, of Hohenzollern Sigmaringen, was invited to the throne. He was a relative of the king of Prussia; and, when he accepted the crown, it was a real grievance to France. Leopold was withdrawn from the candidacy; but this matter was made the pretext for the Franco-Prussian war now raging on the soil of France.

"But we read history in the newspapers for the latest details; and only last month the *Cortes* elected Amedeo, second son of the king of Italy, king of Spain. He has accepted the crown, and departed for his kingdom. We can wish him a prosperous reign; but in a country like Spain he will find that a crown is not a wreath of roses. I will not detain you longer, young gentlemen."

The professor bowed, and descended from his rostrum. Most of the students had given good attention to his discourse; for they desired to understand the history of the country they were about to visit.

Since Professor Mapps finished his lecture in the port of Barcelona, King Amedeo, after two long years of fruitless struggling with the enemies of Spain's peace and prosperity, renounced the crown for himself, his children, and successors. Nearly a year later Alfonso XII. was proclaimed king of Spain, and now occupies the throne. While the country was looking for a king, the third Carlist war was begun, — the last two led by the son of the original Don Carlos, — but it was a failure.

CHAPTER V.

A SUDDEN DISAPPEARANCE.

WHILE Professor Mapps was giving his lecture, or his "talk" as he preferred to call it, in the grand saloon of the steamer, quite a number of boats were pulling around the steamer, and the other vessels of the squadron, some of them containing boatmen looking for a job, and others, people who were curious to see the ship and her consorts. The several craft were not men-of-war or merchantmen; and they seemed to excite a great deal of curiosity. Not a few of the boats came up to the gangway, their occupants asking permission to go on board; but they were politely refused by the officers in charge.

Some of the boats carried lateen, or leg-of-mutton sails, which are used more than any other on the Mediterranean. A long yard, or spar, is slung at an angle of forty-five degrees, on a short mast, so that one-fourth of the spar is below and the rest above the mast. The sail is triangular, except that the part nearest to the tack is squared off. It is attached to the long yard on the hypothenuse side. On the larger craft, the sail is hauled out on the long spar, sliding on hanks, or rings. It is a picturesque rig; and some of the students who had a taste for boating were anxious to try their skill in handling a sail of this kind.

One of these feluccas, with two gentlemen in the stern, seemed to be more persistent than the others to obtain admission for its occupants on board of the Prince. Her huge sail was brailed up, and she had taken a berth at the gangway of the steamer. Peaks, the adult boatswain of the ship, obeyed his orders to the letter, and would not permit any one to put foot on the deck. One of the gentlemen who came off in her had ascended the accommodation steps, and insisted upon holding a parley with Peaks; but as the old salt understood only a few words of Spanish, and the stranger did not speak English, they did not get ahead very well. The boatswain resolutely but good-naturedly refused to let the visitor pass him, or to disturb the lecture by sending to the saloon for some one to act as interpreter. The gentleman obstinately declined to give up his point, whatever it was, and remained at the gangway till the students were dismissed from the exercise.

When the lecture was finished, Mr. Lowington came out of the saloon; and, as he passed the gangway, Peaks touched his cap, and, informed him that a Spaniard on the steps insisted upon coming on board.

"I don't understand his lingo, and can't tell what he is driving at," added Peaks.

"Somebody that wishes to visit the ship, probably," replied the principal.

"I have turned back more than fifty, but this one won't be turned back," continued Peaks, as Mr. Lowington stepped up to the gangway.

As soon as the Spanish gentleman saw him, he raised his hat, and addressed him in the politest terms, begging pardon for the intrusion. The principal invited him to come on board, and then immediately directed the people of the Josephine and Tritonia to return to their vessels. While the Tritonias were piping over the side, Mr. Lowington gave his attention to the visitor.

"Have you a student in your ship by the name of Enrique Raimundo?" asked the Spanish gentleman, after he had properly introduced the subject of his visit.

Mr. Lowington spoke Spanish, having learned it when he was on duty as a naval officer in the Mediterranean; but, as he had been out of practice for many years, he was not as fluent in the language as formerly. But he understood the question, and so did Raimundo, who happened to pass behind the principal, in company with Scott, at this interesting moment. Possibly his heart rose to his throat, as he heard his name mentioned; at any rate, after the history he had narrated to Scott, he could not help being greatly disturbed by the inquiry of the stranger. But he had the presence of mind to refrain from any demonstration, and went over the side into the cutter with his companions. If his handsome olive face was paler than usual, no one noticed the fact.

Mr. Lowington was a prudent man in the management of the affairs of the students under his care. When he heard the inquiry for the second master of the Tritonia, whom he knew to be a Spaniard, he at once concluded that the visitor was a friend or a relative of the young man. But it was no part of his policy to deliver over his pupils to their friends and relatives without fully understanding what he was doing. Persons claiming such relations might lead the students astray. They might be the agents of some of his rogues on board, who had resorted to this expedient to obtain a vacation on shore.

"Are you a relative of Raimundo?" was the first question the principal proposed to the stranger.

"No, I am not; but"—

Mr. Lowington failed to understand the rest of the reply made by the gentleman, for here his Spanish was at fault. The visitor was not a relative of Raimundo. If he had answered in the affirmative, the principal would have directed the Tritonia's boats to remain, so that the visitor could see the young man, if upon further explanation it was proper for him to do so. If the gentleman was not a relative, it was not advisable to disturb the routine of the squadron to oblige him. He could see Raimundo the next day, when he went on shore. The boats of the Josephine and the Tritonia were therefore permitted to return without any delay.

"*No hablo mucho Español*" (I do not speak much Spanish), said Mr. Lowington, laughing; "*y no comprendo*" (and I do not understand).

He then with the utmost politeness, as required in all intercourse with Spanish gentlemen, invited the visitor into the grand saloon, and sent for Professor Badois, the instructor in modern languages, to assist at the interview. The gentleman proved to be Don Francisco Castro, an *abogado*, or lawyer, who represented Don Alejandro, the lawful guardian of Enrique Raimundo. He claimed the body of his client's ward, the second master of the Tritonia. Even Professor Badois had some difficulty in comprehending the legal terms used by the *abogado;* but so much was made clear to the principal.

"I don't understand this business," said he. "I received the young man from Manuel Raimundo, his uncle in New York, who has always paid his tuition fees; and I hold myself responsible to him for the safe keeping of my pupil."

"Ah, but you are in Spain, and the young man is a Spaniard, subject to Spanish law," added Don Francisco, with a bland smile. "All the evidence will be presented to you, and you will be fully justified in giving up the young man."

Mr. Lowington was very much disturbed. He knew nothing of the circumstances of the case beyond what the lawyer told him; and he was very much perplexed by the situation. He called Dr. Winstock, who spoke Spanish even more fluently than Professor Badois, and asked his advice.

"If Don Alejandro is the lawful guardian of Raimundo, how happens the young man to be a resident of New York?" asked the surgeon, after the case had been fully explained to him.

The lawyer shrugged his shoulders, but smiled as blandly as ever.

"Don Manuel, the uncle of the boy, stole him from his guardian when he left his native land," said Don Francisco. "You see, the young man has a fortune of five million *reales;* and no doubt Don Manuel wants to get this money or a part of it."

"But Manuel Raimundo is one of the richest wine-merchants of New York," protested the principal.

The subject was discussed for half an hour longer. Don Francisco said he had sent agents to New York to obtain possession of the boy, and had kept the run of the squadron from the day the ward of his client had entered as a student. He had taken no action before, because he had been assured that the vessels would visit Spain, where there would be no legal difficulties in the way of securing his client's ward. The lawyer made a very plain case of it, and was entirely fair in every thing he proposed. He would not take Raimundo out of the vessel by force unless compelled to do so. The whole matter would be settled in the proper court, and the young man should have the best counsel in Spain.

"Very well, Don Francisco. I am much obliged to you for the courtesy with which you have managed your case so far," said Mr. Lowington. "I will employ counsel to-morrow to look up the matter in the interest of my pupil."

"But the young man, — what is to be done with him in the mean time?" asked the lawyer.

"He will be safe on board of the Tritonia."

"Pardon me, sir; but I have been looking for the boy too many years to let him slip through my fingers now," interposed Don Francisco earnestly, but with his constant smile. "If he hears that I am looking for him, he will keep out of my way, as he has done for several years."

"Do you wish to make a prisoner of him?" inquired the principal.

"No, no! By no means, — no prison! He shall have the best room in my house; but I must not lose sight of him."

"That would be taking possession of the young man without regard to any thing I may wish to do for him. I do not like that arrangement," added Mr. Lowington.

The courteous *abogado* seemed to be troubled. He did not wish to do any thing that would not be satisfactory to the "distinguished officer" before him; but, after considerable friendly argument, he proposed a plan which was accepted by the principal. The person who had come off in the boat with him was an *alguacil*, or constable, who had been empowered to arrest Don Alejandro's ward. Would the principal allow this official to remain on board of the vessel with Raimundo, and keep an eye on him all the time? Mr. Lowington did not object to this arrangement. He would go with Don Francisco to the Tritonia, where the situation could be explained to Raimundo, and the *alguacil* should occupy a state-room with his charge, if he desired. The principal treated his guest with distinguished consideration; and the first cutter was lowered to convey him to the Tritonia. Dr. Winstock accompanied the party; the twelve oars of the first cutter dropped into the water with mechanical precision, to the great admiration of the Spanish gentlemen; and the boat darted off from the ship's side.

In a moment the cutter was alongside the Tritonia, and the party went on board of her. Most of the officers were on the quarter-deck, and Mr. Lowington looked among them for the second master. All hands raised their caps to the principal as soon as he appeared on the deck.

"Captain Wainwright, I wish to see Mr. Raimundo," said he to the young commander. "Send for him, if you please."

"Mr. Raimundo," repeated the captain, touching his cap. "Mr. Richards, pass the word for Mr. Raimundo."

The first master, who had been designated, went to look for the young Spaniard. His name was repeated all over the deck, and through the cabin and steerage; but Raimundo did not respond to the call. A vigorous search was made in every part of the vessel; yet the second master was still missing. Don Francisco's constant courtesy seemed to be somewhat shaken. Inquiries were made of all the other officers in regard to the second master. They had seen him on the deck after the return of the boats from the Prince. Scott had left him in the cabin, half an hour before; but he had not the least idea what had become of him. Don Francisco spoke French and Italian; and he examined O'Hara in the latter, and several other officers in the former language.

Mr. Lowington explained that he had sent no one to the Tritonia to inform Raimundo that he was wanted; and the *alguacil*, who had remained in the felucca all the time till he took his place in the first cutter, assured the lawyer that no one had gone from the steamer to the schooner after all the boats left.

The principal and the vice-principal were as much perplexed as the lawyer. None of them could alter the fact that Raimundo was missing; and they were utterly unable to account for his mysterious disappearance. All of them were confident that the absentee would soon be found; and the *abogado* returned to the shore, leaving the *alguacil* in the Tritonia to continue the search.

CHAPTER VI.

A LOOK AT BARCELONA.

THE sudden disappearance of Raimundo produced the greatest astonishment on board of the Tritonia, and not less among those who knew him best in the other vessels of the squadron. His character had been excellent since he first joined the academy squadron. No one believed he had run away for the mere sake of escaping the study and discipline of his vessel, or for the sake of "a time" on shore. The *abogado's* business was explained to Mr. Pelham on board of the Tritonia, but to no others. Raimundo was gone without a doubt; but when, where, or how he had disappeared, was a profound mystery.

The excellent character of Raimundo, and the fact that he was a universal favorite, were strongly in his favor; and no one was disposed to render a harsh judgment in regard to his singular conduct. The officers talked it over in the cabin, the seamen talked it over in the steerage. The students could make nothing of the matter; and it looked to them very much like the usual cases of running away, strange as it seemed to them that a fellow like Raimundo, who had been a model of good conduct on board, should take such a step.

Of course Scott was an exception to the general rule. Though he knew not where his friend had gone, he understood why he had disappeared; for Raimundo had told him what he had heard on board of the American Prince, and he was fully satisfied that the stranger had come for him.

"I think the matter is fully explained," said Professor Crumples, in the state-room. "A demand has been made on the principal for Raimundo; and straightway Raimundo disappears. It is plain enough to me that the young man knew the lawyer was after him."

"But how could he know it?" demanded Professor Primback.

"That I cannot explain; but I am satisfied that a student like Raimundo would not run away. He has not gone for a frolic, or to escape his duty: he is not one of that sort," persisted Professor Crumples.

"I think you are right, Mr. Crumples," added the vice-principal. "Raimundo was a bad boy, or at least full of mischief and given to a lark, before he joined the institution; but for more than a year his deportment has been perfectly exemplary. He has been a model since I have had charge of this vessel. I have found that those who have really reformed are often stiffer and more determined in their zeal to do right than many who have never left the straight path of duty. I may say that I know this fact from experience. I am satisfied that Raimundo had some very strong motive for the step he has taken. But what you say, Mr. Crumples, suggests a little further inquiry into the matter."

The vice-principal spoke Spanish, and he immediately sent for the *alguacil* to join the trio in the state-room.

"Had the boats belonging to this vessel left the steamer when Don Francisco went on board of her?" asked Mr. Pelham as the Spanish officer entered the room.

"No, sir: not a boat had left the steamer when Don Francisco was permitted to go on the deck of the steamer," replied the *alguacil* promptly. "He waited on the steps, at the head of which the big officer stood, for more than an hour; and I was in the boat at the foot of the steps all the time. I counted eight boats made fast to the boom; and I am sure that no one left the steamer till after Don Francisco had been admitted on board. I saw all the boys get into these boats, and pull away to this vessel and the other."

"Then Don Francisco was on the deck of the steamer at the same time that our ship's company were there," added Mr. Pelham.

"No doubt of that," replied the *alguacil*, who appeared to desire that no suspicion of foul play on the part of the officers or the principal should be encouraged.

"Now, if I could find any one who noticed the conduct of Raimundo on board of the steamer, we might get at something," continued the vice-principal.

"I think you can easily find such a one," suggested Professor Crumples. "Lieutenant Scott and Raimundo are fast friends; they are in the same quarter-watch, and appear to be great cronies."

"I was thinking of him when you spoke.— Mr. Scott," called the vice-principal, when he had opened the door of the state-room.

Scott was in the cabin, and presented himself at the door. He was requested to come in, and the door was closed behind him.

"Were you with Raimundo on board of the steamer?" asked Mr. Pelham.

Scott was fully determined not to do or say any thing that would injure his friend, even if he were sent to the brig for his fidelity to the absent shipmate; and he hesitated long enough to consider the effect of any thing he might say.

"We are all friends of Raimundo, and do not wish to harm him," added the vice-principal. "You have already said you did not know where Raimundo was."

"I do not."

"Do you object to answering the question I asked?"

"I do not," replied Scott, who had by this time made up his mind that the truth could not harm his friend. "I was with Raimundo all the time he was on board of the steamer. We went in the same boat, and returned together."

"Did you notice the gentleman that came on board of the Tritonia with Mr. Lowington?"

"I did. He was on deck here half an hour, or more."

"Did you see him on board of the American Prince?"

"I did. He spoke to the principal just as Raimundo and I passed behind him."

"Behind whom?"

"Behind the principal. I looked the gentleman in the face while he was speaking to Mr. Lowington."

"Do you know what he said?"

"I can walk Spanish, but I can't talk Spanish; and so I couldn't understand him."

"You don't know what he said, then?"

Scott hesitated again.

"I don't say that."

"But you intimated that you did not understand Spanish."

"I do know what the gentleman said as I passed him," replied Scott.

"How could you know, without understanding the language he spoke?"

"Raimundo told me what he said; and he could understand Spanish if I could not."

"Ah, indeed! Raimundo told you! Well, what did he tell you the gentleman said?" asked the vice-principal earnestly.

"He told me he heard the gentleman ask the principal if he had a student under his care by the name of Enrique Raimundo: that's all he heard, and that's all he told me about the gentleman," replied Scott, who had said so much because he believed that this information would do his absent shipmate more good than harm.

"That explains it all," added Mr. Pelham; and he informed the *alguacil* what Scott had said.

This was all the vice-principal had expected to show by Scott; and he was entirely satisfied with the information he had obtained, not suspecting that the third lieutenant knew any thing more about the matter. Mr. Pelham and the rest of the party asked Scott some more questions in regard to the conduct of the absentee after he came on board of the Tritonia; but

Raimundo had taken care that his friend should know nothing at all about his intended movements, and the lieutenant was as ignorant of them as any other person on board. To his intense relief he was dismissed without having betrayed the confidence of his friend in the slightest degree.

Scott knew the whole story of the young Spaniard; and he was confident that the principal and the vice-principal, if not the professors, had learned at least Don Alejandro's side of it from the stranger; and he felt that he was relieving his friend from the charge of being a runaway, in the ordinary acceptation of the term, by showing that Raimundo knew that some one was after him.

The exciting topic was discussed by all hands till the anchor-watch was set, and the rest of the ship's company had turned in. Even Bill Stout and Bark Lingall in the brig had heard the news, for Ben Pardee had contrived to communicate it to them on the sly; and they discussed it in whispers, as well as another more exciting question to them, after all hands below were asleep. Bill was fully determined to repeat the wicked experiment which had so providentially failed that day.

"Bark is willin'," added that worthy, when the plan had been fully considered.

The *alguacil* visited every part of the vessel, attended by the vice-principal, before he retired for the night. The next morning, all hands were mustered on deck, and the search was repeated. This time the hold was visited; but no sign of the fugitive could be found. The *alguacil* protested that he was sure no attempt had been made by any person on board to conceal the absentee; for every facility had been afforded him to see for himself.

Breakfast had been ordered at an early hour; for it was understood that all hands were to go on shore, and see what little there was to be seen in Barcelona. Before the meal was finished, the principal came on board with Don Francisco. The *alguacil* reported to his employer what he had done, and described the thorough search which had been made for the missing ward. The principal offered to do any thing the lawyer would suggest in order to find Raimundo. No one could imagine how he had left the vessel, though it seemed to be a settled conviction with all that he had left. Don Francisco could suggest nothing; but he insisted that the *alguacil* should remain on the vessel, to which the principal gladly assented.

Don Francisco was sent on shore in good style in the first cutter of the Prince; and, as soon as breakfast was over in the Tritonia, the principal directed that all hands should be mustered in the waist.

"Young gentlemen," said Mr. Lowington, as soon as the students had assembled, "I spent last evening, and the greater part of last night, in devising a plan by which all hands in the fleet may see the most interesting portions of Spain and Portugal."

This announcement was received with a demonstration of applause, which was permitted and even enjoyed by the faculty; for it had long before been proved that the boys were honest and sincere in their expressions of approbation, and that they withheld their tribute when they were not satisfied with the announcement, or the programme, whatever it was. The principal bowed in acknowledgment of the applause.

"I am well aware that some of the interior towns of Spain possess more interest than any on the seacoast; and therefore I have decided that you shall see both. You will spend to-morrow in seeing Barcelona, which may easily be seen in one day by those who do not wish to make a critical survey of the country. To-night the ship's company of the American Prince will depart for Saragossa; and will visit Burgos, Valladolid, the Escurial, Madrid, Toledo, Badajos, and thence through Portugal to Lisbon, from which they may go to Cintra and other places. They will reach Lisbon in about two weeks. To-morrow morning the ship's company of the Tritonia and that of the Josephine will be sent in the steamer direct to Lisbon, from which place they will make the tour, reversed, back to Barcelona. The ship's company of the American Prince will return to Barcelona in their own vessel, which will wait for them at Lisbon. When all hands are on board again, the squadron will sail along the coast, visiting Valencia, Alicante, Carthagena, Malaga, Gibraltar, and Cadiz; and another interior trip will be made to Granada, Cordova, and Seville. This plan will enable you to see about the whole of Spain. Then we shall have visited nearly every country in Europe. To-day will be used in coaling the steamer, and you will go on shore as soon as you are ready."

This speech was finished with another demonstration of applause; and the principal immediately returned to the Prince, alongside of which several coal-barges had already taken their places. The students had put on their go-ashore uniforms, and were in readiness to take a nearer view of the city. The officers and crew of the Prince had packed their bags for the two weeks' trip through Spain, and her boats were now pulling to the landing-place near the foot of the *Rambla*. Those of the Josephine and Tritonia soon folfowed them.

The *alguacil* remained on board of the Tritonia. He had a recent photograph of Raimundo, obtained in New York by Don Alejandro's agent; and he was confident that the fugitive had not left the vessel with the rest of the students. As it was necessary for the adult boatswain and carpenter, Marline and Rimmer, to go on shore with the boats in order to take charge of them, the two prisoners in the brig were left in care of the head steward. When the vessel was deserted by all but the cooks and stewards, the *alguacil* made another diligent search for the ward of his employer, but with no better success than before. He tried to talk with Salter, the chief steward; but that individual did not know a word of Spanish, and he did not get ahead very fast. In the course of an hour, he seemed to be disgusted with his occupation, and, calling a shore boat, he left the Tritonia. Probably Don Rancisco had directed him to use his own judgment as to the time he was to remain on board.

Mr. Salter was the chief steward of the Tritonia, and he had a great deal of business of his own to attend to, so that he could not occupy himself very closely in looking after the marines in the brig. He was obliged to make up his accounts, which were required to be as accurately and methodically kept as though the vessel were a man-of-war. His desk was in the cabin, for he was an officer of no little consequence on board. Though the passage-way between the cabin and the steerage was open, he could not see, from the place where he was seated, what the prisoners were about, or hear their conversation. They had their books in the brig, though they did not study their neglected lessons. But what they said and what they did must be reserved till a later time in the day; for it would not be fair to leave all the good students to wander about Barcelona without any attention.

The boats landed, and for the first time the young voyagers stood on the soil of Spain. Captain Wainwright, Scott, and O'Hara were among those who were permitted to take care of themselves, while not a few were in charge of the vice-principals and the professors. Those who were privileged to go where they pleased without any supervision chose their own companions. Scott and O'Hara were inclined to train in the same company; and Captain Sheridan and Lieutenant Murray of the steamer, with whom both of them had been formerly very intimate, hailed them as they came on shore. The four formed a party for the day. It was a very desirable party too, for the reason that Dr. Winstock, an old traveller in Spain, as indeed he was in all the countries of Europe, was as great a crony of Sheridan as he once had been of Paul Kendall, the first captain of the Josephine, and a commander of the Young America. The surgeon shook hands with Scott and O'Hara, and then led the way to the *Rambla*, which is the broad avenue extending through the centre of the city.

"Barcelona, I suppose you know, young gentlemen,

is the second city in Spain in population, and has nearly or quite two hundred thousand inhabitants," said the doctor, as the party entered the *Rambla*. "It is by far the most important commercial city, and is quite a manufacturing place besides. There are several cotton, silk, and woollen mills outside of the walls; and ten years ago the imports of cotton from the United States were worth nearly five millions of dollars."

"What do you call our country in Spanish, doctor?" asked Sheridan.

"*Los Estados Unidos de America*," replied Dr. Winstock. "By the way, O'Hara, do you speak Spanish?"

"No, sir: I spake only Oyrish and Oytalian," laughed the fourth lieutenant of the Tritonia.

"Though Spanish and Italian are very much alike, each of them seems to be at war with the other. Ford, in Murray's Hand-book for Spain, says that a knowledge of Italian will prove a constant stumbling-block in learning Spanish. I found it so myself. Before I came to Spain the first time I could speak the language very well, and talked it whole evenings with my professor. Then I took lessons in Italian; but I soon found my Spanish so confused and confounded that I could not speak it at all."

"Then I won't try to learn Spanish," added O'Hara.

"Here is the post-office on your right, and the *Teatro Principal* on the left; but it is not the principal theatre at the present time."

"This street — I suppose they would call it a boulevard in Paris — is not unlike '*Unter den Linden*' in Berlin," said Murray. "It has the rows of trees in the middle."

"But the time to visit the *Rambla* is just before night on a pleasant day, when it is crowded with people. Barcelona is not so thoroughly Spanish as some other cities of Spain — Madrid and Seville, for instance. The people are quite different from the traditional Spaniard, who is too dignified and proud to engage in commerce or to work at any honest business; while the Catalans are an industrious and thriving people, first-rate sailors, quick, impulsive, and revolutionary in their character. They are more like Frenchmen than Spaniards."

"There is a square up that narrow street," said Sheridan.

"That's the *Plaza Real*, — Royal Square, — surrounded by houses with arcades, like the *Palais Royal* in Paris. In the centre of it is a fine monument, dedicated to the Catholic kings, as distinguished from the Moorish sovereigns, and dedicated to Ferdinand and Isabella; and you remember that Catalonia became a part of Aragon, and was annexed to Castile by the marriage of their respective sovereigns. This is the *Rambla del Centro*, for this broad avenue has six names in its length of three-quarters of a mile. Here is the *Calle Fernando* on our right, which is the next street in importance to the *Rambla*, and, like it, has several names for its different parts. Now we have the *Teatro del Lico* on our left, which is built on the plan of *La Scala* at Milan, and is said to be the largest theatre in Europe, seating comfortably four thousand people."

Dr. Winstock continued to point out the various objects of interest on the way; but most of them were more worthy to be looked at than to be written about.

The party walked the entire length of the *Rambla* to the *Plaza de Cataluña*, which is a small park, with a fountain in the centre. Taking another street, they reached a point near the centre of the city, where the cathedral is located. It is a Gothic structure, built in the fourteenth and fifteenth centuries. In 1519 Charles V. presided in the choir of this church over a general assembly of the Knights of the Golden Fleece. Under the high altar is the crypt or tomb of St. Eulalia, the patron saint of the city. She suffered martyrdom in the fourth century; and it is said that her remains were discovered five hundred years after her death, by the sweet odor they emitted. Her soul ascended to heaven in the visible form of a dove.

Near the cathedral, on the *Plaza de la Constitucion*, or Constitution Square, are the Town Hall and the Parliament House, in which the commons of Catalonia met before it became a part of the kingdom of Aragon. Between this square and the *Rambla* is the church of *Santa Maria del Pino*, Gothic, built a little later than the cathedral. Its name is derived from a tradition that the image of the Virgin was found in the trunk of a pine-tree, and because this tree is the emblem of the Catholic faith, ever green and ever pointing to heaven. On the altars of two of its chapels, Jews were allowed to take an oath in any suit with a Christian, or to establish the validity of a will, and for similar purposes. In another church Hebrews are permitted to take oath on the Ten Commandments, placed on an altar.

The party visited several other churches, and finally reached the great square near the head of the port, on which are located the Royal Palace, the Exchange, and the Custom House; but there is nothing remarkable about them. There are fifty fountains in the city, the principal of which is in the palace square. It is an allegorical representation of the four provinces of Catalonia.

"There is not much to see in Barcelona," said Dr. Winstock, as they walked along the sea-wall, in the resort called the *Muralla del Mar*. "This is a commercial city, and you do not see much that is distinctively Spanish. Commerce with other nations is very apt to wear away the peculiarities of any people."

"But where are the Spaniards? I don't think I have seen any of them," added Sheridan.

"Probably most of the people you have met in our walk were Spaniards," replied the doctor.

"Don't we see the national costume?"

"You will have to go to a bull-fight to see that," laughed the surgeon; "and then only the men who take part in the spectacle will wear the costume. The audience will be dressed in about the same fashion you have seen all over Europe. Perhaps if you go over into Barceloneta you will find some men clothed in the garb of the Catalans."

"Shall we see a bull-fight?" asked Scott.

"Not in Barcelona. I suppose, if there should be an opportunity, the principal would allow all who wished to see it to do so; for it is a Spanish institution, and the traveller ought not to leave Spain without seeing one. But it is a sickening sight; and, after you have seen one or two poor old horses gored to death by the bull, you will not care to have any more of it. The people of this city are not very fond of the sport; and the affair is tame here compared with the bull-fights of Madrid and Seville."

At three o'clock those of the party who belonged to the steamer departed for Saragossa. Scott and O'Hara wandered about the city the rest of the day, visiting Barceloneta, and taking an outside view of the bull-ring, or *Plaza de Toros*, which is about the same thing as in all the other large cities of the country. They dined at a French restaurant in the *Rambla*, where they did not go hungry for the want of a language. At an early hour they returned to the Tritonia, where they were to spend another night before their departure in the American Prince.

CHAPTER VII.

FIRE AND WATER.

"WHAT'S going on, Bark?" asked Bill Stout, as all hands were called to go on shore; and perhaps this was the hundredth time this question had been put by one or the other of the occupants of the brig since the ship's company turned out that morning.

"All hands are going on shore," replied Bark Lingall. "I hope they will have a good time; and I am thankful that I am not one of them, to be tied to the coat-tail of Professor Primback."

The marines knew all about the events that had transpired on board of the vessel since she anchored, including the strange disappearance of Raimundo. Ben Pardee had contrived to tell them all they wanted to know, while most of the students were on deck. But he and Lon Gibbs had not been informed of the conspiracy to burn the Tritonia. Bark had simply told them that "something was up," and they must do some mischief to get committed to the brig before they could take a hand in the game. Lon and Ben had talked the matter over between themselves, and were ready to do as required till the orders came for the Josephines and the Tritonias to proceed to Lisbon in the Prince. The voyage in the steamer had too many attractions to permit them to lose it. They had done better in their lessons than Bill and Bark, who had purposely neglected theirs.

"I should not object to the voyage in the Prince," said Bark.

"Nor I, if I had known about it; but it is too late now to back out. We are in for it, — in the brig. We shall have a better chance to get off when all the professors are away," added Bill.

"There don't appear to be any one taking care of us just now," said Bark, after he had looked through the bars of the prison, and satisfied himself that no one but themselves was in the steerage. "Marline had to go on shore with the crowd to take care of the boats; and so had the carpenter."

"Some one has the care of us, I know," replied Bill. "But I can soon find out."

Bill Stout began to pound on the slats of the cage; and the noise soon brought the chief steward to the brig.

"What are you about in there?" demanded Mr. Salter.

"I want to see Mr. Marline or Mr. Rimmer," replied Bill, meekly enough.

"They are both gone on shore to take charge of the boats, and won't be back till night," added Salter. "What do you want?"

"I want a drink of water: I am almost choked," answered Bill.

"You don't want Mr. Rimmer for that," said Salter, as he left the brig.

In a moment he returned with a pitcher of water, which he handed into the cage through the slide. Having done this, he returned to the cabin to resume his work.

"I'll bet he is alone on board!" exclaimed Bill, as soon as Salter had gone.

"I think not," replied Bark.

"Why did he bring the water himself, then?"

"I don't know; perhaps the stewards are all on deck."

"No: he always lets most of his men go on shore when we are in port. I don't believe there is more than one of them on board," continued Bill, with no little excitement in his manner.

"I heard some one walking on deck since the boats went off. It may have been Salter; but I am sure he is not alone on board."

"No matter, if there are only two or three left. Now is our time, Bark!" whispered Bill Stout.

"We may be burnt up in the vessel: we are locked into the brig," suggested Bark.

"No danger of that. When the fire breaks out, Salter will unlock the door of the cage. If he don't we can break it down."

"What then?" queried Bark. "Every boat belonging to the vessel is gone, and we might get singed in the scrape."

"Nonsense, Bark! At the worst we could swim ashore to that old lighthouse."

"Well, what are we going to do then? We wear the uniform of the fleet, and we shall be known wherever we go," added the more prudent Bark.

"You have money enough, and so have I. All we have to do is to buy a suit of clothes apiece, and then we shall be all right."

They discussed the matter for half an hour longer. Bark was willing to admit that the time for putting the villanous scheme in operation was more favorable than any that was likely to be afforded them in the future. Though the professors were all on shore, they believed they could easily keep out of their way in a city so large as Barcelona.

"Suppose Salter should come into the steerage when you are down in the hold?" suggested Bark.

"That would be bad," replied Bill, shaking his head. "But we must take some risk. We will wait till he comes in to take a look at us, and then I will do the job. He won't come in again for half an hour; for I suppose he is busy in the cabin, as he always is while we are in port."

They had to wait half an hour more before the chief steward came into the steerage. Though he intended to be a faithful officer, Mr. Salter was wholly absorbed in his accounts, and he did not like to leave them even for a moment. He went into the steerage far enough to see that both of the prisoners were safe in the cage, and hastened back to his desk.

"We are all right now," whispered Bill, as he bent down to the scuttle that led into the hold.

"If you make any noise at all the chief steward will hear you," replied Bark, hardly less excited than his companion in villany.

Bill raised the trap-door with the utmost care. As he made no noise, Mr. Salter heard none. Bill had his matches all ready, with the paper he had prepared for the purpose. He had taken off his shoes, so as to make no noise on the steps. He was not absent from the brig more than two minutes, and Salter was still absorbed in his accounts. Bark carefully adjusted the scuttle when Bill came up; and he could smell the burning straw as he did so.

Bill put on his shoes with all the haste he could, without making any noise; and both the conspirators tried to look as though nothing had happened, or was about to happen. They were intensely excited, of course, for they expected the flames would burst up through the cabin floor in a few moments. Bark looked over the slats of the cage to find where the weakest of them were, so as to be ready, in case it should be necessary, to break out.

"Do you smell the fire?" asked Bill, when his anxiety had become so great that he could no longer keep still.

"I did smell it when the scuttle was off; but I don't smell it now," replied Bark.

"What was that noise?" asked Bill.

Both of them had heard it, and it seemed to be in the hold. They could not tell what it was like, only that it was a noise.

"What could it be?" mused Bill. "It was in the hold, and not far from the foot of the ladder."

"Perhaps it was the noise of the fire," suggested Bark. "It may have burned away so that one of the boxes tumbled down."

"That must have been it," replied Bill, satisfied with this plausible explanation. "But why don't the fire break out? It is time for it to show itself, for fire travels fast."

"I suppose it has not got a-going yet. Very likely the straw and stuff is damp, and does not burn very freely."

"It will be a sure thing this time, for I saw the blaze rising when I came up the ladder," added Bill.

"And I saw it myself also."

"But it ought to be a little hot by this time," replied Bill, who began to have a suspicion that every thing was not working according to the programme.

"You know best how you fixed things down below. The fire may have burned the straw all up without lighting the ceiling of the vessel."

At least ten minutes had elapsed since the match had been applied to the combustibles, and it was certainly time that the fire should begin to appear in the steerage. But there was no fire, and not even the smell of fire, to be perceived. The conspirators were astonished at the non-appearance of the blaze; and after waiting ten minutes more they were satisfied that the fire was not making any progress.

"It is a failure again," said Bark Lingall. "There will be no conflagration to-day."

"Yes, there will, if I have to set it a dozen times," replied Bill Stout, setting his teeth firmly together. "I don't understand it. I certainly saw the blaze before I left the hold; and I couldn't have done the job any better if I had tried for a week."

"You did it all right, without a doubt; but a fire will not always burn after you touch it off," answered Bark, willing to console his companion in his failure.

"I will go down again, and see what the matter is, at any rate. If I can't get up a blaze in the hold, I will see what I can do in one of the mess-rooms," added Bill stoutly.

"How can you get into one of the mess-rooms?" asked Bark. "You forget that we are locked into the brig."

"No, I don't forget it; but you seem to forget that we can go down into the hold, and go up by the forward scuttle into the steerage."

"You are right, Bill. I did not think of that," said Bark. "And you can also go aft, and up by the after scuttle into the cabin. I remember now that there are three ways to get into the hold."

"I haven't forgot it for a moment," added Bill, with something like triumph in his tones. "I am going down once more to see why the blaze didn't do as it was expected to do."

"Not yet, Bill. Wait till Salter has been into the steerage again."

"It isn't twenty minutes since he was here; and he will not come again for half an hour at least."

Bill Stout felt that he had done enough, and had proved that he knew enough, to entitle him to have his own way. Raising the scuttle, he descended into the hold. He did not dare to remain long, lest the chief steward should come into the steerage, and discover that he was not in the brig. But he remained long enough to ascertain the reason why the fire did not burn; and, filled with amazement, he returned to communicate the discovery he had made to his fellow-conspirator. When he had closed the trap, and turned around to confront Bark, his face was the very picture of astonishment and dismay.

"Well, what's the matter, Bill?" asked Bark, who could not help seeing the strange expression on the countenance of his shipmate.

"Matter enough! I should say that the Evil One was fighting against us, Bark," replied his companion.

"I should say that the Evil One is fighting on the other side, if on either," added Bark. "But what have you found?"

"The fire is out, and the straw and other stuff feels just as though a bucket of water had been thrown upon it. At any rate, it is wet," answered Bill.

"Nonsense! no water could have been thrown upon it."

"How does it happen to be wet, then?"

"The hold of a vessel is apt to be a damp place."

"Damp! I tell you it was wet!" protested Bill; and the mysterious circumstance seemed to awe and alarm him.

"Certainly no water could have been thrown upon the fire," persisted Bark.

"How happens it to be wet, then? That's what I want to know."

"Do you think any water was thrown on the straw?"

"I don't see how it could have been; but I know it was wet," replied Bill.

"Very likely the dry stuff burned off, and the wet straw would not take fire," suggested Bark, who was good for accounting for strange things.

"That may be; I did not think of that," mused Bill. "But there is a pile of old dunnage on the starboard side, and some more straw and old boxes and things there; and I will try it on once more. I have got started, and I'm going to do the job if I hang for it."

"Wait till Salter has been in again before you go below," said Bark.

Bill was content to wait. To his desire for freedom, was added the feeling of revenge for being committed to the brig when all hands were about to make a voyage in the Prince. He was determined to destroy the Tritonia, — more determined than when he first attempted the crime. In a short time the chief steward made another visit to the steerage, and again returned to the cabin.

"Now is my time," said Bill, when he was satisfied that Salter had reached the cabin.

"Be careful this time," added Bark, as he raised the scuttle.

"I shall be careful, but I shall make a sure thing of it," replied Bill, stepping upon the narrow ladder, and descending.

Bill Stout was absent full five minutes this time; and, when he returned to the brig, he had not lighted the train that was to complete the destruction of the Tritonia.

"I had no paper, and I could not make a blaze," said he. "Have you a newspaper about you, Bill?"

"No, I have not: I do not carry papers around with me."

"What shall I do? I can't light the rubbish without something that is entirely dry."

"Here," answered Bark, picking up one of the neglected text-books on the floor. "You can get as much paper as you want out of this book."

"But that won't do," replied Bill. "I thought you were a very prudent fellow."

"So I am."

"If I should miss fire again, and this book or any part of it should be found in the pile, it would blow the whole thing upon us."

"Tear out a lot of the leaves; and they will be sure to be burnt, if you light them with the match."

As no other paper could be obtained, Bill consented to tear out some of the leaves of the book, and use them for his incendiary purpose. Bark declared that what was left of it would soon be in ashes, and there was nothing to fear as to its being a telltale against them. Once more Bill descended into the hold; and, as he had made every thing ready during his last visit, he was absent only long enough to light the paper, and thrust it into the pile of combustibles he had gathered. He had placed several small sticks of pine, which had been split to kindle the fire in the galley, on the heap of rubbish, in order to give more body to the fire when it was lighted. He paused an instant to see the flame rise from the pile, and then fled up the ladder.

"Hurry up!" whispered Bark at the scuttle. "I hear Salter moving about in the cabin."

But the trap-door was returned to its place before the chief steward appeared; and he only looked into the steerage.

"The job is done this time, you may bet your life!" exclaimed Bill, as he seated himself on his stool, and tried to look calm and self-possessed.

"I saw the blaze," added Bark. "Let's look down, and see if it is going good."

"No, no!" protested Bill earnestly. "We don't want to run a risk for nothing."

Both of the young villains waited with throbbing hearts for the bursting out of the flames, which they thought would run up the ceiling of the vessel, and communicate the fire to the berths on the starboard side of the steerage. Five minutes — ten minutes — a quarter of an hour, they waited for the catastrophe; but no smoke, no flame, appeared. Bill Stout could not understand it again. Another quarter of an hour they waited, but less confidently than before.

"No fire yet, Bill," said Bark, with a smile.

"I don't know what it means," replied the puzzled incendiary. "You saw the fire, and so did I; and I can't see why the blaze don't come up through the deck."

"It is very odd, Bill; and I can't see through it any better than you can," added Bark. "It don't look as though we were to have a burn to-day."

"We are bound to have it!" insisted Bill Stout. "I shall try next time in one of the mess-rooms."

"With all the pains and precautions to prevent fire on board, it seems that the jolly craft won't burn. No fellow has been allowed to have a match, or even to take a lantern into the hold; and now you can't make the vessel burn when you try with all your might."

"The Evil One is working against us," continued Bill, who could make no other explanation of the repeated failures.

"If he is, he is on the wrong side; for we have done nothing to make him desert us," laughed Bark. "We certainly deserve better of him."

"I am going below to see what was the matter this time," added Bill, as he raised the trap-door.

Bark offered no opposition to his purpose, and Bill went down the ladder. He was not gone more than a couple of minutes this time; and when he returned he looked as though he had just come out of the abode of the party who was working against him. He seemed to be transfixed with wonder and surprise; and for a moment he stood in silence in the presence of his fellow-conspirator.

"What's the matter with you, Bill? You look like a stuck pig that has come back to haunt the butcher," said Bark, trying to rally his associate. "Did you see any spirits in the hold? This is a temperance ship, and the principal don't allow any on board."

"You may laugh, Bark, if you like; but I believe the evil spirit is in the hold," replied Bill impressively.

"What makes you think so, Bill?"

"The pile of rubbish is as wet as water can make it. Do you suppose there is any one in the hold?"

"Who could be there?" demanded Bark.

"I don't know; but it seems to me some one is down there, who puts water on the fire every time I light it. I can't explain it in any other way."

"Nonsense! No one could by any possibility be in the hold. If any one of the stewards had gone down, we should have seen him."

After more discussion neither of the conspirators was willing to believe there was any person in the hold. It was not a place a man would be likely to stay in any longer than he was compelled to do so. It was partially ventilated by a couple of small shafts, and very dimly lighted by four small panes of heavy glass set in the cabin and steerage floors, under the skylights. It was not more than four feet high where the greatest elevation was had; that is, between the dunnage that covered the ballast, and the timbers on which the floors of the between-decks rested. It was not a desirable place for any one to remain in, though there was nothing in it that was destructive to human life. It was simply a very dingy and uncomfortable retreat for a human being.

"I am going to try it on just once more," said Bill Stout, after his suspicions of a supernatural interference had subsided. "I know there was water thrown on the pile of rubbish. It seems to me the Evil One must have used a fire-engine on the heap, after I had lighted the fire. But I am going to know about it this time, if I am condemned to the brig for the rest of my natural life. There is quite a pile of old boxes and cases split up in the hold, ready for use in the galley. I am going to touch off this heap of wood, and stand by till I see it well a-going. I want you to shut the door when I go down next time; for Salter will not come in for half an hour or more. I am going to see what puts the fire out every time I light it."

"But suppose Salter comes into the steerage, and finds you are not here: what shall I say to him?"

"Tell him I am in the hold, — any thing you please. I don't care what becomes of me now."

Bill Stout raised the trap-door, and descended; and, in accordance with the instructions of that worthy, Bark closed it as soon as his head disappeared below the steerage floor. Bill lighted up the pile of kindling-wood ; and then, with a quantity of leaves he had torn from the book, he set fire to the heap of combustibles. The blaze rose from the pile, and promised that the result that the conspirators had been laboring to produce would be achieved. True to the plan he had arranged, Bill waited, and watched the blaze he had kindled ; but the fire had scarcely lighted up the gloomy hold, before a bucket of water was dashed on the pile of wood, and the flames were completely extinguished. There was somebody in the hold, after all ; and Bill was almost paralyzed when he realized the fact.

The fire was put out ; and the solitary fireman of the hold moved aft. Bill watched him, and was unable to determine whether he was a human being, or a spirit from the other world. But he was desperate to a degree he had never been before. He stooped down over the extinguished combustibles to ascertain whether they were really wet, or whether some magic had quenched the flame which a minute before had promised to make an end of the Tritonia. The water still hung in drops on the kindling-wood. He stirred up the wood, and lighted another match, which he applied to the dryest sticks he could find.

"What are you about, you villain ? Do you mean to burn the vessel ? " demanded a voice near him, the owner of which instantly stamped out the fire with his feet.

The mystery was solved ; for Bill recognized the voice of Raimundo, whose mysterious disappearance had excited so much astonishment on board of the vessel.

CHAPTER VIII.

SARAGOSSA AND BURGOS.

THE ship's company of the American Prince departed from Barcelona at three o'clock in the afternoon, for Saragossa, or Zaragoza as the Spaniards spell it. At first the route was through a beautiful and highly cultivated country, and then into the mountains. By five o'clock it was too dark to see the landscape; and the students, tired after the labors of the day, were disposed to settle themselves into the easiest positions they could find, and many of them went to sleep.

At Manresa the train stopped for supper, which was all ready for the students when they arrived. Mr. Lowington had employed four experienced couriers for the double tour across the peninsula. One was to precede each of the two parties to engage accommodations, and make terms with landlords, railroad agents, and others; and one was to attend each party to render such service as might be required of him. The journeys were all arranged beforehand, so that trains were to have extra cars, and meals were to be ready at stations and hotels.

The train arrived at Saragossa just before four o'clock in the morning. The cars, or carriages as they are called in Europe, were precisely like those in use in

England. Only six persons were put in each compartment; and the boys contrived various plans to obtain comfortable positions for sleeping. Some of them spread their overcoats on the floor for beds, using their bags for pillows; and others made couches on the seats. Most of them were able to sleep the greater part of the night. But the *Fonda del Universo* was prepared for their reception, and they were glad enough to turn into the fifty beds ready for them.

At nine o'clock all hands were piped to breakfast. The meal was served in courses, and was essentially French. Some of the waiters spoke French; but there was really no need of saying any thing, for each dish of the bill of fare was presented to every person at the table. After the meal, the students were assembled in the large reading-room, — the hotel had been recently built, — and Professor Mapps was called upon by the principal to say something about Saragossa, in order that the tourists might know a little of the history of the place they were visiting. The instructor took a convenient position, and began his remarks: —

"The old monks used to write history something after the manner of the Knickerbocker's History of New York; and they put it on record that Saragossa was founded by Tubal, nephew of Noah; but you will not believe this. The city probably originated with the Phœnicians, and was a place of great importance in the time of Julius Cæsar, who saw its military value as commanding the passage of the Ebro, and built a wall around it. It was captured by the Suevi in 452, and taken from them by the Goths fourteen years later. In the eighth century the Moors obtained possession of the city, and held it till the twelfth, when it was conquered by Alfonso of Aragon. It contains many relics of the Roman and Moorish works.

"Saragossa has been the scene of several noted sieges, the most famous of which was that of 1808, when the French captured the place after the most desperate resistance on the part of the Aragonese. The brave defenders of the city had no regular military organization, and were ill-provided with arms and ammunition. The people chose for a leader a young man whose name was Palafox: he was as brave as a lion, but not versed in military science. The siege lasted sixty-two days, and the fighting was almost incessant. It was 'war to the knife' on the part of the Aragonese, and they rejected all overtures to surrender. Famine made fearful havoc among them, and every house was a hospital. Even the priests and the women joined in the strife. I dare say you have all heard of the 'Maid of Saragossa,' who is represented in pictures as a young woman assisting in working a gun in the battle. Her name was Augustina; and she was a very pretty girl of twenty-two. Her lover was a cannonneer, and she fought by his side. When he was mortally wounded, she worked the gun herself. You will find something about her in 'Childe Harold.'

"At length the French got into the town; but the conflict was not finished, for the people fought for twenty-one days more in the streets. Fifteen thousand were either dead or dying when the French entered the city. At last the authorities agreed to surrender, but only on the most honorable terms. It has been estimated, that, out of a population of one hundred and fifty thousand, fifty-four thousand perished in battle or by famine and pestilence."

After these brief remarks, the party separated, and divided up into small squads to see the city as they pleased. As usual, Captain Sheridan and Murray joined themselves to Dr. Winstock, who was as much at home in Saragossa as he was in Paris.

"You will find that this city is thoroughly Spanish; and doubtless you will see some of the native costumes," said the doctor, as they left the hotel.

"But this hotel is as much French as though it were in France," added Murray, who desired when in Spain to do as the Spaniards did, so as to learn what they do.

"That is very true; but we shall come to the true Spanish hotel in due time, and I have no doubt you will get enough of it in a very short time," laughed Dr. Winstock. "There are three classes of hotels in Spain, though at the present time they are all about the same thing. A *fonda* is a regular hotel; a *posada* is the tavern of the smaller country towns; and a *venta* is a still lower grade of inn. A drinking-shop, which we sometimes call a 'saloon' in the United States, is a *ventorro* or a *ventorillo;* and a *taberna* is a place where smoking and wine-drinking are the business of their frequenters. A *parador* is a hotel where the diligences stop for meals, and may also be a *fonda.*"

"A *fonda* is a hotel," said Sheridan; "and we may not be able to remember any more than that."

"When you see the names I have given you on the signs, you will understand what they mean. But our business now is to see this city. Like Barcelona, it has one principal wide street extending through the middle of it: all the other avenues are nothing more than lanes, very narrow and very dirty. It is on the Ebro, and has a population of some eighty thousand people."

"How happens it that this place is not colder? It is in about the same latitude as New York City; and now, in the month of December, it is comfortably warm," said Sheridan.

"These valleys have a mild climate; and the vine and olive are their principal productions. It is not so on the high table-land in the centre of Spain. At Madrid, for instance, the weather will be found to be quite cold at this time. The weather is so bitter there sometimes that the sentinels on guard have to be changed every quarter of an hour, as they are in danger of being frozen to death."

The party walked first to the great square, in the centre of which is a public fountain. They paused to look at the people. Most of the men wore some kind of a mantle or cloak. This garment was sometimes the Spanish circular cloak, worn with a style and grace that the Spaniard alone can attain. That of the poorer class was often nothing but a striped blanket, which, however, they slung about them with no little of the air of those who wore better garments. They were generally tall, muscular, but rather bony fellows, with an expression as solemn as though they were doing duty at a funeral. Some of them wore the broad-brimmed *sombrero;* some had handkerchiefs wound around their heads, like turbans; and others sported the ordinary hat or cap.

The party could not help laughing when they saw, for the first time, a priest wearing a hat which extended fore and aft at least three feet, with the sides rolled up close to the body. Everybody was dignified, and moved about at a funeral pace.

At the fountain women and girls were filling the jars of odd shape with water, and bearing them away poised on one of their hips or on the head. Several donkeys were standing near, upon which their owners were loading the sacks of water they had filled.

"Bags of water!" exclaimed Murray.

"They do not call them bags, but skins," said the doctor. "You can see the legs and neck of the animal, which are very convenient in handling them. These skins are more easily transported on the backs of the donkeys than barrels, kegs, or jars could be. Many kinds of wine are transported in these skins, which could hardly be carried on the back of an animal in any other way. Except a few great highways, Spain is not provided with roads. In some places, when you ride in a carriage, you will take to the open fields; and very rough indeed they are sometimes."

The party proceeded on their walk, and soon reached the Cathedral of San Salvador, generally called *El Seo;* a term as applicable to any other cathedral in Aragon as to this one. It is a sombre old structure: a part of it is said to have been built in the year 290; and pious people have been building it till within three hundred and fifty years of the present time. There are some grand monuments in it; among them that of Arbues, who was assassinated for carrying out the decrees of the Inquisition. The people of Aragon did not take kindly to this institution; but the murder was terribly avenged, and the Inquisition established its authority in the midst of the tumult it had excited. Murillo, the great Spanish painter, made the assassination of Arbues the subject of one of his principal pictures.

Saragossa has two cathedrals, the second of which is called *El Pilar*, because it contains the very pillar on which the Virgin landed when she came down from heaven in one of her visits to Spain. It appears that St. James — Santiago in Spanish — came to Spain after the crucifixion of the Saviour, in the year 40, to preach the gospel to the natives. When he had got as far as Saragossa, he was naturally tired, and went to sleep. In this state the Virgin came to him with a message from the Saviour, requiring him to build a chapel in honor of herself. She stood on a jasper pillar, and was attended by a multitude of angels. St. James obeyed the command of the heavenly visitor, and erected a small chapel, only sixteen feet long and half as wide, where the Virgin often attended public worship in subsequent years. On this spot, and over the original chapel, was built the present church. On the pillar stands a dingy image of the Virgin, which is said to be from the studio of St. Luke, who appears to have been both a painter and a sculptor. It is clothed in the richest velvet, brocade, and satin, and is spangled with gold and diamonds. It cures all diseases to which flesh is heir; for which the grateful persons thus healed have bestowed the most costly presents. It is little less than sacrilege to express any disbelief in this story of the Virgin, or in the miracles achieved by the image.

Dr. Winstock and his young companions went from the churches, to take a walk in the older part of the city. The narrow streets reminded them of Constantinople, while many of the buildings were similar, the upper part projecting out over the street. The balconies were shaded with mats, like the parti-colored draperies that hang from the windows in Naples. Many of the houses were of the Moorish fashion, with the *patio*, or court-yard, in the centre, with galleries around it, from which admission to the various apartments is obtained. Saragossa has a leaning tower built of brick, which was the campanile, or belfry, of the town.

The party of the surgeon spent the rest of the day in a walk through the surrounding country, crossing the Ebro to the suburb of the city. Near the bridge they met a couple of ladies who wore the mantilla, a kind of veil worn as a head-dress, instead of the bonnet, which is a part of the national costume of Spain. All over Spain this fashion prevails, though of course the modes of Paris are adopted by the most fashionable ladies of the capital and other cities.

At four o'clock the ship's company dined at the hotel, and then wandered about the city at will till dark. They were advised to retire at an early hour, and most of them did so. They were called at half-past four in the morning, and at six were on the train. At half-past eight they were at Tudela, the head of navigation on the Ebro. At quarter past one they were at Miranda, on the line from Bayonne to Madrid, where dinner was waiting for them. This meal was decidedly Spanish, though it was served in courses. The soup was odorous of garlic, which is the especial vice of Spanish cookery to those who have an aversion to it. Then came the national dish, the *olla podrida*, a kind of stew made of every kind of meat and every kind of vegetable, not omitting a profusion of garlic. Some of the students declared that it was "first-rate." A few did not like it at all, and more were willing to tolerate it. We do not consider it "bad to take." The next dish was calves' brains fried in batter, which is not national, but is oftener had at the hotels than *olla podrida*. The next course was mutton chops, followed by roast chicken, with a salad. The dessert was fruit and raisins. On the table was plenty of *Val de Peñas* wine, which the students were forbidden to taste.

At half-past two the tourists departed, and at twenty minutes to six arrived in the darkness at Burgos. The port watch went to the *Fonda del Norte*, and the starboard to the *Fonda Rafaela*. The doctor and the captain were at the latter, and it was more like the inns of Don Quixote's time than any that Sheridan had seen. It had no public room except the *comedor*, or dining-room. The hotel seemed to be a number of buildings thrown together around a court-yard, on one side of which was the stable. Sheridan and Murray were shown to a room with six other students, but the apartment contained four beds. It was large enough for four more, being not less than thirty feet long, and half as wide. It was comfortably furnished, and every thing about it was clean and neat. The establishment was not unlike an old-fashioned country tavern in New England.

Dinner, or, as the students called it, supper, was served at six o'clock. The meal was Spanish, being about the same as the one they had taken at Miranda. Instead of the *olla podrida* was a kind of stew, which in the days of Gil Blas would have been called a *ragout.*

"This isn't a bad dinner," said Murray, when they had finished the third course.

"It is a very good one, I think," replied Sheridan.

"I have been reading books of travel in Spain for the last two weeks, most of them written by Englishmen; and I had come to the conclusion that we should be starved to death if we left the ship for more than a day or two. The writers found a great deal of fault with their food, and growled about garlic. I rather like garlic."

"The doctor says the English are very much given to grumbling about every thing," added Sheridan. "I don't think we shall starve if we are fed as well as we have been so far."

"Our room is as good as we have found in most of the hotels in other countries. So far, the trains on the railroads have been on time instead of an hour late, as one writer declared they always were."

"If one insists upon growling, it is easy enough to find something to growl at."

In the evening some of the party strolled about town, but it was as quiet as a tomb; for the rule in Spain is, "Early to bed, and late to rise." But the students were out of bed in good time in the morning, and taking a view of the city. They found a very pretty promenade along the little river Arlanzon, whose waters find their way into the Duero; and at a considerable distance from it obtained a fine view of the great cathedral. It is impossible to obtain any just view of it, except at a distance, on account of the mass of buildings which are huddled around it, and close to it. But the vast church towers above them all, and presents to the eye a forest of spires great and small. Near the river, in an irregular *plaza*, is an old gateway, which is quite picturesque. The structure looks like a castle, with round towers at the corners, and circular turrets. On the front are a number of figures carved in stone.

Breakfast was served at half-past ten, and dinner at six, at the *Fonda;* but special tables were set for the students at more convenient hours. A Spanish meal could not be agreeable to nice and refined American people. The men often sit with their hats on, and between the courses smoke a cigarette, or *cigarillo* in Spanish. They converse in an energetic tone, but are polite if addressed, though they mind their own business severely, and seem to be devoid of curiosity — or at least are too dignified to stare — in regard to strangers. The food is very odorous of onions and garlic, and in the smaller inns consists largely of stews or ragouts, generally of mutton or kidneys. New cheese, not pressed, is sometimes an item of the bill of fare. *Val de Pañas* wine is furnished free all over Spain at the *table d'hote*; but it always tastes of the skins in which it is transported, and most Americans who partake of it think it is poor stuff. Great quantities of it are exported to Bordeaux, where it is manufactured into claret.

After breakfast, the students were assembled to enable Professor Mapps to tell them something about the history of the city, to which he added a very full account of the Cid. Of his remarks we can give only an abstract.

Burgos is one of the most famous cities of Castile, of which it was at one time the capital. The name comes from the same word as "Burg," and means a fortified eminence; and such it is, being on the watershed between the basins of the Ebro and the Duero. It was founded in 884 by a Castilian knight. It was the birthplace of Ferdinand Gonzales, who first took the title of Count of Castile, shook off the yoke of Leon, and established the kingdom of Castile. The city is on the direct line to Madrid from Paris. The French captured the place in 1808; and it was twice besieged and taken by the Duke of Wellington in the peninsular war.

The Cid is the popular hero of Spain, and especially of the people of Burgos. He was the King Arthur of Spain, and there is about as much romance in his history as in that of the British demigod. The Cid Campeador, "knight champion," was born about 1040, and died when he was not much over fifty. His name was Rodrigo Ruy Diaz; and his marvellous exploits are set forth in the "Poem of the Cid," believed to have been written in the twelfth century. It is the oldest poem in the Spanish language. His first great deed was to meet the Count Gomez, who had grossly insulted the Cid's aged father, in a fair fight in the field, and utterly vanquish him, cutting off his head. The old man was unable to eat from brooding over his wrong; but, when Ruy appeared with the head of the slain count, his appetite was restored. By some he is said to have married Ximena, the daughter of his dead adversary. Great was the fame of the Cid's prowess after this exploit. Shortly after this event, five Moorish kings, with a powerful force, entered Castile; and the Cid roused the country to oppose their progress, and fell upon the enemy, routing the five kings with great slaughter, and making all of them his prisoners. Then he fought for King Ferdinand against the Aragonese, and won all that was in dispute. When France demanded the homage of his king, he entered that country, and won a victory which settled the question of homage for all time. After this event he did considerable domestic fighting when Castile was divided among the sons of the dead sovereign; and was finally banished by the new king. He departed with his knights and men-at-arms, and took up a strong position in the territory of the Moors, where he made war, right and left, with all the kingdoms of the peninsula except his own country, which he had the grace to except in his conquests. He took Valencia, where he seems to have established himself. His last exploit in the flesh was the capture of Murviedro. Then he died, and was buried in Valencia.

Now that the Cid, who had been the scourge of the Moors, was dead, the Christians could no longer hold out against the infidels, and were in danger of losing what they had gained. In this emergency they clothed the corpse of the dead hero in armor, and fastened it on his war-steed, placing his famous sword in his hand. Thus equipped for battle, the dead Cid was led into the field in the midst of the soldiers. The very sight of him struck terror to the hearts of the Moslems, and the defunct warrior won yet another battle. He was marched through the land, the enemy fleeing before him in every direction, to Burgos. He seems not to have been buried when he got there, but was embalmed and placed in a chair of state, where he went into the business of working miracles. His long white beard fell upon his breast, his sword was at his side, and he seemed to be alive rather than dead. One day a Jew, out of bravado, attempted to take hold of his venerable beard, when the Cid began to draw his sword, whereat the Jew was so frightened that he fainted away. When he recovered he at once became a Christian. The Cid was a fiery man, and did not hesitate to slap the face of a king or the pope, if he was angry. Even after he was dead, and sitting in his chair, he sometimes lost his temper; and Ximine found it expedient to bury him, in order to keep him out of trouble.

The students went to the cathedral first. It is a vast pile of buildings, and is considered one of the finest churches in Europe. There is an immense amount of fine and delicate work about it, which cannot be described. The dome is so beautiful that Philip II. said it was the work of angels rather than men. The choir is quite a lofty enclosure, which obstructs the view from the pavement. The archbishop's palace, and the cloister, on one side, seem to be a part of the church. It contains, as usual, a great many chapels, each of which has its own treasures of art or antiquity. In one of them is the famous Christ of Burgos, which is said to have been made by Nicodemus after he and Joseph of Arimathea had buried the Saviour. As usual, it was found in a box floating in the sea. The hair, beard, eyelashes, and the thorns, are all real; and a French writer says the skin of the figure is human. The image works miracles without number, sweats on Friday, and even bleeds at times; and is held in the highest veneration by the people.

In another chapel is the coffer of the Cid, an old worm-eaten chest bound with iron. When the champion was banished by the king, as he wanted to go off with flying colors, and was in need of a large sum of money, he filled this chest with sand and stones, and, without allowing them to look into it, assured a couple of rich Jews that it was full of gold and jewels. They took his word for it (strange as such a transaction would be in modern times), and loaned the money he needed. When he had captured Valencia, he paid the loan, and exposed the cheat he had put upon them. Of course they were willing to forgive him after he had paid the money.

The next point of interest with the students was the town hall, where they were permitted to look upon the bones of the Cid and his wife, which are kept in a box, with a wire screen over them to prevent any heathen from stealing them. The bones are all mixed up, and no one can tell which belong to the Cid and which to his wife.

At noon Dr. Winstock procured an antiquated carriage at the hotel stable, and took Sheridan and Murray out into the country. After a ride of a couple of miles they reached Miraflores, which is a convent founded by John II., and finished by Isabella I. Its church contains the royal tomb in which John II. is buried, and is one of the finest things of the kind in the world, the sculpture being of the most delicate character. Several other Castilian kings are buried in this place.

The little party took the carriage again, intending to visit the Monastery of San Pedro de Cardeña. There was no road, only an ill-defined track across the fields; and very rough fields they were, covered with rocks so thick that the vehicle often had to pass over many of them. The passengers were terribly shaken up. On the way they occasionally met a peasant riding on or leading a mule or donkey loaded with various commodities carried in panniers. They were interesting as a study.

San Pedro is nothing but a ruin. It was established in the fifth century; and in the ninth the Moors destroyed the edifice, and killed two hundred monks who lived in it. It was rebuilt; and, being the favorite convent of the Cid, he requested that he might be buried in it. The monument is in a side chapel, and looks as though it had been whitewashed at no very remote period. The doctor read the inscription on the empty tomb. A dirty peasant who joined the party as soon as they got out the carriage followed them at every step, almost looking into their mouths when they spoke.

When the party started to return, things began to be very lively with them. First Sheridan rubbed his legs; then Murray did so; and before long the doctor joined in the recreation.

"What's the matter?" asked the surgeon, laughing.

"I don't know; but my legs feel as though I had an attack of the seven-years' itch," replied the captain with a vigorous attempt to reach and conquer the difficulty.

"That's just my case," added Murray, with an equally violent demonstration.

"I don't understand it," continued the captain.

"I do," answered the surgeon, vigorously rubbing one of his legs.

"What is it?" asked Sheridan, suspecting that they all had some strange disease.

"*Cosas de España*," laughed the doctor.

"But that is Spanish; and I don't understand the lingo."

"A *cosa de España* is a 'thing of Spain;' fleas are things of Spain; and that is what is the matter with you and me. The lining of this carriage has been repaired by covering it in part with cloth with a long nap, which is alive with fleas."

"The wicked flea!" exclaimed Murray.

"He goeth about in Spain, seeking whom he may devour," added the doctor.

When they reached the hotel, supper was ready; but they did not want any just then, for no one feels hungry while a myriad of fleas are picking his bones. Garments were taken off, and brushed on the inside; the skin was washed with cologne-water; and the party were happy till they took in a new supply.

At about eleven at night, the ship's company took the train south, and at quarter past eight the next morning were at *El Escorial*.

CHAPTER IX.

THE HOLD OF THE TRITONIA.

RAIMUNDO was in the hold of the Tritonia. He had made for himself a hiding-place under the dunnage in the run, by removing a quantity of ballast, and arranging a number of empty casks so as to conceal his retreat from any who might search the hold for him. The task had been ingeniously accomplished; and those who looked for him had examined every hole and corner above the ballast, that could possibly hold a person of his size; and they had no suspicion that there was room even for a cat under the dunnage.

The young Spaniard had fully considered his situation before he ventured into the waters of Spain. He was fully prepared for the event that had occurred. The plan of his hiding-place was his own; but he knew that he could not make it, or remain in it for any considerable time, without assistance. If he spent a week or even three days in his den, he must have food and drink. He did not believe the squadron would remain many weeks in Spanish waters; and it was his purpose to stay in the hold during this time, if he found it necessary to do so. A confederate was therefore indispensable to the success of the scheme.

Certain work required to be done in the hold, such as getting up stores and keeping every thing in order, was divided among the stewards. Those employed in the cabin attended to the after-hold, and those in the steerage to the fore-hold. One of the former was a Cuban mulatto, a very bright fellow, who spoke Spanish as well as English. Raimundo had become quite intimate with him, because they both spoke their native tongue, which it was pleasant to each to hear, and the steward had become very fond of him. His name was Hugo; and Raimundo was confident the man would be his friend in the emergency.

During study hours, the vice-principal and the professors were employed in the steerage. When the quarter-watch to which the young Spaniard belonged was off duty, instead of spending his time on deck as his companions did in fine weather, he remained in the cabin, which at times was entirely deserted. He found that Hugo was willing to listen to him; and by degrees he told him his whole story, as he had related it to Scott, and disclosed the plan he intended to adopt when his uncle or his agents should put in a claim for him. Hugo was ready and anxious to take part in the enterprise. There could be no doubt in regard to his fidelity, for the steward would have perilled his life in the service of the young Spaniard.

At a favorable time they visited the hold together; and Raimundo indicated what was to be done in the preparation of the hiding-place. Both of them worked at the job. The ballast taken from the hold was carefully distributed in other places under the dunnage. Hugo had charge of the after-hold, and his being there so much excited no suspicion.

When the ship's company returned, after the lecture, Raimundo waited in the cabin till he was alone with Hugo; for all hands were on deck, observing the strange scenes around them. He then descended to the hold, and deposited himself in the den prepared for him. His faithful confederate had lined it with old garments and pieces of sail-cloth, so that the place was not as uncomfortable as it might have been. The " mysterious disappearance " had been duly effected.

Hugo carried food and drink to his charge in the morning, and left a pail of water for his ablutions, if he chose to make them. Of course the steward was very nervous while the several searches were in progress; but, as he spoke Spanish, he was able to mislead the *alguacil*, even while he professed to desire that every part of the vessel should be examined. Hugo not only provided food and water for the self-made prisoner, but he informed him, when he could, what was going on; so that he knew when all hands had gone on shore, and was duly apprised of the fact that the Josephines and Tritonias were to proceed to Lisbon in the Prince. But the steward dared not remain long in the hold, while Salter was in the cabin. Raimundo wanted to get on board of the steamer that day or night, if it were possible; but the chances were all against him.

Hugo assured him that it would be entirely safe for him to leave his hiding-place, as he could easily keep out of the way of any chance visitor in the hold, and he would notify him if another search was likely to be made. Availing himself of this permission, Raimundo crawled out of his hole. It was a relief to his limbs to stretch them; and he exercised himself as freely as he could. While he was thus engaged, he saw the fore-scuttle opened, and some one come down. The fugitive stepped behind the mainmast. He saw the figure of one of the students, as he judged that he was from his size, moving stealthily in the gloom of the place. In a moment more, he rushed up the steps, and disappeared. In an instant afterwards, Raimundo saw a flame flash up from the pile of rubbish.

The vessel was on fire, or she soon would be; for there was fire near her timbers. Grasping the bucket of water Hugo had left for his ablutions, he poured enough on the fire to extinguish it, and then retreated to the covert of the mainmast. A second time the incendiary-match was applied; and again the fugitive put it out with the contents of the pail. For the third time the incendiary pile that was to doom the beautiful Tritonia to destruction was lighted; and this time the wretch who applied the match evidently intended to remain till the flames were well under way. The fugitive was greatly disturbed; for, if he showed himself to the incendiary, he would betray his secret, and expose his presence. But he could not hesitate to save the vessel at whatever consequences to himself; and, as soon as he saw the blaze, he rushed aft, accosted the villain, and stamped out the fire, for he had entirely emptied the pail.

"What are you about, you villain? Do you mean to burn the vessel?" demanded Raimundo, who did not yet know who the incendiary was.

Bill Stout was startled, not to say overwhelmed, by

this unexpected interference with his plans. He recognized the second master, whose mysterious disappearance had excited so much astonishment. But he was prompt to see, that, if Raimundo had detected him in a crime, he had possession of the fugitive's secret. Somebody on shore wanted the second master, and an officer had come on board for him. Perhaps he was guilty of some grave misdemeanor, and for that reason would not allow himself to be caught; for none of the students except Scott knew why the young Spaniard was required on shore. Bill Stout did not care: he only saw that it was an even thing between himself and Raimundo.

"Who are you?" asked the fugitive, when he had waited a moment for an answer to his first question.

"I advise you not to speak too loud, Mr. Raimundo, unless you wish to have the chief steward know you are here," replied Bill, when he had recovered his self-possession, and taken a hurried view of the situation.

"Stout!" exclaimed Raimundo, identifying the familiar voice.

But he spoke in a low tone, for he was not disposed to summon Mr. Salter to the hold, though he had felt that he sacrificed himself and his plan when he showed himself to the incendiary.

"That's my name," replied the young villain.

"I understand what you were scheming at in your watch on deck. Lingall, Pardee, and Gibbs are your associates in this rascality," added Raimundo.

Stout, who was not before aware that he had been watched by the second master or by any other officer, was rather taken aback by this announcement; but he promptly denied that the students named were concerned in the affair.

"Lingall is with you, I know. I see how you have managed the affair. He is your companion in the brig, which was built over the midship scuttle," continued Raimundo. "But why do you desire to burn the vessel?"

"Because I want to get out of her," replied Bill sullenly. "But I can't stop here to talk."

"Do you really mean to burn the Tritonia?"

"That's what I did mean; but, since you have found me out, I shall not be likely to do it now."

"Whatever you do, don't do that. You are in the waters of Spain now, and I don't know but you would have to be tried and punished for it in this country."

Bill Stout had no idea of being tried and punished for the crime in any country; and he had not even considered it a crime when he thought of the matter. He did not expect to be found out when he planned the job: villains never expect to be. But he was alarmed now; and the deed he had attempted seemed to be a hundred times more wicked and dangerous than at any time before.

"I can't stop here: Salter will miss me if I do," added Bill, moving up the ladder.

"Wait a minute," interposed Raimundo, who was willing to save himself from exposure if he could.

"I'll come down again, after a while," answered Bill, as he opened the scuttle, and got into the brig.

"Why did you stay down so long?" demanded Bark Lingall nervously.

"It's all up now, and we can't do any thing," replied Bill sullenly, as he seated himself on his stool, and picked up one of his books.

"What's the matter?"

"We are found out."

"Found out!" exclaimed Bark; and his heart rose into his throat at the announcement. "How can that be?"

"I was seen doing it."

"Who saw you?"

"You couldn't guess in a month," added Bill, who fixed his gaze on his book while he was talking.

"Didn't I hear you speaking to some one in the hold, Bill?" asked Bark, as he picked up a book, in order to follow the studious example of his companion.

"I was speaking to some one," replied Bill.

"Who was it?"

"Raimundo; and he knew that you were concerned in the job without my mentioning your name;" and Bill explained what had passed between himself and the second master.

"Raimundo!" exclaimed Bark, in a musing manner. "Then he mysteriously disappeared into the hold."

"He did; and he has us where the hair is short," added Bill.

"And perhaps we have him where the hair is long enough to get hold of. All we have to do is to tell Salter, when he comes to look at us, that Raimundo is in the hold."

"We won't do it; and then Raimundo won't say we set the vessel on fire," protested Bill.

"Wait a bit, Bill. He is a spooney, a chaplain's lamb. He may keep still till he gets out of his own scrape, whatever it may be, and then **blow on us** when he is safe himself."

"I don't know: I shall see him again after Salter has paid us another visit."

The chief steward came into the steerage a few minutes later; and seeing both of the prisoners engaged in study, as he supposed, he probably believed the hour of reformation had come. As soon as he had gone, Bill opened the scuttle again, and went down into the hold; but he was unwilling to leave the brig for more than a few moments at a time, lest some accident should betray his absence to the chief steward. He arranged a plan by which he could talk with Raimundo without danger from above. Returning to the brig, he lay down on the floor, with a book in his hand, so that his head was close to the scuttle. Bark was seated on the floor, also with a book in his hand, in such a position as to conceal the trap-door, which was raised a few inches, from the gaze of Mr. Salter, if he should happen suddenly to enter the steerage. Raimundo was to stand on the steps of the ladder, with his head on a level with the cabin floor, where he could hear Bill, and be heard by him.

"I think we can't afford to quarrel," said Bill magnanimously. "We are all in the same boat now. I suppose you are wanted on shore for some dido you cut up before you left your home."

"I did nothing wrong before I left my home," replied Raimundo; and it galled him terribly to be obliged to make terms with the rascals in the brig. "My trouble is simply a family affair; and, if captured, I shall be subjected to no penalty whatever."

"Is that all?" asked Bill, sorry it was no worse.

"That's all; but for reasons I don't care to explain, I do not wish to be taken back to my uncle in Barcelona. But I will give myself up before I will let you burn the Tritonia," replied Raimundo, with no little indignation in his tones.

"Of course, as things stand now, we shall not burn the vessel," added Bill: "we will make a fair trade with you."

"I shall make no trades of any kind; but I leave you free to do what you think best, and I shall remain so myself," said Raimundo, who was too high-toned to bargain with fellows wicked enough to burn the beautiful Tritonia. "It is enough that I wish to get away from this city."

"If you clear out, you won't blow on us," added Bill, willing to put the best construction on the statement of the second master.

"I promise nothing; but this I say: if you burn the Tritonia, whether I am on board or a thousand miles away, I will inform the principal who set the fire."

"Of course we should not do any thing of that sort now," added Bark, whose head was near enough to the scuttle to enable him to hear all that was said.

"I shall be obliged to keep out of the way of all on board, for the present at least," said Raimundo.

"We are satisfied with that," replied Bill, who seemed to be in haste to reach some other branch of the subject.

"Very well: then there is nothing more to be said," answered Raimundo, who was quite willing to close the interview at this point.

The conspirators were not so willing; for the chance of escape held out to them by the burning of the vessel was gone, and they were very much dissatisfied with the situation. It would be madness to repeat the attempt to destroy the vessel; and the future looked very unpromising. All hands were going off on a very desirable cruise in the steamer. Ben Pardee and Lon Gibbs had apparently deserted them when tempted by the voyage to Lisbon. They had a dismal prospect of staying in the brig, under the care of Marline and Rimmer, for the next three weeks.

The second master had plenty of time to think over his arrangements for the next week or two; and he was not much better satisfied with the immediate prospect for the future, than were the occupants of the brig. His accommodations were far less comfortable than theirs; and the experience of a single night had caused him to fear that he might take cold and be sick. Besides, he had not calculated that the Tritonia was to lie at this port for two or three weeks, thus increasing the danger and discomfort of his situation. If he had to abandon his hiding-place, he preferred to take his chances at any other port rather than Barcelona. It was more than probable that Marline and Rimmer would overhaul the hold, and re-stow the boxes and barrels while the vessel was at anchor; and possibly the principal had ordered some repairs at this favorable time.

His chance of getting on board of the Prince before she sailed was too small to afford him any hope. The change the principal had made in the programme interfered sadly with his calculations. Mr. Lowington had made this alteration in order to enable the students to visit the northern and central parts of the peninsula before the weather became too cold to permit them to do so with any degree of comfort. The fugitive was willing, therefore, to change his plans if it was possible.

"Hold on a minute," interposed Bill Stout, when Raimundo was about to descend the ladder. "What are you going to do with yourself while the vessel lies here for the next three weeks?"

"I shall have to keep out of sight in the hold," replied the second master.

"But you can't do that. You will starve to death."

"I have looked out for that."

Though Bill Stout asked some questions on this point, Raimundo declined to say in what manner he had provided for his rations.

"Do you know who are in charge on board now?" asked Bill.

"Only Mr. Salter and one of the stewards," replied the fugitive.

"Why don't you use your chance while Marline and Rimmer are ashore, and leave the vessel? You can get away without being seen."

"I can't get out of the vessel without going through the cabin where Mr. Salter is," answered Raimundo; but the suggestion gave him a lively hope.

"Yes, you can: you can get out by the fore-scuttle, go over the bow, and roost on the bobstay till a shore boat comes along," added Bill. "Only you musn't let the steward see you. Salter is in the cabin, and he won't know any thing about it."

Raimundo was grateful for the suggestion, though he was not willing to acknowledge it, considering the source from which it came. Hugo would help him, instead of being a hinderance. The steward would call a boat, and have it all ready for him when he got out of the vessel. He could even keep Mr. Salter in the cabin, while he made his escape, by engaging his attention in some matter of business.

"I will see what I can do," said the fugitive as he left the ladder.

He went aft to the cabin ladder, and raised the scuttle an inch. Hugo was setting the table for Mr. Salter's lunch. He saw the trap-door raised, and he immediately went below for a jar of pickles. In five minutes Raimundo had recited his plan to him. In five minutes more Hugo had a boat at the bow of the Tritonia, waiting for its passenger. At half-past twelve, Hugo called Mr. Salter to his lunch; and, when this gentleman took his seat at the table, Hugo raised the trap, and slammed it down as though it had not been in place before. Raimundo understood the signal.

The fugitive went forward, and ascended to the deck by the fore-scuttle. He was making his way over the bow when he found that he was followed by Bill Stout and Bark Lingall.

"What are you doing here?" demanded Raimundo, astonished and annoyed at the action of the incendiaries.

"We are going with you," replied Bill Stout. "Over with you! if you say a word, we will call Salter."

Raimundo dropped into the boat that was waiting for him, and the villains from the brig followed him.

CHAPTER X.

THE ESCURIAL AND PHILIP II.

BEFORE the train stopped, the students obtained a fair view of the Escurial, which is a vast pile of buildings, located in the most desolate place to be found even in Spain. The village is hardly less solemn and gloomy than the tremendous structure that towers above. The students breakfasted at the two *fondas* in the place; and then Mr. Mapps, as usual, had something to say to them: —

"The Escurial, or *El Escorial* as it is called in Spanish, is a monastery, palace, and church. The name is derived from *scoriæ*, the refuse of iron-ore after it is smelted; and there were iron-mines in this vicinity. The full name of the building is '*El Real Sitio de San Lorenzo el Real del Escorial*,' or, literally, 'The Royal Seat of St. Lawrence, the Royal, of the Escurial.' It was built by Philip II. in commemoration of the battle of St. Quentin, in 1557, won by the arms of Philip, though he was not present at the battle. He had made a vow, that, if the saint gave him the victory, he would build the most magnificent monastery in the world in his honor. St. Lawrence was kind enough to accommodate him with the victory; and this remarkable pile of buildings was the result. Philip redeemed his vow, and even did more than this; for, in recognition of the fact that the saint was martyred on a gridiron, he built this monastery in the form of that useful cooking implement. As you see, the structure is in the form of a square; and, within it, seventeen ranges of buildings cross each other at right angles. The towers at each corner are two hundred feet high; and the grand dome in the centre is three hundred and twenty feet high.

"The total length of the building is seven hundred and forty feet, by five hundred and eighty feet wide. It was begun in 1563, when Philip laid the corner-stone with his own hands; and was completed twenty-one years later. It cost, in money of our time, fifteen millions of dollars. It has four thousand windows; though you may see that most of them are rather small. The church, which is properly the chapel of the monastery, is three hundred and seventy-five feet long, and contains forty chapels. The high altar is ninety feet high, and fifty feet wide, and is composed of jasper. Directly under it is the royal tomb, in which are laid the remains of all the sovereigns of Spain from Charles V. to the present time. The Spaniards regard the Escurial as the eighth wonder of the world. It is grand, solemn, and gloomy, like Philip who built it. In the mountain, a mile and a half from the Escurial, is a seat built of granite, which Philip used to occupy while watching the progress of the work."

The students separated, dividing into parties to suit

themselves. All the available guides were engaged for them; and in a few minutes the interior of the church presented a scene that would have astonished the gloomy Philip if he could have stepped out of his shelf below to look at it, for a hundred young Americans — from the land that Columbus gave to Castile and Leon — was an unusual sight within its cold and deserted walls.

"I suppose you have read the lives of Charles V. and Philip II.," said Dr. Winstock, as he entered the great building with his young friends.

Both of them had read Robertson and Prescott and Irving; and it was because they were generally well read up that the doctor liked to be with them.

"It isn't of much use for any one who has not read the life of Philip II. to come here: at least, he would be in the dark all the time," added the doctor.

"I have seen it stated that Charles V. and his mother, Crazy Jane, both wanted a convent built which should contain a burial-place for the royal family," said Sheridan.

"That is true. All of them were very pious, and inclined to dwell in convents. Charles V. showed his taste at his abdication by retiring to Yuste," replied the surgeon.

"The architecture of the building is very plain."

"Yes, — simple, massive, and grand."

"Like Philip, as Professor Mapps said."

"It took him two years to find a suitable spot for the building," said the doctor.

"I don't think he could have found a worse one," laughed Murray.

"But he found just the one he wanted; and he did not select it to suit you and me. Look off at those mountains on the north, — the Guadarramas. They tower above Philip's mausoleum, but they do not belittle it. The region is rough but grand: it is desolate; but that makes it more solemn and impressive. It is a monastery and a tomb that he built, not a pleasure-house."

"But he made a royal residence of it," suggested Murray.

"For the same reason that his father chose to end his days in a monastery. Philip would be a wild fanatic in our day; but he is to be judged by his own time. He was really a king and a monk, as much one as the other. When we go into the room where he died, and where he spent the last days of his life, and recall some of his history there, we shall understand him better. I don't admire his character, but I am disposed to do justice to him."

The party entered the church, called in Spanish *templo:* it is three hundred and twenty feet long, and it is the same to the top of the cupola.

"The interior is so well proportioned that you do not get an adequate idea of the size of it," said the doctor. "Consider that you could put almost any church in our own country into this one, and have plenty of room for its spire under that dome. It is severely plain; but I think it is grand and impressive. The high altar, which I believe the professor did not make as large as it really is, is very rich in marbles and precious stones, and cost about two hundred thousand dollars."

"That's enough to build twenty comfortable country

churches at home," added Murray. "And this whole building cost money enough to build fifteen thousand handsome churches in any country. Of course there are plenty of beggars in Spain."

"That is the republican view of the matter," replied Dr. Winstock. "But the builder of this mighty fabric believed he was serving God acceptably in rearing it; and we must judge him by his motive, and consider the age in which he lived. Observe, as Mr Ford says in his hand-book, that the pantheon, or crypt where the kings are buried, is just under the steps of the high altar : it was so planned by Philip, that the host, when it was elevated, might be above the royal dead. Now we will go into the *relicario.*"

"I think I have seen about relics enough to last me the rest of my lifetime," said Sheridan.

"You need not see them if you do not wish to do so," laughed the surgeon. "This is a tolerably free country just now, and you can do as you please."

But the captain followed his party.

"The French carried away vast quantities of the treasures of the church when they were engaged in conquering the country. But they left the bones of the saints, which the pious regard as the real treasures. Among other things stolen was a statue presented by the people of Messina to Philip III., weighing two hundred pounds, of solid silver, and holding in its hand a gold vessel weighing twenty-six pounds; besides forty-seven of the richest vases, and a heavy crown set with rubies and other precious stones," continued Dr. Winstock, consulting a guide-book he carried in his hand. "This book says there are 7,421 relics here now, among which are ten whole bodies, 144 heads, 306 whole legs and arms; here is one of the real bars of the gridiron on which St. Lawrence was martyred, with portions of the broiled flesh upon it; and there is one of his feet, with a piece of coal sticking between the toes."

"But where did they get that bar of the gridiron?" asked Murray earnestly. "St. Lawrence was broiled in the third century."

"I don't know," replied the doctor. "You must not ask me any questions of that kind, for I cannot answer them."

The party returned to the church again; and the surgeon called the attention of his companions to the oratorios, one on each side of the altar, which are small rooms for the use of the royal persons when they attend the mass.

"The one on the left is the one used by Philip II.," added the doctor. "You see the latticed window through which he looked at the priest. Next to it is his cabinet, where he worked and where he died. We shall visit them from the palace."

After looking at the choir, and examining the bishop's throne, the party with a dozen others visited the pantheon, or royal tomb. The descent is by a flight of marble steps, and the walls are also of the same material. At the second landing are two doors, that on the left leading to the "*pantheon de los infantes*," which is the tomb of those queens who were not mothers of sovereigns of Spain, and of princes who did not sit on the throne. There are sixty bodies here, including Don Carlos, the son of Philip, Don John of Austria, who asked to be buried here as the proper reward for his services, and other persons whose names are known to history.

After looking at these interesting relics of mortality, the tourists descended to the pantheon, which is a heathenish name to apply to a Christian burial-place erected by one so pious as Philip II. It is octagonal in form, forty-six feet in diameter and thirty-eight feet high. It is built entirely of marble and jasper. It contains an altar of the same stone, where mass is sometimes celebrated. These mortuary chapels were not built by Philip II., who made only plain vaults; but by Philip III. and Philip IV., who did not inherit the taste for simplicity of their predecessor on the throne. Around the tomb are twenty-six niches, all of them made after the same pattern, each containing a sarcophagus, in most of which is the body of a king or queen. On the right of the altar are the kings, and on the left the queens. All of them are labelled with the name of the occupant, as "Carlos V.," "Filipe II.," "Fernando VII.," &c.

"Can it be possible that we see the coffins of Charles V. and Philip II.?" said Sheridan, who was very much impressed by the sight before him.

"There is no doubt of it," replied the doctor.

"I can hardly believe that the body of Philip II. is in that case," added the captain. "I see no reason to doubt the fact; but it seems so very strange that I should be looking at the coffin of that cold and cruel king who lived before our country was settled, and of whom I have read so much."

"I think before you leave Spain you will see something that will impress you even more than this."

"What is it?"

"I will not mention it yet; for it is better not to anticipate these things. All the kings of Spain from Charles V. are buried here, except Philip V. and Ferdinand VI."

"What an odd way they have here of spelling Charles and Philip!" said Murray. "These names don't look quite natural to me."

"Carlos Quinto is the Spanish for Charles Fifth; and Ferdinand Seventh is Fernando Septimo, as you see on the urn. But our way of writing these things is as odd to the Spaniards as theirs is to us. The late queen and her father, when they came to the Escurial, used to hear mass at midnight in this tomb."

"That was cheerful," added Sheridan.

"They had a fancy for that sort of thing. Maria Louisa, Philip's wife, scratched her name on one of these marble cases with her scissors."

The party in the pantheon returned to the church to make room for another company to visit it. Dr. Winstock and his friends ascended the grand staircase, and from the top of the building obtained a fine view of the surrounding country, which at this season was as desolate and forbidding as possible. After this they took a survey of the monastery, most of which has the aspect of a barrack. They looked with interest at some of the portraits among the pictures, especially at those of Philip and Charles V. In the library they glanced at the old manuscripts, and at the catalogue in which some of Philip's handwriting was pointed out to them.

They next went to the palace, which is certainly a

mean abode for a king, though it was improved and adorned by some of the builder's successors. Philip asked only a cell in the house he had erected and consecrated to God; and so he made the palace very simple and plain. Some of the long and narrow rooms are adorned with tapestries on the walls; but there is nothing in the palace to detain the visitor beyond a few minutes, except the apartments of Philip II. They are two small rooms, hardly more than six feet wide. One of them is Philip's cabinet, where he worked on affairs of state; and the other is the oratory, where he knelt at the little latticed window which commanded a view of the priests at the high altar of the church. The old table at which he wrote, the chair in which he sat, and the footstool on which he placed his gouty leg, are still there. The doctor, who had been here before, pointed them out to the students.

"It almost seems as though he had just left the place," said Sheridan. "I don't see how a great king could be content to spend his time in such a gloomy den as this."

"It was his own fancy, and he made his own nest to suit himself," replied the doctor. "He was writing at that table when the loss of the invincible armada was announced to him. It is said he did not move a muscle, though he had wasted eighteen years of his life and a hundred million ducats upon the fleet and the scheme. He was kneeling at the window when Don John of Austria came in great haste to tell him of the victory of Lepanto; but he was not allowed to see the king till the latter had finished his devotions."

"He was a cool old fellow," added Murray.

"When he was near the end, he caused himself to be carried in a litter all over the wonderful building he had erected, that he might take a last look at the work of his hands," continued the doctor. "He was finally brought to this place, where he received extreme unction; and, having taken leave of his family, he died, grasping the crucifix which his father had held in his last moments."

The party passed out of the buildings, and gave some time to the gardens and grounds of the Escurial. There are some trees, a few of them the spindling and ghostly-looking Lombardy poplars; but, beyond the immediate vicinity of the "eighth wonder," the country is desolate and wild, without a tree to vary the monotony of the scene. The doctor led the way down the hill to the *Casita del Principe*, which is a sort of miniature palace, built for Charles IV. when he was a boy. It is a pretty toy, containing thirty-three rooms, all of them of reduced size, and with furniture on the same scale. It contains some fine pictures and other works of art.

The tourists dined, and devoted the rest of the day to wandering about in the vicinity of the village. Some of them walked up to the *Silla del Rey*, or king's chair, where Philip overlooked the work on the Escurial. At five o'clock the ship's company took the slow train, and arrived at Madrid at half-past seven, using up two hours and a half in going thirty-two miles.

"I am sorry it is too dark for you to see the country," said the doctor, after the train started.

"Why, sir, is it very fine?" asked Sheridan.

"On the contrary, it is, I think, the most desolate

region on the face of the globe; with hardly a village, not a tree, nothing but rocks to be seen. It reminds me of some parts of Maine and New Hampshire, where they have to sharpen the sheep's noses to enable them to feed among the rocks. The people are miserable and half savage; and it is said that many of them are clothed in sheepskins, and live in burrows in the ground, for the want of houses; but I never saw any thing of this kind, though I know that some of the gypsys in the South dwell in caves in the sides of the hills. Agriculture is at the lowest ebb, though Spain produces vast quantities of the most excellent qualities of grain. Like a portion of our own country, the numerous valleys are very fertile, though in the summer the streams of this part of Spain are all dried up. The gypsys camp in the bed of the Manzanares, at Madrid. Alexandre Dumas and his son went to a bull-fight at the capital. The son was faint, as you may be, and a glass of water was brought to him. After taking a swallow, he handed the rest to the waiter, saying, 'Portez cela au Manzanares: cela lui fera plaisir.' (Carry that to the Manzanares: it will give it pleasure)."

"Good for Dumas, *fils!*" exclaimed Murray.

"There is a prejudice against trees in Spain. The peasants will not plant them, or suffer them to grow, except those that bear fruit; because they afford habitations for the birds which eat up their grain. Timber and wood for fuel are therefore very scarce and very dear in this part of the country. But this region was not always so barren and desolate as it is now. In the wars with the Moors, both armies began by cutting down the trees and burning the villages. More of this desolation, however, was caused by a very remarkable privilege, called the *mesta*, granted to certain of the nobility. It gave them the right of pasturage over vast territories, including the Castiles, Estremadura, and La Mancha. It came to be a legal right, and permitted immense flocks of sheep to roam across the country twice a year, in the spring and autumn. In the time of Philip II., the wandering flocks of sheep were estimated at from seven to eight millions. They devoured every thing before them in the shape of grass and shrubs. This privilege was not abolished till 1825."

"I should think Philip and the rest of the kings who lived at the Escurial would have had a nice time in going to and from the capital," said Sheridan. "He did not have a palace-car on the railroad in those days."

"After Philip's day they did not live there a great deal of the time, not so much because it was inconvenient as because it was a gloomy and cheerless place. They used to make it a rule to spend six weeks of the year there; though the last of the sovereigns did not live there at all, I believe. But they had good roads and good carriages for their time. The Spaniards do not make many roads; but what they do make are first-class. I am sorry we do not go to Segovia, though there is not much there except the cathedral and the Roman aqueduct, which is a fine specimen. But you have seen plenty of these things. Six miles from Segovia is La Granja, or the Grange, which is sometimes called the palace of San Ildefonso. It is a *real sitio*, or royal residence, built by Philip V. It is a summer retreat, in the midst of pine forests four thousand feet above the sea-level. We went through Valladolid in the night. Columbus died there, you remember; and Philip II. was born there; but there is nothing of great interest to be seen in the city."

When the train arrived at Madrid, a lot of small omnibuses, holding about eight persons each, were waiting for the company; and they were driven to the *Puerta del Sol*, where the principal hotels are located. Half of the party went to the *Grand Hotel de Paris*, and the other half to the *Hotel de los Principes*. Dr. Winstock and his *protégés* were quartered at the former.

On shore no distinction was made between officers and seamen, and no better rooms were given to the former than to the latter. As two students occupied one wide bed, they were allowed to pair off for this purpose. It so happened that the captain and the first lieutenant had one of the worst rooms in the house. After they had gone up two pairs of stairs, a sign on the wall informed them that they had reached the first story; and four more brought them to the seven-by-nine chamber, with a brick floor, which they were to occupy. The furniture was very meagre.

In Spain hotels charge by the day, the price being regulated by the size and location of the room. Such as that we have just described was thirty-five *reales*. A good sized inside room, two flights nearer the earth, was fifty *reales*, with an increase of five *reales* for an outside room looking into the street. The table was the same for all the guests. The price per day varies from thirty to sixty *reales* in Spain, forty being the most common rate at the best hotels out of Madrid. From two to four *reales* a day is charged for attendance, and one or two for candles. Two dollars a day is therefore about the average rate. Only two meals a day are served for this price, — a breakfast at ten or eleven, and dinner at six.

It is the fashion in Spain, for an individual or company to conduct several hotels in different cities. The Fallola brothers run the grand Hotel de Paris in Madrid, the ones with the same name in Seville and in Cadiz, and the Hotel Suiza in Cordova; and they are the highest-priced hotels on the peninsula, and doubtless the best. The company that manages the Hotel de Los Principes in Madrid also have the Rizzi in Cordova, the Londres in Seville, the Cadiz in Cadiz, and the Siete Suelos in Granada, in which the prices are more moderate. The Hotel Washington Irving at Granada, and the Alameda in Malaga, are under the same management, and charge forty-four and forty *reales* a day respectively, besides service and lights. Though Spain is said to be an expensive country to live in, these prices in 1870 were only about half those charged in the United States.

Railroad fares are about two cents and a half a mile, second-class; and about a third higher, first-class. A one-horse carriage for two costs forty cents an hour in Madrid; and for four persons, two horses, fifty cents. A very handsome carriage, with driver and footman in livery, may be had for five dollars a day.

After supper the students walked about the *Puerta del Sol*, and took their first view of the capital of Spain.

CHAPTER XI.

THE CRUISE IN THE FELUCCA.

RAIMUNDO was very much disgusted when he found that Bill Stout and Bark Lingall were to be the companions of his flight. Thus far he had felt that his conduct was justifiable. His uncle Manuel had taught him to believe that his guardian intended to "put him out of the way." Don Alejandro had not actually attempted to do any thing of this kind, so far as was known; and no case could be made out against him. Don Manuel did not mean that he should have an opportunity to attempt any thing of the kind. Certainly it was safer to keep out of his way, than to tempt him to do a deed which his own brother believed he was capable of doing. Raimundo thought Don Manuel was right: indeed, he could remember enough of Don Alejandro's treatment of him before he left Barcelona, to convince him of his guardian's intentions.

But when he found himself in the boat, escaping from the Tritonia with two of the worst "scalliwags" of the crew, the case seemed to present a different aspect to him. He realized that he was in bad company; and he felt contaminated by their presence. Yet he did not see how he could help himself. The only way he could get out of the scrape was to surrender to the chief steward, and in due time be handed over to the agent of his guardian. Whether he was correct or not in his estimate of his uncle's character, he was sincere in his belief that Don Alejandro intended to do him harm, even to the sacrificing of his life. Independently of his personal fears, he did not think it would be right to give himself up to one who might be tempted to do an evil deed. He concluded to make the best of the situation, and as soon as possible to get rid of his disagreeable companions.

"Where shall we go, Raimundo?" asked Bill Stout, as confidentially as though he had been a part of the enterprise from the beginning.

"We must go on shore, of course," replied the young Spaniard, who was not yet sufficiently reconciled to the situation to be very cordial.

More than this, he had not yet considered what his course should be when he had left the vessel; but it occurred to him, as Bill asked the question, that the *alguacil*, whose action had been fully reported to him by Hugo, might be watching the vessel from the shore. Raimundo looked about him to get a better idea of the situation. The wind was from the north-west, which swung the Prince so that she lay between the Tritonia and the landing-place, and hid her hull from the view of any one on the city side.

"I think we had better not land at any of the usual places," suggested Bark. "Marline, Rimmer, and all the rest of the forward officers, are in charge of the boats at the principal landing."

"I had no idea of going to the city. It would not

be safe for me to show my face there," answered Raimundo; and he directed the boatman to pull to the Barceloneta side of the port, and in such a direction as to keep in the shadow of the vessels of the fleet.

The man offered to land them at a more convenient place; but Raimundo insisted upon going to the point indicated. Very likely the boatman suspected that his passengers were not leaving the vessel to which they belonged in a perfectly regular manner; but probably this would not make any difference to him, as long as he was well paid for his services. Presently the boat grounded on some rocks at the foot of the sea-wall, which rose high above them. As usual the boatman was anxious to obtain another job; and he offered to take them to any point they wished to go to.

"I will take you back to your ship when you are ready to go," continued the man with a smile, and a twinkle of the eye, which was enough to show that he did not believe they intended to return.

Raimundo replied that they had no further use for the boat that day.

"I have a big boat like that," persisted the man, pointing to a felucca which was sailing down the bay.

The craft indicated was about thirty feet long, and carried a large lateen sail.

"Where is she?" asked Raimundo, with interest.

The man pointed up the harbor, and said he could have her ready in a few minutes.

"Do you go out to sea in her?"

"Oh, yes! go to Majorca in her," replied the boatman, quite excited at the prospect of a large job.

"Can you take us to Tarragona in her?" continued

the young Spaniard, to whom the felucca suggested the best means of getting away from Barcelona.

"Certainly I can: there is no trouble about it."

"How much shall you charge to take us there?"

"It is fifteen leagues to Tarragona," replied the boatman, who proceeded to magnify the difficulties of the enterprise as soon as the price was demanded.

"Very well: we can go by the railroad," added Raimundo, who fully comprehended the object of the man.

"Your officers will see you if you go into the city," said the boatman, with a cunning smile.

There was no longer any doubt that the fellow fully comprehended the situation, but the fugitive saw that he would not betray them; for, if he did, he would lose the job, which he evidently intended should be a profitable one.

"Name your price," he added; and he was willing to pay liberally for the service he desired.

"Five hundred *reales*," answered the man.

"Do you think we have so much money?" laughed the fugitive. "We can't make a bargain with you."

"What will you give?" asked the boatman.

"Two hundred *reales*."

After considerable haggling, the bargain was struck at three hundred *reales*, or fifteen dollars; and this was less than the fugitive had expected to pay. The rest of the arrangements were readily made. Filipe, for this was the name he gave, was afraid his passengers would be captured while he went for his felucca; and, keeping in the shadow of the sea-wall, he pulled them around the point on which the old light-house stands, and landed them on some rocks under the wall.

In this position they could not be seen from the vessels of the fleet, or from the landing-place on the other side, while the high wall concealed them from any person on the shore who did not take the trouble to look over at them.

"We shall want something to eat," said Raimundo, as the boatman was about to leave them. "Take this, and buy as much bread and cold meat as you can with it."

Raimundo handed him three dollars in Spanish silver, which Hugo had obtained for him. The large sum of money he had was in Spanish gold, obtained in Genoa. He had a few dollars in silver left for small expenses.

"What are we here for?" asked Bill Stout, who, of course, had not understood a word of the conversation of his companion and the boatman.

Both he and Bark had asked half a dozen times what they were talking about; but Raimundo had not answered them.

"What has been going on between you and that fellow all this time?" asked Bill, in a tone so imperative that the young officer did not like it at all.

"I have made a bargain with him to take us to Tarragona," replied Raimundo coldly.

"And did not say a word to Bark and me about it!" exclaimed Bill.

"If you don't like it you need not go. I did not invite you to come with me."

"Did not invite me!" sneered Bill. "I know you didn't; but we are in the party, and want you to understand that we are no longer under your orders. You needn't take it upon yourself to make arrangements for me."

"I made the arrangement for myself, and I don't ask you to go with me," answered Raimundo with dignity.

"Come, come! Bill, dry up!" interposed Bark. "Do you want to make a row now before we are fairly out of the vessel?"

"I got out of the vessel to get clear of those snobs of officers, and I am not going to have one of them lording it over me here."

"Nonsense! He hasn't done any thing that you can find fault with," added Bark.

"He has made a trade with that boatman to take us somewhere without saying a word to us about it," blustered Bill. "I want to put a check on that sort of thing in the beginning."

"He has done just the right thing. If we had been alone we could not have managed the matter at all."

"I could have managed it well enough myself."

"You can't speak a word of Spanish, nor I either."

"I don't even know where that place is — Dragona — or whatever it is," growled Bill.

"I am not to blame for your ignorance," said Raimundo. "You heard every thing that was said; and, if you don't like it, I am willing to get along without you."

"Come, Bill; we must not get up a row. Raimundo has done the right thing, and for one I am very much obliged to him," continued Bark.

"He might have told us what he was about," added Bill, somewhat appeased by the words of his fellow-conspirator.

"We had no time to spare; and he could not stop to tell the whole story twice over."

"Where is the place we are going to?" demanded Bill in the same sulky tone.

"Tarragona, a seaport town, south of here. How far is it, Mr. Raimundo?"

"About fifty miles."

"Will you tell us now, if you please, what arrangements you made with the boatman?" continued Bark, doing his best to smooth the ruffled feelings of the young Spaniard.

"Certainly I will; but I want to say in the first place that I had rather return to the Tritonia at once than be bullied by Stout or by anybody else. I don't put on any airs, and I mean to treat everybody like a gentleman. I am a Spaniard, and I will not be insulted by any one," said Raimundo, with as much dignity as an hidalgo in Castile.

"I didn't mean to insult you," said Bill mildly.

"Let it pass; but, if it is repeated, we part company at once, whatever the consequences," added Raimundo, who then proceeded to explain what had passed between Filipe and himself.

The plan was entirely satisfactory to Bark; and so it was to Bill, though he had not the grace to say so. The villain had an itching to be the leader of whatever was going on himself; and he was very much afraid that the late second master of the Tritonia would usurp this office if he did not make himself felt in the beginning. He was rather cowed by the lofty stand Raimundo had taken; and he had come to the conclusion that he had better wait till the expedition was a little farther along before he attempted to assert himself again.

"Have you any money?" asked Raimundo, when he had finished his explanation.

"Yes. Both of us have money; and we will pay our share of the cost of the boat," replied Bark, who was ten times more of a man than his companion in mischief.

"Is it Spanish money?"

"No, not any of it. I have seven English sovereigns in gold, and some silver. Bill has twelve sovereigns. I can draw over eighty pounds on my letter of credit; and Bill can get fifty on his."

"I only wanted to know what ready money you had," added Raimundo. "You must not say a word about money when we get into the felucca."

"Why not?" asked Bill, in his surly way, as though he was disposed to make another issue on this point.

"I don't know the boatman; and it is very likely he may have another man with him. There he comes, and there is another man with him," replied Raimundo, as the felucca appeared off the light-house. "If you should show them any large sum of money, or let them know you had it, they might be tempted to throw us overboard for the sake of getting it. Of course, I don't know that they would do any thing of the kind; but it is best to be on the safe side."

"Some of these Spaniards would cut a man's throat for half a dollar," added Bill.

"So would some Americans; and they do it in New York sometimes," replied Raimundo warmly. "I repeat it: don't say a word about money."

"The men in the boat cannot understand us if we do," suggested Bark.

"They may speak English, for aught I know."

"The one you talked with could not."

"I don't know about that. I did not try him in English. We must all pretend that we have very little money, whether we do it in English or in Spanish. When Filipe — that's his name — asked me five hundred *reales* for taking us to Tarragona, I said that I had not so much money."

"And that was a lie; wasn't it?" sneered Bill.

"If it was, it is on my conscience, and not yours; and it may be a lie that will save your life and mine," answered Raimundo sharply.

"I don't object to the lie; but I thought you, one of the parson's lambs, did object to such things," chuckled Bill.

"I hate a lie: I think falsehood is mean and ungentlemanly; but I believe there is a wide difference between a lie told to a sick man, or to prevent a boatman from being tempted to cut your throat, and a lie told to save you from the consequences of your own misconduct."

"Well, you needn't preach: we are not chaplain's lambs," growled Bill.

"Neither am I," added Raimundo. "I am what they call a Christian in Spain, and that is a Roman Catholic. But here is the felucca. Now mind what I have said, for your own safety."

Filipe ran the bow of his craft up to the rocks on which the fugitives were standing, and they leaped on board of her. The boatman's assistant shoved her off, and in a moment more she was driving down the harbor before the fresh breeze. The second man in the boat was not more than twenty years old, while Filipe was apparently about forty-five. He introduced his companion as his son, and said his name was John (*Juan*).

At the suggestion of Raimundo, the fugitives coiled themselves away in the bottom of the felucca, so that no inquisitive glass on board of the vessels or on the shore should reveal their presence to any one that wanted them. In this position they had an opportunity to examine the craft that was to convey them out of the reach of danger, as they hoped and believed. She was not so large as the craft that Filipe had pointed out as the model of his own; but she carried two sails, and was decked over forward so as to form quite a roomy cuddy. She was pointed at both ends, and sailed like a yacht. It was about one o'clock when the party went on board of her, and at her present rate of speed she would reach her destination in six or seven hours. She had the wind on her beam, and the indications were that she would have it fair all the way. There was not a cloud in the sky, and there was every promise of fair weather for the rest of the day. When the felucca had passed Monjuich, the party ventured to move about the craft, as they were no longer in danger of being seen from the city or the fleet; but they took the precaution to keep out of sight when they passed any other craft which might report them to their anxious friends in Barcelona.

"What have you got to eat, Filipe?" asked Raimundo, when the felucca was clear of the city.

"Plenty to eat and drink," replied the skipper.

"Let me see what you have, for I am beginning to have an appetite."

"RAIMUNDO DID NOT HESITATE TO STRIKE HIM DOWN." Page 172.

Juan was directed to bring out the hamper of provisions his father had purchased. Certainly there were enough of them; but the quality was any thing but satisfactory. Coarse black bread, sausages that looked like Bolognas, and half a dozen bottles of cheap wine, were the principal articles in the hamper. The whole could not have cost half the money given to the boatman. But Filipe insisted that he had paid a *peseta* more than the sum handed him.

Raimundo inquired into this matter more because he was anxious to know about the character of the man than because he cared for the sum expended. He felt that he was, in a measure, in this man's power; and he desired to ascertain what sort of a person he had to deal with. If he was not wicked enough to cut the throats of his passengers, or to throw them overboard for their money, he might betray them when there was no more money to be made out of them. The inquiry was not at all satisfactory in its results. Filipe had cheated him on the provisions; and Raimundo was confident that he would do so in other matters to the extent of his opportunities.

The food tasted better than it looked; and Raimundo made a hearty meal, as did all the others on board, including the boatmen. Raimundo would not drink any of the wine; but his companions did so quite freely, in spite of his caution. He noticed that Filipe urged them to drink, and seemed to be vexed when he could not induce him to taste the wine.

"Where are you going when you get to Tarragona?" asked the boatman, when the collation was disposed of.

"I think I shall go to Cadiz, and join my ship when she arrives there," replied Raimundo.

"To Cadiz!" exclaimed Filipe. "How can you go to Cadiz when you have no money?"

Raimundo saw that he had said too much, and that the skipper wished to inquire into his finances.

"I shall get some money in Tarragona," he replied; but he did not deem it prudent to mention his letter of credit.

Filipe continued to ply him with questions, which he evaded answering as well as he could. He did his best to produce the impression on his mind that he had no money. The boatman asked him about his companions, whether they could not let him have all the money he wanted to enable him to reach Cadiz. Why did they leave their ship if they had no money? How did he expect to get money in Tarragona?

"How do I know that you will pay me if you are so poor?" demanded Filipe, evidently much vexed at the result of his inquiry.

"I have money enough to pay you, and a few dollars more," replied Raimundo.

"I don't know: I think you had better pay me now, before I go any farther."

"No, I will not pay you till we get to Tarragona," replied the young Spaniard.

"I don't know that you have money enough to pay me," persisted the boatman.

Raimundo took from his pocket the three isabelinos he had reserved for the purpose of paying for the boat, with the silver he had left, and showed them to the rapacious skipper.

"That will convince you that I have the money," said he, as he returned the gold and silver to his pocket.

He resolutely refused to pay for the boat till her work was done. By this time Bill and Bark, overcome by the wine they had drunk, were fast asleep in the cuddy where they had gone at the invitation of the boatman. Raimundo was inclined to join them; but the skipper was a treacherous fellow, and it was not prudent to do so. After all the man's efforts to ascertain what money he had, he was actually afraid the fellow would attack him, and attempt to search his pockets. There were brigands in Spain,—at least, a party had been recently robbed by some in the south; and there might be pirates as well. So confident was the passenger of the evil intentions of Filipe, that he believed, if he was not robbed, it would be because the man supposed he had no more money than he had shown him. He kept his eye on a spare tiller in the boat, which he meant to use in self-defence if the occasion should require.

Just before dark Bill and Bark, having slept off the effect of the wine, awoke, and came out of the cuddy. Filipe proposed that they should have supper before dark, and ordered Juan to bring out the hamper. Raimundo did not want any supper, and refused to eat or drink. Bark and Bill were not hungry, and also declined. Then the skipper urged them to drink.

"Don't taste another drop," said Raimundo earnestly. "That man means mischief."

"Do you mean to insult me?" demanded Filipe, fixing a savage scowl upon Raimundo.

It was plain enough now that the man understood English, though he had not yet spoken a word of it, and had refused to answer when spoken to in that language. At the same time he left the helm, which Juan took as though he was beside his father for that purpose. Raimundo leaped from his seat, with the tiller in his hand; for he had kept his place where he could lay his hand upon it.

"Stand by me!" shouted he to his companions.

Filipe rushed upon Raimundo, and attempted to seize him by the throat. The young officer struck at him with the tiller, but did not hit him. He dodged the blow; but it fanned his wrath to the highest pitch. Raimundo saw him thrust his hand into his breast-pocket; and he was sure there was a knife there. He raised his club again; but at this instant Bark Lingall threw his arms around the boatman's throat, and, jamming his knees into his back, brought him down on his face in the bottom of the boat.

"Hold him down! don't let him up!" cried Raimundo.

Bark was a stout fellow; and he held on, in spite of the struggles of the Spaniard. At this moment Juan left the tiller, and rushed forward to take a hand in the conflict, now that his father had got the worst of it. He had a knife in his hand, and Raimundo did not hesitate to strike him down with the heavy tiller; and he lay senseless in the bottom of the felucca. The young officer then went to the assistance of Bark Lingall; and, in a few minutes more, they had bound the skipper hand and foot, and lashed him down to the floor.

CHAPTER XII.

SIGHTS IN MADRID.

AFTER an early breakfast — early for Spain — the students were assembled in a large hall provided by the landlord; and Professor Mapps gave the usual lesson relating to the city they were visiting : —

"The population of Madrid has fallen off from about four hundred thousand to the neighborhood of three hundred thousand. The city was in existence in the tenth century, but was not of much account till the sixteenth, when Charles V. took up his residence here. Toledo was at that time the capital, as about every prominent city of Spain had been before. In 1560 Philip III. made Madrid the sole capital of the country; and it has held this distinction down to this day, though Philip II. tried to move it to Valladolid. It is twenty-two hundred feet above the level of the sea; and the cutting off of all the trees in the vicinity — and I may add in all Spain — has injuriously affected the climate. This region has been said to have but two seasons, — 'nine months of winter, and three months of hell.' If it is very cold in winter, it is probably by comparison with the southern part of the peninsula. Like many other cities of Spain, Madrid has been captured by the English and the French."

Though the professor had much more to say, we shall report only these few sentences. The students hastened out to see the city; and the surgeon took the captain and the first lieutenant under his wing, as usual. They went into the *Puerta del Sol*,— the Gate of the Sun. Most of the city in early days lay west of this point, so that its eastern gate was where the centre now is. As the sun first shone on this gate, it was called the gate of the sun. Though the gate is gone, the place where it was located still retains the name. It is nearly in the shape of an ellipse; and most of the principal streets radiate from it. It usually presents a very lively scene, by day or by night. It is always full of pedlers of matches, newspapers, lottery-tickets, and other merchandise.

"Where shall we go?" said the doctor.

"We will leave that to you," replied Sheridan. "You know the ropes in this ship, and we don't."

"I think we will go first to the royal palace; and we had better take a *berlina*, as they call it here."

"A *berlina?* Is it a pill?" asked Murray.

"No; it is a carriage," laughed the doctor. "Do you see that one with a tin sign on the corner, with '*se alquila*' painted on it? That means that the vehicle is not engaged."

The *berlina* was called, and the party were driven down the *Calla del Arenal* to the palace. It is a magnificent building, one of the finest in Europe, towering far above every thing else in the city. It is the most sightly structure in Madrid. In front of it is the *Plaza del Oriente*, and in the rear are extensive gardens, reaching down to the Manzanares. On the right of it are the royal stables, and on the left is the royal armory.

"When I was in Madrid, in the time of the late queen, no one was admitted to the palace because some vandal tourists had damaged the frescos and marbles," said Dr. Winstock. "But for the last year it has been opened. Your uniform and my passport will open the doors to us."

"What has the uniform to do with it?" asked Murray.

"A uniform is generally respected in Europe; for it indicates that those who wear it hold some naval or military office."

"We don't hold any such office," added Sheridan.

"But you are officers of a very respectable institution."

As the doctor anticipated, admission was readily obtained; and the trio were conducted all over the palace, not excepting the apartments of the late queen. There is nothing especially noteworthy about it, for it was not unlike a score of other palaces the party had visited.

In the stables, the party saw the state coaches; but, as they had seen so many royal carriages, they were more interested in an American buggy because it looked like home. The doctor pointed out the old coach in which Crazy Jane carried about with her the body of her dead husband. The provisional government had sold off most of the horses and mules. In the yard is a bath for horses.

From the stables the trio went to the armory, which contains many objects of interest. The suits of armor are kept as clean and nice as they were when in use. Those worn by Charles V. and Philip II. were examined with much care; but there seemed to be no marks of any hard knocks on them. At the head of the room stands a figure of St. Ferdinand, dressed in regal robes, with a golden crown on the head and a sword in the hand, which is borne in solemn procession to the royal chapel by priests, on the 29th of May, and is kept there two weeks to receive the homage of the people.

In another room is a great variety of articles of historic interest, among which may be mentioned the steel writing-desk of Charles V., the armor he wore when he entered Tunis, his camp-stool and bed, and, above all, the steel armor, ornamented with gold, that was worn by Columbus. In the collection of swords were those of the principal kings, the great captain, and other heroes.

"There is the armor of Isabella, which she wore at the siege of Granada," said the doctor.

"Did she fight?" asked Murray.

"No more than her husband. Both were sovereigns in their own right; and it was the fashion to wear these things."

"Very likely she had this on when Columbus called to see her at Granada," suggested Sheridan.

"I don't know about that. I fancy she did not wear it in the house, but only when she presented herself before the army," replied the doctor.

The party spent a long time in this building, so interested were the young men in viewing these memorials of the past grandeur of Spain. After dinner they went to the naval museum, which is near the armory.

It contains a great number of naval relics, models of historic vessels, captured flags, and similar mementos of the past. The chart of Columbus was particularly interesting to the students from the New World. There are several historical paintings, representing scenes in the lives of Cortes, Pizarro, and De Soto. A portrait of Columbus is flanked on each side by those of the sovereigns who patronized him.

"This is a beautiful day," said Dr. Winstock, as they left the museum. "They call it very cold here, when the mercury falls below the freezing point. It does not often get below twenty-four, and seldom so low as that. I think the glass to-day is as high as fifty-five."

"I call it a warm day for winter," added Sheridan.

"But the air of this city is very subtle. It will kill a man, the Spaniards say, when it will not blow out a candle. I think we had better take a *berlina*, and ride over to the *Prado*. The day is so fine that we may possibly see some of the summer glories of the place."

"What are they?" asked Murray.

"To me they are the people who walk there; but of course the place is the pleasantest when the trees and shrubs are in foliage."

A *berlina* was called, and the party drove through the *Calle Mayor*, the *Puerta del Sol*, and the *Calle de Alcala*, which form a continuous street, the broadest and finest in Madrid, from the palace to the Prado, which are on opposite sides of the city. A continuation of this street forms one end of the *Prado;* and another of the *Calle de Atocha*, a broad avenue reaching from the *Plaza Mayor*, near the palace, forms the other end.

These are the two widest streets of Madrid. The *Calle de Alcala* is wide enough to be called a boulevard, and contains some of the finest buildings in the city.

"That must be the bull-ring," said Sheridan, as the party came in sight of an immense circular building. "I have read that it will hold twelve thousand people."

"Some say sixteen thousand; but I think it would not take long to count all it would hold above ten thousand. Philip V. did not like bull-fights, and he tried to do away with them; but the spectacle is the national sport, and the king made himself very unpopular by attempting to abolish it. As a stroke of policy, to regain his popularity, he built this *Plaza de Toros*. It is what you see; but it is open to the weather in the middle; and all bull-fights are held, '*Si el tiempo no lo impide*' (if the weather does not prevent it). This is the *Puerta de Alcala*," continued the doctor, pointing to a triumphal arch about seventy feet high, built by Charles III. "The gardens on the right are the '*Buen Retiro*,' pleasant retreat. Now we will turn, and go through the *Prado*, though all this open space is often called by this name."

"But what is the 'pleasant retreat'?"

"It is a sort of park and garden, not very attractive at that, with a pond, a menagerie, and an observatory. It is not worth the trouble of a visit," added the doctor, as he directed the driver to turn the *berlina*.

"I have often seen a picture of that statue," said Sheridan, as they passed a piece of sculpture representing a female seated on a chariot drawn by lions.

"That is the Cybele."

"Who is she?"

"Wife of Saturn, and mother of the gods," replied Sheridan.

"This is the *Salon del Prado*," continued the doctor, as the carriage turned to the left into an avenue two hundred feet wide. "There are plenty of people here, and I think we had better get out and walk, if you are not too tired; for you want to see the people."

The *berlina* was dismissed, and the party joined the throng of *Madrileños*. Dr. Winstock called the attention of his young friends to three ladies who were approaching them. They wore the mantilla, which is a long black lace veil, worn as a head-dress, but falling in graceful folds below the hips. The ladies — except the high class, fashionable people — wear no bonnets. The mantilla is a national costume, and the fan is a national institution among them. They manage the latter, as well as the former, with peculiar grace; and it has even been said that they flirt with it, being able to express their sentiments by its aid.

"But these ladies are not half so pretty as I supposed the Spanish women were," said Murray.

"That only proves that you supposed they were handsomer than they are," laughed Sheridan.

"They are not so handsome here as in Cadiz and Seville, I grant," added the doctor; "but still I think they are not bad looking."

"I will agree to that," replied Murray. "They are good-looking women, and that's all you can say of them."

"Probably you have got some extravagant ideas about Spanish girls from the novels you have read," laughed the doctor; "and it is not likely that your ideal beauty will be realized, even in Cadiz and Seville. Here is the *Dos de Mayo*."

"Who's she?" asked Murray, looking rather vacantly at a granite obelisk in the middle of an enclosed garden.

"It is not a woman," replied the doctor.

"Excuse me; I think you said a dose of something," added Murray.

"That monument has the name of '*El Dos de Mayo*,' which means 'the second of May.' It commemorates a battle fought on this spot in 1808 by the peasants, headed by three artillerymen, and the French. The ground enclosed is called 'The Field of Loyalty.'"

"What is this long building ahead?" inquired Sheridan.

"That's the Royal Museum, which contains the richest collection of paintings in Europe."

"Isn't that putting it pretty strong, after what we have seen in Italy and Germany?" asked Sheridan.

"I don't say the largest or the best-arranged collection in Europe, but the richest. It has more of the old masters, of the best and most valuable pictures in the world, than any other museum. We will go there to-morrow, and you can judge for yourselves."

"Of course we are competent to do that," added Murray with a laugh.

"We haven't been to any churches yet, doctor," said Sheridan.

"There are many churches in Madrid, but none of any great interest. The city has no cathedral."

"I am thankful for that!" exclaimed Murray. "I have seen churches enough, though of course I shall go to the great cathedrals when we come to them."

"You will be spared in Madrid. Philip II. was asked to erect one; but he would appropriate only a small sum for the purpose, because he did not wish any church to rival that of the Escurial."

"I am grateful to him," added Murray.

"The Atocha church contains an image which is among the most venerated in Spain. It works miracles, and was carved by St. Luke."

"Another job by St. Luke!" exclaimed Murray.

"That is hardly respectful to an image whose magnificent dress and rich jewels would build half a score of cheap churches."

"Are there any theatres in Madrid, doctor?" asked Murray.

"Of course there are; half a dozen of them. The principal is the Royal Theatre, near the palace, where the performance is Italian opera. It is large enough to hold two thousand; but there is nothing Spanish about it. If you want to see the Spanish theatre you must go to some of the smaller ones. As you don't understand Spanish, I think you will not enjoy it."

"I want to see the customs of the country."

"The only custom you will see will be smoking; and you can see that anywhere, except in the churches, where alone, I believe, it is not permitted. Everybody smokes, even the women and children. I have seen a youngster not more than five years old struggling with a *cigarillo;* and I suppose it made him sick before he got through with it; at least, I hope it did, for the nausea is nature's protest against the practice."

"But do the ladies smoke?"

"Not in public; but in private many of them do. I have seen some very pretty girls smoking in Spain."

"I don't remember that I have seen a man drunk in Spain," said Sheridan.

"Probably you have not; I never did. The Spaniards are very temperate."

This long talk brought the party back to the hotel just at dark. The next day was Sunday; but many of the students visited the churches, though most of them were willing to make it a day of rest, in the strictest sense of the word. On Monday morning, as the museum did not open till one o'clock, the doctor and his *protégés* took a *berlina*, and rode out to the palace of the Marquis of Salamanca, where they were permitted to explore this elegant residence without restraint. In one of the apartments they saw a large picture of the Landing of the Pilgrims, by a Spanish artist; and it was certainly a strange subject. Connected with the palace is a museum of antiquities quite extensive for a private individual to own. The Pompeian rooms contain a vast quantity of articles from the buried city.

"Who is this Marquis of Salamanca?" asked Sheridan, as they started on their return.

"He is a Spanish nobleman, a grandee of Spain I suppose, who is somewhat noted as a financier. He has invested some money in railroads in the United States. The town of Salamanca, at the junction of the Erie and Great Western, in Western New York, was named after him," replied Dr. Winstock.

"I have been through the place," added Sheridan.

"This is not a very luxurious neighborhood," said Murray, when they came to one of those villages of poor people, of which there were several just outside of the city.

"Generally in Europe the rich are very rich, and the poor are very poor. Though the rich are not as rich in Spain as in some other countries, there is no exception to the rule in its application to the poor. These hovels are even worse than the homes of the poor in Russia. Wouldn't you like to look into one of them?

"Would it be considered rude for us to do so?" asked Sheridan.

"Not at all. These people are not so sensitive as poor folks in America; but, if they are hurt by our curiosity, a couple of *reales* will repair all the damages."

"Is this a *château en Espagne?*" said Murray. "I have read about such things, but I never saw one before."

"*Châteaux en Espagne* are castles in the air, — things unreal and unsubstantial; and, so far as the idea of comfort is concerned, this is a *château en Espagne*. When we were in Ireland, an old woman ran out of a far worse shanty than this, and, calling it an Irish castle, begged for money. In the same sense we may call this a Spanish castle."

The carriage was stopped, and the party alighted.

"You see, the people live out-doors, even in the winter," said the doctor. "The door of this house is wide open, and you can look in."

The proprietor of the establishment stood near the door. He wore his cloak with as much style as though he had been an hidalgo. Under this garment his clothes were ragged and dirty; and he wore a pair of spatter-dashes, most of the buttons of which were wanting, and it was only at a pinch that they staid on his ankles. His wife and four children stopped their work, or their play, as the case was, and gazed at the unwonted visitors.

"*Buenos dias, caballero,*" said the doctor, as politely as though he had been saluting a grandee.

The man replied no less politely.

"May we look into your house?" asked the doctor.

"*Esta muy a la disposicion de usted,*" replied the *caballero* (it is entirely at your disposal).

This is a *cosa de España*. If you speak of any thing a Spaniard has, he makes you a present of it, be it his house or his horse, or any thing else; but you are not expected to avail yourself of his generosity. It would be as impolite to take him at his word as it would be for him not to place it "at your disposal."

The house was of one story, and had but one door and one window, the latter very small indeed. The floor was of cobble-stones bedded in the mud. The little window was nothing but a hole; there was no glass in it; and the doctor said, that, when the weather was bad, the occupants had to close the door, and put a shutter over the window, so that they had no light. The interior was divided into two rooms, one containing a bed. Every thing was as simple as possible. The roof of the shanty was covered with tile which looked like broken flower-pots. In front, for use in the summer, was an attempt at a veranda, with vines running up the posts.

The doctor gave the smallest of the children a *peseta*, and bade the man a stately adieu, which was answered with dignity enough for an ambassador. The party drove off, glad to have seen the interior of a Spanish house.

"Why did you give the money to the child instead of the father?" asked Sheridan.

"I suppose your experience in other parts of Europe would not help you to believe it, but the average Spaniard who is not a professional beggar is too proud to receive money for any small favor," replied the doctor. "I have had a *peseta* indignantly refused by a man who had rendered me a small serviee. This is as strange as it is true, though, when you come to ride on a *diligencia*, you will find that driver, postilion, and *zagal* will do their best to get a gratuity out of you. I speak only of the Spaniard who does you a favor, and not those with whom you deal; but, as a general rule, the people are too proud to cheat you."

"They are very odd sort of people," added Murray. "There is one shovelling with his cloak on."

"Not an unusual sight. I have seen a man ploughing in the field with his cloak on, and that on a rather warm day. You notice here that the houses are not scattered as they are with us; but even these shanties are built in villages," continued the doctor.

"I noticed that the houses were all in villages in all the country we have come through since we left Barcelona," said Murray.

"Can you explain the reason?"

"I do not see any reason except that is the fashion of the country."

"There is a better reason than that. In early days the people had to live in villages in order to be able to defend themselves from enemies. In Spain the custom never changes, if isolated houses are even safe at the present time."

"What is that sheet of paper hanging on the balcony for?" asked Murray. "There is another; and now I can see half a dozen of them." The *berlina* was within a short distance of the *Puerta del Sol*.

"A sheet of white paper in the middle of the balcony signifies that the people have rooms to let; if at the corner, they take boarders."

The party arrived at the hotel in season for dinner; and, when it was over, they hastened to the *Museo*, or picture-gallery. The building is very long, and of no particular architectural effect. It has ten apartments on the principal floor, in which are placed the gems of the collection. In the centre of the edifice is a very long room which contains the burden of the paintings. There are over two thousand of them, and they are the property of the Crown. Among them are sixty-two by Rubens, fifty-three by Teniers, ten by Raphael, forty-six by Murillo, sixty-four by Velasquez, twenty-two by Van Dyck, forty-three by Titian, thirty-four by Tintoretto, twenty-five by Paul Veronese, and hundreds by other masters hardly less celebrated.

The doctor's party spent three hours among these pictures, and they went to the museum for the same time the next day; for they could better appreciate these gems than most of the students, many of whom were not willing to use a single hour in looking at them. Our party visited the public buildings, and took many rides and walks in the city and its vicinity, which we have not the space to report. On Wednesday morning the ship's company started for Toledo.

CHAPTER XIII.

AFTER THE BATTLE IN THE FELUCCA.

WE left the second master of the Tritonia and the two runaway seamen in a rather critical situation on board of the felucca. We regret the necessity of jumping about all over Spain to keep the run of our characters; but we are obliged to conform to the arrangement of the principal, — who was absolute in his sway, — and follow the young gentlemen wherever he sends them. Though Mr. Lowington was informed, before his departure with the ship's company of the Prince, of the escape of Raimundo and the two "marines," he was content to leave the steps for the recovery of the runaways to the good judgment of the vice-principal in charge of the Tritonia.

Raimundo had managed his case so well that the departure of the three students from the vessel was not discovered by any one on board or on shore. If the *alguacil* was on the lookout for his prisoner, he had failed to find him, or to obtain any information in regard to him. The circumstances had certainly favored the escape in the highest degree. The distance across the harbor, the concealment afforded by the hulls of the vessels of the fleet, and the shadow of the sea-wall under which the fugitives had placed themselves, had prevented them from being seen. Indeed, no one could have seen them, except from the deck of the Tritonia or the Josephine; and probably those on board of the latter were below, as they were on the former.

Of course Mr. Salter, the chief steward of the Tritonia, was very much astonished when he found that the prisoners had escaped from the brig. Doubtless he made as much of an excitement as was possible with only one of his assistants to help him. He had no boat; and he was unable to find one from the shore till the felucca was well out of the harbor. Probably Hugo was as zealous as the occasion required in the investigation of the means by which the fugitives had escaped; but he was as much astonished as his chief when told that Bill Stout and Bark Lingall were gone. The brig was in its usual condition, with the door locked; but the unfastened scuttle soon disclosed the mode of egress selected by the rogues. Mr. Pelham, assisted by Mr. Fluxion, vice-principal of the Josephine, did all they could to find the two "marines," without any success whatever; but they had no suspicion that the second master, who had disappeared the night before, was one of the party.

The next morning all hands from the two consorts were sent on board of the American Prince. Mr. Fluxion was the senior vice-principal, and had the command of the vessel. The ship's company of the Josephine formed the starboard, and that of the Tritonia the port watch. The officers took rank in each grade according to seniority. Mr. Fluxion was unwilling to sail until he had drilled this miscellaneous ship's company in their new duties. He had a superabundance of officers, and it was necessary for them to know their places. In the morning he had telegraphed to the principal at Saragossa, in regard to the fugitives; and the order came back for him to sail without them. Mr. Lowington was not disposed to waste much of his time in looking for runaways: they were pretty sure to come back without much assistance. At noon the Prince sailed for Lisbon; and all on board of her were delighted with the novelty of the new situation. As it is not necessary to follow the steamer, which safely arrived at Lisbon on the following Sunday morning, we will return to Raimundo and his companions.

Filipe, struggling, and swearing the heaviest oaths, was bound hand and foot in the bottom of the felucca, and lashed to the heel of the mainmast. Juan lay insensible in the space between the cuddy and the mainmast, where he had fallen when the young Spaniard hit him with the spare tiller. The boat had broached to when the helm was abandoned by the boatman's son, to go to the assistance of his father. Of course Raimundo and Bark were very much excited by this sudden encounter; and it had required the united strength of both of them to overcome the boatman, though he was not a large man. Bill Stout had done nothing. He had not the pluck to help secure Filipe after he had been thrown down, or rather dragged down, by Bark.

As soon as the victory was accomplished, Raimundo sprang to the helm, and brought the felucca up to her course again. His chest heaved, and his breathing was so violent as to be audible. Bark was in no better condition; and, if Juan had come to his senses at that moment, he might have conquered both of them.

"Pick up that knife, Lingall," said Raimundo, as soon as he was able to speak.

He pointed to the knife which the boatman had dropped during the struggle; and Bark picked it up.

"Now throw it overboard," added the second master. "We can handle these men, I think, if there are no knives in the case."

"No; don't do that!" interposed Bill Stout. "Give it to me."

"Give it to you, you coward!" replied Raimundo. "What do you want of it?"

"I will use it if we get into another fight. I don't like to tackle a man with a knife in his hand, when I have no weapon of any kind," answered Bill, who, when the danger was over, began to assume his usual bullying tone and manner.

"Over with it, Lingall!" repeated Raimundo sharply. "You are good for nothing, Stout: you had not pluck enough to touch the man after your friend had him down."

Bark waited for no more, but tossed the knife into the sea. He never "took any stock" in Bill Stout's bluster; but he had not suspected that the fellow was such an arrant coward. As compared with Raimundo, who had risen vastly in his estimation within the last few hours, he thoroughly despised his fellow-conspirator. If he did not believe it before, he was satisfied now, that the gentlest and most correct students could also be the best fellows. However it had been before, Bill no longer had any influence over him; while he was ready to obey the slightest wish of the second master, whom he had hated only the day before.

"See if you can find the other knife, — the one the young man had," continued Raimundo.

"I see it," replied Bark; and he picked up the ugly weapon.

"Send it after the other. The less knives we have on board, the better off we shall be," added the second master "I don't like the habit of my countrymen in carrying the *cuchilla* any better than I do that of yours in the use of revolvers."

"I think it was stupid to throw away those knives, when you have to fight such fellows as these," said Bill Stout, as he glanced at the prostrate form of the older boatman, who was writhing to break away from his bonds.

"Your opinion on that subject is of no value just now," added Raimundo contemptuously.

"What do you say, Bark?" continued Bill, appealing to his confederate.

"I agree with Raimundo," answered Bark. "I don't want to be mixed up in any fight where knives are used."

"And I object just as much to knifing a man as I do to being knifed," said Raimundo. "Though I am a Spaniard, I don't think I would use a knife to save my own life."

"I would," blustered Bill.

"No, you wouldn't: you haven't pluck enough to do any thing," retorted Bark. "I advise you not to say any thing more on this subject, Stout."

At this moment Filipe made a desperate attempt to free himself; and Bill retreated to the forecastle, evidently determined not to be in the way if another battle took place. Bark picked up the spare tiller the second master had dropped, and prepared to defend himself. Another club was found, and each of those who had the pluck to use was well prepared for another attack.

"Lie still, or I will hit you over the head!" said Bark to the struggling skipper, as he flourished the tiller over him.

But the ropes with which he was secured were strong and well knotted. Bark was a good sailor, and he had done this part of the work. He looked over the fastenings, and made sure that they were all right.

"He can't get loose, Mr. Raimundo," said he.

"But Juan is beginning to come to his senses," added the second master. "He has just turned half over."

"I hope he is not much hurt: we may get into a scrape if he is."

"I was just thinking of that. But I don't believe he is very badly damaged," added Raimundo. "If the old man can't get away, suppose you look him over, and see what his condition is."

Bark complied with this request. Filipe seemed to be interested in this inquiry; and he lay quite still while the examination was in progress. The young sailor found a wound and a considerable swelling on the side of Juan's head; but it was now so dark that he could not distinctly see the nature of the injury.

"Have you a match, Mr. Raimundo?" he asked.

"I have not. We were not allowed to have matches on board the Tritonia," replied the second master.

"*Tengo pajuelas*," said Filipe. "*Una linterna en el camarote de proa.*"

"What does he say?" inquired Bark, glad to find that the skipper was no longer pugnacious.

"He says he has matches, and that there is a lantern in the cuddy," replied Raimundo. "Here, Stout, look in the cuddy, and see if you can find a lantern there."

Bill had the grace to obey the order, though he was tempted to refuse to do so. He found the lantern, for he had seen it while he lay in the cuddy. He brought it to Bark, and took the lamp out of the globe.

"You will find some matches in Filipe's pockets," added Raimundo.

"I have matches enough," answered Bill.

"I forgot that you used matches," said the second master; "but I am glad you have a chance to make a better use of them than you did on board of the Tritonia."

"You needn't say any thing! You are the first officer that ever run away from that vessel," growled Bill, as he lighted a match, and communicated the blaze to the wick of the lamp.

It was a kerosene-lamp, just such as is used at home, and probably came from the United States. Bark proceeded to examine the wound of Juan, and found it was not a severe one. The young man was rapidly coming to himself, and in a few minutes more he would be able to take care of himself.

"I think we had better move him into the cuddy,"

suggested Bark. "We can make him comfortable there, and fasten him in at the same time."

"That's a capital idea, Lingall; and if Stout will take the helm I will help you move him," answered Raimundo.

"I will help move him," volunteered Bill.

"I supposed you were afraid of him," added the second master. "He has about come to himself."

Juan spoke then, and complained of his head. Bark and Bill lifted him up, and carried him to the cuddy, where they placed him on the bed of old garments upon which they had slept themselves during the afternoon. Bark had some little reputation among his companions as a surgeon, probably because he always carried a sheet of court-plaster in his pocket, and sometimes had occasion to attend to the wounds of his friends. Perhaps he had also a taste for this sort of thing; for he was generally called upon in all cases of broken heads, before the chief steward, who was the amateur surgeon of the Tritonia, was summoned. At any rate, Bark, either from genuine kindness, or the love of amateur surgical dressing, was not content to let the wounded Spaniard rest till he had done something more for him. He washed the injury in fresh water, closed the ugly cut with a piece of court-plaster, and then bound up the head of the patient with his own handkerchief.

The wounded man tried to talk to him; but he could not understand a word he said. If his father spoke English, it was certain that the son did not. When he had done all this, Bark relieved Raimundo at the helm, and the latter went forward to talk with the patient, who was so quiet that Bark had not thought of fastening the door of the cuddy.

"I am well now," said Juan, "and I want to go out."

"You must not go out of this place; if you do, we shall hit you over the head again," replied the second master sternly.

"Where is my father?" asked the patient.

"He is tied hand and foot; and we shall tie you in the same way if you don't keep still and obey orders," added Raimundo. "Lie still where you are, and no harm shall be done to you."

Raimundo, taking the lantern with him, left the cuddy, and fastened it behind him with the padlock he found in the staple. Putting the key in his pocket, he made an examination into the condition of Filipe, with the aid of the lantern. He found him still securely bound, and, better than that, as quiet as a lamb.

"How is my son?" asked he.

"He is doing very well. We have dressed his wound, and he will be as well as ever in a day or two," replied Raimundo.

"*Gracias, muchos gracias!*" exclaimed the prisoner.

"If we had been armed as you were, he might have lost his life," added Raimundo, moving aft to the helm. "I think we are all right, Lingall."

"I am very glad of it. We came very near getting into a bad scrape," replied Bark.

"It is bad enough as it is. I have been afraid of something of this kind ever since we got well out of the port of Barcelona," continued the second master. "The villain asked me so many questions about my money that my suspicions were excited, and I was on the watch for him. Then he was so anxious that we should drink wine, I was almost sure he meant mischief."

"I am very sorry I drank any wine. It only makes my head ache," replied Bark penitently.

"I have heard my uncle speak of these men; and I know something about them."

"The wine did not make my head ache," said Bill.

"That's because there is nothing in it," answered Raimundo, who could not restrain his contempt for the incendiary.

"But I do not understand exactly how the fight was begun," said Bark. "The first I knew, the boatman sprang at you."

"That's the first I knew, though I was on the lookout for him, as I had been all the afternoon. He understood what I meant when I told you this man means mischief."

"But he told you he could not speak English."

"Most of the boatmen speak more or less English: they learn it from the passengers they carry. He wanted to know whether we had money before he did any thing. He was probably satisfied that we had some before he attempted to assault us."

"I know you have money," cried Filipe, in English; and he seemed to be more anxious to prove the correctness of his conclusion than to disprove his wicked intentions.

"You have not got any of it yet," replied Raimundo.

"But I will have it!" protested the villain.

"You tempt me to throw you and your son overboard," said Raimundo sternly, in Spanish.

"Not my son," answered the villain, suddenly changing his tone. "He is his mother's only boy."

"You should have thought of that before you brought him with you on such business."

The boatman, for such a villain as he was, seemed to have a strange affection for his son; and Raimundo was almost willing to believe he had not intended till some time after they left the port to rob his passengers. Perhaps, with the aid of the wine, he had expected an easy victory; for, though the students were all stout fellows, they were but boys.

"I will not harm you if you do not injure my boy," pleaded Filipe.

"It is not in your power to harm us now; for we have all the power," replied the second master.

"But you are deserters from your ship. I can tell where you are," added Filipe, with something like triumph in his tones.

"We expect you to tell all you know as soon as you return."

"I can do it in Tarragona: they will arrest you there if I tell them."

"We are not afraid of that: if we were, we should throw you and your son overboard."

Filipe did not like this side of the argument, and he was silent for some time. It must be confessed that Raimundo did not like his side any better. The fellow could inform the police in Tarragona that the party were deserters, and cause them to be sent back to Barcelona. Though this was better than throwing the boatman and his son overboard, which was only an idle threat, it would spoil all his calculations, and defeat all his plans. He studied the case for some time, after he had explained to Bark what had passed between himself and Filipe in Spanish.

"You want more money than you were to receive for the boat; do you, Filipe?" asked he.

"I have to pay five hundred *reales* on this boat in three days, or lose it and my small one too," replied the boatman; and the passenger was not sure he did not invent the story as he went along. "I am not a bad man; but I want two hundred *reales* more than you are to pay me."

"Then you expect me to pay what I agreed, after what has happened, do you?"

"You promised to pay it."

"And you promised to take me to Tarragona; and you have been trying to murder me on the way," exclaimed Raimundo indignantly.

"Oh, no! I did not mean to kill you, or to hurt you; only to take two hundred *reales* from you," pleaded the boatman, with the most refreshing candor.

"That's all; is it?"

The villain protested, by the Virgin and all the saints in the Spanish calendar, that he had not intended any thing more than this; and Raimundo translated what he said to his companion.

"There are a lot of lights on a high hill ahead," said Bill Stout, who had been looking at the shore, which was only a short distance from them.

"That must be Tarragona," replied the second master, looking at his watch by the light of the lantern. "It is ten minutes of seven; and we have been six hours on the trip. I thought it would take about this time. That must be Tarragona; it is on a hill eight hundred feet high."

"We have been sailing very fast, the last three hours," added Bark. "But how are we to get out of this scrape?"

"I will see. Keep a sharp lookout on the starboard, Lingall; and, when you see a place where you think we can make a landing, let me know.—Can you steer, Stout, and keep her as she is?"

"Of course I can steer. I don't give up to any fellow in handling a boat," growled Bill.

Raimundo gave him the tiller; but he watched him for a time, to see that he made good his word. The bully did very well, and kept the felucca parallel with the shore, as she had been all the afternoon.

"There is a mole makes out from the shore," continued the active skipper to Bark, who had gone forward of the foremast to do the duty assigned to him.

"Ay, ay! I can see it," replied Bark.

"I think we need not quarrel, Filipe," said Raimundo, bending over the prisoner, and unloosing the rope that bound his hands to the mast; but they were still tied behind him. "We are almost into Tarragona, and what we do must be done quickly."

"Don't harm Juan," pleaded Filipe.

"That will depend on yourself, whether we do or not," replied Raimundo, as fiercely as he could speak. "We are not to be trifled with; and Americans carry pistols sometimes."

"I will do what you wish," answered Filipe.

"I will give you what I agreed, and two hundred

reales besides, if you will keep still about our being deserters; and that is all the money we have."

"*Gracias!* I will do it!" exclaimed the boatman. "Release me, and I will land you outside of the mole, and not go near the town to speak to any person."

"I am afraid to trust you."

"You can trust a Catalan when he promises;" and Filipe proceeded to call upon the Virgin and the saints to witness what he said.

"Where can we land?" asked the second master.

The boatman looked over the rail of the felucca; and, when he had got his bearings, he indicated a point where a safe landing might be made. It was not a quarter of a mile distant; and Filipe said the mainsail ought to be furled. Raimundo picked up the spare tiller, — for, in spite of the Catalan's oath and promise, he was determined to be on the safe side, — and then unfastened the ropes that bound the prisoner.

"If you play me false, I will brain you with this club, and pitch your son into the sea!" said Raimundo, as tragically as he could do the business.

"I will be true to my promise," he replied, as he brailed up the mainsail.

"You see that your money is ready for you as soon as you land us," continued Raimundo, as he showed the villain five *Isabelinos* he held in one hand, while he grasped the spare tiller with the other.

"*Gracias!*" replied Filipe, who was possibly satisfied when he found that he was to make the full sum he had first named as his price; and it may be that he was tempted by the urgency of his creditor to rob his passengers.

"Have your pistol ready, Lingall!" added Raimundo, as the boatman, who had taken the helm from Bill, threw the felucca up into the wind, and her keel began to grate on the rocks.

"Ay, ay!" shouted Bark.

The boat ran her long bow up to the dry land, and hung there by her bottom. Raimundo gave the five hundred *reales* to Filipe, and sprang ashore with the tiller in his hand. Calling to Bark, they shoved off the felucca, and then ran for the town.

CHAPTER XIV.

TOLEDO, AND TALKS ABOUT SPAIN.

TOLEDO is about fifty-six miles from Madrid. As the principal had laid out a large day's work, it became necessary to procure a special train, as the first regular one did not reach Toledo till after eleven o'clock. The special was to leave at six; and it was still dark when the long line of small omnibuses that conveyed the company to the station passed through the streets.

"What is the matter with that man?" asked Sheridan, attracted by the cries of a man on the sidewalk with a sort of pole in his hand.

"That's a watchman," replied the doctor.

"What's he yelling about?"

"'*Las cinco y medio y sereno*' is what he says," added the surgeon. "'Half-past five and pleasant weather' is the translation of his cry. When it rains he calls the hour, and adds '*fluvioso;*' when there is a fire he informs the people on his beat of the fact, and gives the locality of the conflagration, which he gets from the fire-alarm. In some of the southern cities, as in Seville, the watchman indulges in some pious exclamations, 'Twelve o'clock, and may the Virgin watch over our good city!' It used to be the fashion in some of the cities of our country, for the guardian of the night to indulge in these cries to keep himself awake; and I have heard him shout, 'One o'clock and all is well' in Pittsburg."

"I have walked about the *Puerta del Sol* in the evening; but I have not seen a watchman," added Sheridan.

"Probably they do not use the cry early in the night, in the streets where the people are gathered; at least, there seems to be no need of it," replied the doctor. "But I suppose there are a great many things yet in Madrid that you have not seen. For instance, did you notice the water-carriers?"

"I did," answered Murray. "They carry the water in copper vessels something like a soda-fountain, placed upon a kind of saddle, like the porters in Constantinople.

"Some of them have donkeys, with panniers in which they put kegs, jars, and glass vessels filled with water. These men are called '*aguadors*,' and their occupation is considered mean business; the *caballero* whose house we visited would be too proud to be a water-carrier, and would rather starve than engage in it."

The tourists left the omnibuses, and took their places in the cars. As soon as the train had started, as it was still too dark to see the country, the doctor and his friends resumed the conversation about the sights of Madrid.

"Did you go to the *Calle de la Abada?*" asked Dr. Winstock.

"I don't know: I didn't notice the name of any such street," replied Sheridan; and Murray was no wiser, both of them declaring that the Spanish names were too much for them.

"It is not unlike Market Street in Philadelphia, twenty years ago, when the middle of the avenue was filled with stalls in a wooden building."

"I saw that," added Sheridan. "The street led to a market. All the men and women that had any thing to sell were yelling with all their might. They tackled every person that came near."

"I saw the dirt-cart go along this same street," said Murray. "It was a wagon with broad wheels as though it was to do duty in a swamp, with a bell fixed on the forward part. At the ring of the bell, the women came out of their houses, and threw baskets of dirt into the vehicle, which a man in it emptied and returned to them."

"I was in the city in fruit time once, and saw large watermelons sold for four and six *cuartos* apiece, a *cuarto* being about a cent," continued the doctor. "The nicest grapes sold for six *cuartos* a pound. Meat is dear, and so is fish, which has to be brought from ports on the Mediterranean and the Bay of Biscay. Bread is very good and cheap; but the shops you saw were not bakeries: these are off by themselves."

"They don't seem to have any objection to lotteries in Madrid," said Sheridan. "I couldn't move in the great streets without being pestered with the sellers of lottery-tickets."

"There are plenty of them; for the Spaniards wish to make fortunes without working for them."

"Many of the lottery-venders are boys," added Murray. "They called me Señorito."

"They called me the same. The word is a title of respect, which means master. The drawing of a lottery is a great event in the city, and the newspaper is sometimes filled with the premium numbers."

"I did not see so many beggars as I expected, after all I had read about them," said Sheridan. "But I could understand their lingo, when they said, 'For the love of God.'"

"That is their universal cry. You will see enough in the south to make up the deficiency of the capital," laughed the doctor. "They swarm in Granada and Malaga; and you can't get rid of them. In Madrid, as in the cities of Russia, you will find the most of the beggars near the churches, relying more upon those who are pious enough to attend divine service than upon those in the busy part of the city. They come out after dark, and station themselves at any blank wall, where there are no doors and windows, and address the passers-by. By the way, did you happen to see a cow-house?" asked the doctor.

Neither of the two students knew what he meant.

"It is more properly a milk-shop. In the front you will see cups, on a clean white cloth on the table, for those who wish to drink milk on the spot. Behind a barred petition in the rear you will notice a number of cows, some with calves, which are milked in the presence of the customers, that they may know they get the genuine article."

"Don't they keep any pump-handle?" asked Murray.

"I never saw any," laughed the surgeon. "The customers are allowed to put in the water to their own taste, which I think is the best arrangement."

"I saw plenty of cook-shops, like those in Paris," said Sheridan. "In one a cook was frying something like Yankee doughnuts."

"If you got up early enough to visit the breakfast-stalls of the poorer people, you would have been interested. A cheap chocolate takes the place of coffee, which with bread forms the staple of the diet. But the shops are dirty and always full of tobacco-smoke. The higher classes in Spain are not so much given to feasting and dining out as the English and Americans. They are too poor to do it, and perhaps have no taste for such expensive luxuries. The *tertulia* is a kind of evening party that takes the place of the dinner to some extent, and is a *cosa de España*. Ladies and gentlemen are invited, — except to literary occasions, which are attended only by men, — and the evening is passed in card-playing and small talk. Lemonade, or something of the kind, is the only refreshment furnished.

"They go home sober, then," laughed Murray.

"Spaniards always go home sober; but they do not even have wine at the *tertulia*."

"I have heard a great deal said about the *siesta* in Spain; and I have read that the shops shut up, and business ceased entirely, for two or three hours in the middle of the day," said Sheridan; "but I did not see any signs of the suspension of business in Madrid."

"Very many take their *siesta*, even in Madrid; and in the hot weather you would find it almost as you have described it, — as quiet as Sunday," replied the doctor.

"Sunday was about as noisy a day as any in Madrid," added Murray.

"I meant a Sunday at home or in London. When I was here last, the thirty-first day of October came on Sunday; and it was the liveliest day I ever saw in Spain. The forenoon was quiet; for some of the people went to church. At noon there was a cock-fight, attended by some of the most noted men in Spain; and I went to it, though I was thoroughly disgusted both with the sacrilege and the barbarity of the show. At three o'clock came a bull-fight, lasting till dark, in which eight bulls and seven horses were killed. In the evening was the opera, and a great time at all the theatres. I confess that I was ashamed of myself for visiting these places on the sabbath; but I was in Spain to learn the manners and customs of the people, and excused myself on this plea. Monday was the first day of November, which is All Saints' Day. Not a shop was open. The streets were almost deserted; and there was nothing like play to be seen, even among the children. It was like Sunday at home or in London, though perhaps even more silent and subdued. On this day the people visit the cemeteries, and decorate the tombs and graves of the dead with wreaths of flowers and *immortelles*. I pointed out to you the cemetery in the rear of the *Museo*. I visited it on that day; and it was really a very solemn sight."

"I wish I had visited the cemetery," said Sheridan.

"I am sorry you did not; but I did not think of it at the time we were near it. It is a garden surrounded by high walls, like parts of those we saw in Italy. In this wall are built a great many niches deep enough to receive a coffin, the lid of which, in Spain, as in Washington, is *dos d'âne*, or roof-shaped; and the cell is made like it at the top. Besides these catacombs, there are graves and tombs. As in Paris these are often seen with flowers, the toys of children, portraits, and other mementos of the departed, laid upon them."

"I saw a funeral in Geronimo Street yesterday," added the captain. "The hearse was an open one, drawn by four horses covered with black velvet. I followed it to a church, and saw the service, which was not different from what I have seen at home. When the procession started for the grave, it consisted mostly of *berlinas;* and its length increased with every rod it advanced."

"I was told, that, when a person dies in Spain, the friends of the family send in a supply of cooked food, on the supposition that the bereaved are in no condition to attend to such matters," continued the doctor. "But it is light enough now for us to see the scenery."

The country was flat and devoid of interest at first; but it began to improve as the train approached Aranjuez, where the kings have a royal residence, which the party were to visit on the return from Toledo.

"What river is that, Dr. Winstock?" asked Murray.

"*El Tajo,*" replied the doctor, with a smile.

"Never heard of it," added Murray.

"There you labor under one of the disadvantages of a person who does not understand the language of the country in which he is travelling; for you are as familiar with the English name of this river as you are with that of the Rhine," replied the doctor.

"It is the Tagus," added Sheridan. "I know that Toledo is on this river."

"Who could suspect that *El Tah-hoe* was the Tagus?" queried Murray.

"You would if you knew Spanish."

"There is a Spanish *caballero*, mounted on a mule," said Murray, calling the attention of the party to a peasant who was sitting sideways on his steed.

"All of them ride that way," added Sheridan.

"Not all of them do, for there is a fellow straddling his donkey behind two big panniers," interposed the surgeon.

The train continued to follow the river till it reached Toledo. The students got out of the cars, and were directed to assemble near the station in full view of the ancient city. The day was clear and mild, so that it was no hardship to stand in the open air, and listen to the description of the city given by Professor Mapps.

"Toledo, as you can see for yourselves, is situated on a hill, or a series of hills, which rise to a considerable height above the rest of the country. Some of the old Spanish historians say that the city was founded soon after the creation of the world; but better authorities say it was begun by the Romans in the year B. C. 126, which makes it old enough to satisfy the reasonable vanity of the citizens of the place. Of course it was captured by the Moors, and recaptured by the Spaniards; and many of the buildings, and the bridge you see are the work of the Romans and the Moors. Under the Goths, in the seventh century, Toledo became very wealthy and prosperous, and in its best days is said to have had a population of a quarter of a million. It was made the capital of Spain in 567.

Early in the eighth century the Moors obtained possession of the city, and made many improvements. In 1085, after a terrible siege, Alfonso VI. of Castile took it from the Moors, and it was again made the capital. The historians who carry the founding of Toledo almost back to the flood say that the Jews fled from Jerusalem, when it was captured by Nebuchadnezzar, to this city. Be this as it may, there were a great many Hebrews in Toledo in ancient days. They were an industrious people, and they became very wealthy. This people have been the butt of the Christians in many lands, and they were so here. They were persecuted, and their property confiscated; and it is said that the Jews avenged their wrongs by opening the gates of the city to the Moors; and then when the Moors served them in the same way, and despoiled them of their wealth, they admitted the army of Alfonso VI. by the same means. It has since been retained by the Christians. It was the capital and the ecclesiastic head of the nation. The archbishops of Toledo were immensely wealthy and influential.

"One of them was Ximenes, afterward cardinal, the Richelieu of Spain, and one of the most famous characters of history. He was the powerful minister of Ferdinand the Catholic, and the regent of the kingdom in the absence of Charles V. He was a priest who continually mortified his body, and at the same time a statesman of the highest order. He was the confessor of Isabella I. When he was made archbishop of Toledo and head of the Church in Spain, he refused to accept the high honor till he was compelled to do so by the direct command of the pope. When he appeared at court in his monkish robes, looking more like a half-starved hermit than the primate of Spain, the courtiers laughed at him; but he meekly bore the sneers and the scoffs of the light-hearted. He was required by the pope to change his style of living, and make it conform to his high position. He obeyed the order; but he wore the haircloth shirt and frock of the order to which he belonged under his robes of purple. In the elegant apartments of his palace, he slept on the floor with a log of wood for a pillow. He led an expedition against the Moors into Africa, and captured Oran. As regent he maintained the authority of the king against the grandees, and told them they were to obey the king and not to deliberate over his command. By his personal will he subdued the great nobles.

"The Moors brought to Toledo, from Damascus, the art of tempering steel for sword-blades; and weapons from either of these cities have a reputation all over the world. There is a manufactory of swords and other similar wares; and, while some contend that the blades made here are superior to any others, more insist that those made in England are just as good. When the capital was removed to Valladolid, Toledo began to decline; and now it has only fifteen thousand inhabitants. In the days that are past, the Jews and the Moors have been driven out of Spain to a degree that has retarded the prosperity of the country; for both the Hebrews and the Moslems were industrious and thriving races, and added greatly to the wealth of the nation. In religion Ferdinand and Isabella would be considered bigots and fanatics in our time; and their statesmanship would confound the modern student of political economy. But they did not live in our time; and we are grateful to them for the good they did, regardless of their religious or political views.

"The large square structure which crowns the hill is the *Alcazar*, or palace. It is in ruins, but what remains of it is what was rebuilt for the fourth time. It was occupied by the Moorish and Gothic kings, as well as by those of Castile and Leon. The principal sight of the city is the cathedral. It is three hundred and seventy-three feet long, and a little less than two hundred in width. The first church on the spot was begun in the year 587. Among the relics you saw in the Escurial was the entire skeleton of St. Eugenius, the first Archbishop of Toledo, who was buried at St. Denis; and his remains were given to Philip II. by the King of France. He presided at a council held in the original cathedral, which was also visited, Dec. 18, 666, by the Virgin (the hour of the day is not given); and it appears that she made one or more visits at other times. The present church was begun in 1227, and completed in 1493, the year after the discovery of America. One of its chapels is called the Capilla Mosarabe; and perhaps a word about it may interest you. When the Moors captured the city, certain Christians remained, and were allowed to enjoy their own religion; and, being separated from those of the faith, they had a ritual which was peculiarly their own. When the city was restored to the Christians, these people preferred to retain the prayer-book, the customs and traditions, which had come down to them from their own past. The clergy objected, and all efforts to make them adopt the Roman forms were useless. A violent dispute arose, which threatened serious consequences. It was finally decided to settle the question after the manner of the times, by single combat; and each party selected its champion. They fought, and the victory was with the Mosarabic side. But the king Alfonso VI. and the clergy were not satisfied, and, declaring that the means of deciding the case had been cruel and impious, proposed another trial. This time it was to be the ordeal by fire. A heap of fagots was lighted in the *Zocodover*, — the public square near the cathedral, — and the Roman and the Mosarabic prayer-books were committed to the flames. The Roman book was burned to ashes, while the Toledan version remained unconsumed in the fire. There was no way to get around this miraculous decision; and the people of the city retained their ritual. When Ximenes became archbishop he seems to have had more regard than his predecessors for the old ritual, called the Apostolic Mass; and he not only ordained an order of priests for this especial service, but built the chapel I have mentioned. I will not detain you any longer, though there is much more that might be said about this interesting city."

Though the walk was rather long, the omnibuses were scarce, and most of the students were obliged to foot it into the city. The doctor and his travelling pupils preferred this, because they wished to look at the bridge and the towers on the way. They spent some time on the former in looking down into the rapid river, and in studying the structures at either end. The original bridge was built by the Romans, rebuilt by the Moors, and repaired by the Spaniards.

"You have been in the East enough to know that the Orientals are fond of baths and other water luxuries. The Jews brought to Toledo some knowledge of the hydraulics of the Moslems; and they built an immense water-wheel in the river, which Murray says was ninety cubits — at least one hundred and thirty-five feet — high, to force the water up the hill to the city through pipes," said the doctor, as he pointed out the ruins of a building used for this purpose.

"I said it was ninety cubits high?" exclaimed Murray.

"I ought to have said 'Ford,' since he prepared the hand-book of Spain that goes under your name."

"I accept the amendment," laughed Murray.

"And now there are no water-works in Toledo, except such as you see crossing the bridge before us," added the surgeon, as he indicated a donkey with one keg fixed in a saddle, like a saw-horse, and two others slung on each side.

The party passed through the *Puerta del Sol*, which is an old and gloomy tower, with a gateway through it. It is a Moorish structure; and, after examining it, they continued up the slope which winds around the hill to the top, and reached the square to which the professor had alluded. To the students the city presented a dull, deserted, desolate, and inhospitable appearance. It looked as though the people had got enough of the place, and had moved out of town. Though full of treasures for the student of architecture and of antiquity, it had but little interest to progressive Young America.

The party went at once to the cathedral. There is no outside view of it except over the tops of the houses, though portions of it may be seen in different places. The interior was grand to look upon, but too grand to describe; and we shall report only some of Dr. Winstock's talks to his pupils.

"This is the *Puerta del Niño Perdido*, or the Gate of the Lost Child," said he as they entered the church. "The story is the foundation of many a romance of the olden time. The clergy accused the wealthy Hebrews of crucifying, as they did the Saviour, a Christian boy, in order to use his heart in the passover service as a charm against the Inquisition. The gate takes the name from a fresco near it, representing the scene when the lost child was missed. The Jews were charged with the terrible deed, and plundered of their wealth, which was the whole object of the persecution."

The party walked through the grand structure, looked into the choir in the middle, where a service was in progress, and passed through several chapels, stopping a considerable time in the *Capilla Mayor*, where are monuments of some of the ancient kings and other great men.

"This is the tomb of Cardinal Mendoza," said the doctor. "He was an historian, a scholar, and, like Ximenes, a statesman and a warrior. The marble-work in the rear of the altar cost two hundred thousand ducats, or six times as many dollars."

"One hundred and twenty schoolhouses at ten thousand dollars apiece packed into that thing!" exclaimed Murray.

"And Mr. Ford calls it a fricassee of marble!'" laughed the doctor, as they walked into the next chapel. "This is the *Capilla de Santiago*. Do you know who he was?"

"Of course we do. He was the patron saint of Spain, — St. James, one of the apostles," replied Sheridan.

"Do you remember what became of him?"

"He suffered martyrdom under Herod Agrippa," answered the captain.

"The Spaniards carry his history somewhat farther than that event. As they wanted a distinguished patron, and Rome had appropriated Peter and Paul, they contented themselves with James the Elder, the son of Zebedee, and the brother of John. When he was dead, his body was conveyed by some miraculous agency to Jaffa, where it embarked in a boat for Barcelona, the legend informs us. Instead of going on shore, like a peaceable corpse, it continued on its voyage, following the coast of Spain, through the Strait of Gibraltar, to the shore of Galicia, where it made a landing at a place called Padron; or rather the dead-boat got aground there. The body was found by some fishermen, who had the grace to carry it to a cave, where, as if satisfied with its long voyage made in seven days, beating the P. and O. Steamers by a week, it rested peaceably for eight hundred years. At the end of this long period, it seems to have become restless again, and to have caused certain telegraphic lights to be exhibited over the cave. They were seen by a monk, who informed the bishop of the circumstance. He appears to have understood the meaning of the lights, and examined the cave. He found the body, and knew it to be that of St. James; but he has wisely failed to put on record the means by which he identified it. A church was built to contain the tomb of the patron saint; but it was afterwards removed to the church of Santiago, twelve miles distant."

The party crossed the church, and entered the Chapel of San Ildefonso. This saint, a primate of Toledo, was an especial champion of the Virgin, and so won her favor, that she came down from heaven, and seated herself in his chair. She remained during matins, chanting the service, and at its close placed the church robes on his shoulders. The primate's successor undertook to sit down in this chair, but was driven out by angels, which was rather an imputation upon his sanctity. The Virgin repeated the visit several times. St. Ildefonso's body was stolen by the Moors, but it was recovered by a miracle. The sacred vestment the Virgin had placed upon his back was taken away at the same time; but no miracle seems to have been interposed to restore it, though it is said to be in Oviedo, invisible to mortal eyes. In another part of the edifice is the very stone on which the Virgin stepped when she came first to the church. It is enclosed by small iron bars, but the fingers may be inserted so as to press it; and holes are worn into it from the frequent touchings of the pilgrims to this shrine.

"Here are the portraits of all the cardinals, from St. Eugenio down to the present time," said the doctor as they entered the Chapter House. "Cardinal Albornez died in Rome, and the pope desired to send his remains to Toledo. As this was in 1364, there was no regular line of steamers, or an express company, to attend to the transportation: so he offered plenary indulgences to those who would undertake the mission of conveying the body to its distant resting-place. There were plenty of poor people who could not purchase such favors for their souls; and they were glad of the job to bear the cardinal on their shoulders from town to town till they arrived here."

"Where is the chapel the professor told us about?" asked Sheridan.

"We will go to that now."

This chapel, though very rich in church treasures, and one of the most venerated in the cathedral as built to preserve the ancient ritual, contained nothing that engaged the attention of the students, and Mr. Mapps had already told its story. They hardly looked at the image of the Virgin, which is dressed in magnificent costume, covered with gold and jewels, when it is borne in procession on Corpus Christi Day.

"I have seen enough of it," said Murray, as they left the cathedral, and walked to the *Alcazar*.

The old palace was only a reminder of what had been; but the view from its crumbling walls was the best thing about it. The party decided not to visit the sword-factory, which is two miles out of the city; and they went next to the church of *San Juan de los Reyes*. It was a court chapel, and was erected by the Catholic king to commemorate a victory. It is Gothic; but the chains that are hung over the outside of it were all that challenged the interest of the students.

"Those chains were the votive offerings of captives who were released when Granada was taken by Ferdinand and Isabella," said the doctor, when his pupils began to express their wonder. "There are some very fine carvings and frescos in this church."

"I don't care for them," yawned Murray: "I will wait here while you and Sheridan go in." But the captain did not care to go in; and they continued their walk to *Santa Maria la Blanca* and *El Transito,* two churches which had formerly been synagogues. They were very highly ornamented; but by this time the students wanted their dinner more than to see the elaborate workmanship of the Jews or the Moors. They were tired too; for Toledo with its up and down streets is not an easy place to get about in. Some of the boys said it reminded them of Genoa; but it is more like parts of Constantinople, with its steep hills and Moorish houses.

The party dined in various places in the city; and at two o'clock they took the train for Aranjuez, and arrived there in an hour.

"The late queen used to live here three months of the year," said the doctor, as they walked from the station to the palace. "The town is at the junction of the Jarama and the Tagus, and it is really a very pretty place. There is plenty of water. Charles V. was the first of the kings of Spain to make his residence at Aranjuez. A great deal of work has been done here since his time, by his successors."

The students walked through the gardens, and went through the palace. Perhaps the camels kept here were more interesting to the young gentlemen, gorged with six months' sight-seeing in all the countries of Europe, than any thing else they saw at the summer residence of the kings of Spain.

At the station there is a very fair hotel with restaurant, where the party had supper. But they had four hours of weary waiting before the train for *Ciudad Real* would arrive; and most of them tried to sleep, for it had been a long day.

"Better be here than at the junction of this road with that to Toledo," said the doctor, as he fixed himself for a nap. "The last time I was here I did not understand it; and, when I came from Toledo, I got off the train at the junction, which is Castillejo, ten miles from Aranjuez."

"I noticed the place when we went down this morning," replied Sheridan. "The station is little better than a shed, and there is no town there."

"The train was late; and I had to wait there without my supper from eight o'clock till after midnight. It was cold, and there was no fire. I was never more uncomfortable for four hours in my life. The stations in Spain are built to save money, and not for the comfort of the passengers, at least in the smaller places. But we had better go to sleep if we can; for we have to keep moving for nearly twenty-four hours at the next stretch."

Not many of the party could sleep, tired as they were, till they took the train at eleven o'clock. The compartments were heated with hot-water vessels, or rather the feet were heated by them. The students stowed themselves away as well as they could; and soon, without much encouragement to do so, they were buried in slumber.

CHAPTER XV.

TROUBLE IN THE RUNAWAY CAMP.

"WHAT are you running for?" shouted Bill Stout, as Raimundo and Bark Lingall ran ahead of him after the party landed from the felucca. "We are all right now."

Bill could not quite get rid of the idea that he was the leader of the expedition, as he intended to be from the time when he began to make his wicked plans for the destruction of the Tritonia. He had the vanity to believe that he was born to command, and not to obey; and such are generally the very worst of leaders.

"Never mind him, Lingall," said the second master. "When we get to the top of this rising ground we can see where we are."

"I am satisfied to follow your lead," replied Bark.

"If our plans are spoiled, it will be by that fellow," added Raimundo.

But in a few minutes more he halted on the summit of a little hill, with Bark still at his side. Bill was some distance behind; and he was evidently determined to have his own way, without regard to the wishes of the second master. On the rising ground, the lights revealed the position of the city; but the fugitives looked with more interest, for the moment, at the sea. Raimundo had run when he landed, because he saw that the lay of the land would conceal the movements of the felucca from him if he remained where he had come on shore. Perhaps, too, he considered it best to put a reasonable distance between himself and the dangerous boatman. On the eminence they could distinctly see the felucca headed away from the shore in the direction from which she had come when they were on board.

"I was afraid the villain might be treacherous, after all," said Raimundo. "If he had headed into the port of Tarragona, it would not have been safe for us to go there."

"What's your hurry?" demanded Bill Stout, coming up at this moment. "You act as though you were scared out of your wits."

"Shut up, Bill Stout!" said Bark, disgusted with his companion in crime. "If you are going to get up a row at every point we make, we may as well go back to the Tritonia, kiss the rod, and be good boys."

"I haven't made any row," protested Bill. "I couldn't see what you were running for, when no one was after you."

"Raimundo knows what he is about; and, while the thing is going along very well, you set to yelling, so as to let the fellow know where we were, if he took it into his head to follow us."

"Raimundo may know what he is about," snarled Bill; "but I want to know what he is about too, if I am to take part in this business."

"You will not know from me," added Raimundo

haughtily. "I shall not stop to explain my plans to a coward and an ignoramus every time I make a move. We are in Spain; and the country is big enough for all of us. I did not invite you to come with me; and I am not going to be trammelled by you."

"You are a great man, Mr. Raimundo; but I want you to understand that you are not on the quarter-deck of the Tritonia just now; and I have something to say, as well as you," replied Bill.

"That's all! I don't want to hear another word," continued Raimundo. "We may as well part company here and now as at any other time and place."

"Now you can see what you have done, Bill," said Bark reproachfully.

"Well, what have I done? I had as lief be officered on board of the vessel as here, when we are on a time," answered Bill.

"All right; you may go where you please," added Bark angrily. "I am not going about with any such fellow as you are. If I should get into trouble, you would lay back, and let me fight it out alone."

"Do you mean to say, Bark Lingall, that you will desert me, and go off with that spoony of an officer?" demanded Bill, taken all aback by what his friend had said.

"I do mean to say it; and, more than that, I will stick to it," said Bark firmly. "You are both a coward and a fool. Before we are out of the first danger, you get your back up about nothing, and make a row. Mr. Raimundo has been a gentleman, and behaved like a brave fellow. If it hadn't been for him, we should have been robbed of all our money, and perhaps have had our throats cut besides."

"But he got us into the scrape," protested Bill. "He hired that cut-throat to take us to this place without saying a word to us about the business. I knew that fellow was a rascal, and would just as lief cut a man's throat as eat his dinner."

"You knew what he was, did you?"

"To be sure I did. He looked like a villain; and I would not have trusted myself half a mile from the shore with him without a revolver in my pocket," retorted Bill, who felt safe enough now that he was on shore.

"I don't care to hear any more of this," interposed the second master. "It must be half-past seven by this time, and I am going to hurry up to the town. I looked at an old Bradshaw on board, while I was making up my plans, and I noticed that the night trains generally leave at about nine o'clock. There may be one from this place."

"But where are you going?" asked Bark.

"It makes no manner of difference to me where I go, if I only get as far away from Barcelona as possible," replied Raimundo. "The police may have received a despatch, ordering them to arrest us at this place."

"Do you believe they have such an order?" asked Bark, with deep interest.

"I do not believe it; but it may be, for all that. I am confident no one saw the felucca take us off those rocks. I feel tolerably safe. But, when Filipe gets back to Barcelona, he may tell where he took us; and some one will be on my track in Tarragona as early as the first train from the north arrives here."

Raimundo walked towards the town, and Bark still kept by his side. Bill followed, for he had no intention of being left alone by his companions. He thought it was treason on the part of Bark to think of such a thing as deserting him. He felt that he had been the leader of the enterprise up to the time he had got into the boat with the second master; and that he had conducted Bark out of their prison, and out of the slavery of the vessel. It would be rank ingratitude for his fellow-conspirator to turn against him under such circumstances; and he was surprised that Bark did not see it in that light. As for the second master, he did not want any thing more of him; he did not wish to travel with him, or to have any thing to do with him. He was an officer of the Tritonia, one of the tyrants against whom he had rebelled; and as such he hated him. The consciousness that he had behaved like a poltroon in the presence of the officer, while Bark had been a lion in bravery, did not help the case at all. Raimundo despised him, and took no pains to conceal his sentiments.

All Bill Stout wanted was to roam over the country with Bark. In the boat he had imagined the "good times" they would have when free from restraint. They could drink and smoke, and visit the places of amusement in Spain, while the rest of the fellows were listening to lectures on geography and history, and visiting old churches. His idea of life and enjoyment was very low indeed.

After walking for half an hour in the direction of the nearest lights, they reached the lower part of the town;

and the second master concluded that the railroad station must be in this section. He inquired in the street, and found they were quite near it. He was also told that a train would leave for Alicante and Madrid at thirty-five minutes past eight. It was only eight then; and, seeing a store with "*A la Barcelona*" on its sign, he knew it was a clothing-store, and the party entered it. Raimundo bought a long cape coat which entirely concealed his uniform. Bark and Bill purchased overcoats, each according to his taste, that covered up their nautical costume in part, though they did not hide their seaman's trousers. At another shop they obtained caps that replaced their uniform head-pieces.

With their appearance thus changed, they repaired to the station, where Raimundo bought tickets to Valencia. This is a seaport town, one hundred and sixty-two miles from Tarragona. Raimundo was going there because the train went there. His plans for the future were not definitely arranged; but he did not wish to dissolve his connection with the academy squadron. He intended to return to his ship as soon as he could safely do so, which he believed would be when the vessels sailed from Lisbon for the "isles of the sea;" but in this connection he was troubled about the change in the programme which the principal had introduced the day before, of which Hugo had informed him. If the American Prince was to convey the Josephines and the Tritonias to Lisbon, and bring back the Princes,— for the several ships' companies were called by these names, — it was not probable that the squadron would go to Lisbon. All hands would then have visited Portugal and there would be no need of going there again. Raimundo concluded that the fleet would sail on its Atlantic voyage from Cadiz, which would save going three hundred miles to the northward in the middle of winter.

"Do you want first or second class tickets?" asked Raimundo, when they stood before the ticket-office.

"A second class is good enough for me," replied Bill.

"What class do you take?" asked Bark.

"I shall go first class, because I think it will be safer," replied Raimundo. "We shall not meet so many people."

"Then get me a first class," added Bark.

"Two first class and one second," repeated the second master.

"I'm not going alone," snarled Bill. "Get me a first class."

The tickets were procured; and the party took their places in the proper compartment, which they had all to themselves. Bill Stout was vexed again; for, small as the matter of the tickets was, he had once more been overruled by the second master. He felt as though he had no influence, instead of being the leader of the party as he aspired to be. He was cross and discontented. He was angry with Bark for thinking of such a thing as deserting him. He was in just the mood to make another fuss; and he made one.

"I think it is about time for us to settle our accounts with you, Mr. Raimundo;" said Bark, when they were seated in the compartment. "We owe you a good deal by this time."

"*Mr.* Raimundo!" exclaimed Bill, with a heavy emphasis on the handle to the name. "Why don't you call me Mr. Stout, Bark?"

"Because I have not been in the habit of doing so," replied Bark coldly.

"We are not on board the ship now; and I think we might as well stop toadying to anybody," growled Bill.

"About the accounts, Mr. Raimundo," continued Bark, taking no further notice of his ill-natured companion. "How much were the tickets?"

"Ninety-two *reales* each," replied Raimundo. "That is four dollars and sixty cents."

"You paid for the boat and the provisions," added Bark. "We will make an equal division of the whole expense."

"I paid five hundred *reales* for the boat, and sixty for the provisions."

"You paid more than you agreed to for the boat," interposed Bill sulkily. "You are not going to throw my money away like that, I can tell you."

"I hired the boat for my own use, and I am willing to pay the whole of the bill for it," replied Raimundo with dignity.

"That's the sort of fellow you are, Bill Stout!" exclaimed Bark indignantly. — "No matter, Mr. Raimundo; if Bill is too mean to pay his share, I will pay it for him. You shall pay no more than one-third anyhow."

"I am willing to pay my fair share," said Bill, more disturbed than ever to find Bark against him every time. "Then three dollars for that lunch was a swindle."

"I had to take what I could get under the circumstances," added Raimundo; "but you drank most of the wine."

"I was not consulted about ordering it," growled Bill.

"If there ever was an unreasonable fellow on the face of the footstool, you are the one, Bill Stout!" retorted Bark vigorously. "I have had enough of you. — How much is the whole bill for each, Mr. Raimundo?"

"An equal division makes it two hundred and seventy-eight *reales* and a fraction. That is thirteen dollars and sixty cents."

"But my money is in sovereigns."

"Two and a half pence make a *real*. Can you figure that in your head?"

Bark declined to do the sum in his head; but, standing up under the dim light in the top of the compartment, he ciphered it out on the back of an old letter. The train had been in motion for some time, and it was not easy to make figures; but at last he announced his result.

"Two pounds and eighteen shillings, lacking a penny," said he. "Two shares will be five pounds and sixteen shillings."

"That is about what I had made it in my head," added Raimundo.

"Here are six sovereigns for Bill's share and my own," continued Bark, handing him the gold.

"You needn't pay that swindle for me," interposed Bill. "I shall not submit to having my money thrown away like that."

"Of course I shall not take it under these circumstances," replied the second master.

"I am willing to pay for the boat and the provisions," said Bill, yielding a part of the point.

Bark took no notice of him, but continued to press the money upon Raimundo; and he finally consented to take it on condition that a division of the loss should be made in the future if Bill did not pay his full share.

"You want four shillings back: here are five *pesetas*, which just make it," added Raimundo.

"Of course I shall pay you whatever you are out, Bark," said Bill, backing entirely out of his position, which he had taken more to be ugly than because he objected to the bill. "But I don't like this swindle. Here's three sovereigns."

"You need not pay it if you don't want to. I did not mean that Mr. Raimundo should be cheated out of the money," replied Bark.

"Stout," said Raimundo, rising from his seat, "this is not the first time, nor even the tenth, that you have insulted me to-day. I will have nothing more to do with you. You may buy your own tickets, and pay your own bills; and we will part company as soon as we leave this train."

"I think I can take care of myself without any help from you," retorted Bill. — "Here is your money, Bark."

"I won't take it," replied Bark.

"Why not?"

"You have insulted Mr. Raimundo ever since we started from Barcelona; and, after you say you have been swindled, I won't touch your money."

"Are you going back on me, after all I have done for you?" demanded Bill.

"What have you done for me?" asked Bark indignantly; for this was a new revelation to him.

"I got you out of the Tritonia; didn't I?"

"No matter: we will not jaw about any thing so silly as that. I won't touch your money till you have apologized to Mr. Raimundo."

"When I apologize to *Mr.* Raimundo, let me know it, will you?" replied Bill, as he returned the sovereigns to his pocket, and coiled himself away in the corner. "That's not my style."

Nothing more was said; and, after a while, all of the party went to sleep. But Bill Stout did not sleep well, for he was too ugly to be entirely at rest. He was awake most of the night; but, in the early morning, he dropped off again. At seven o'clock the train arrived at Valencia. Bill was still asleep. Raimundo got out of the car; and Bark was about to wake his fellow-conspirator, when the second master interposed: —

"Don't wake him, Lingall, if you please: but come with me. You can return in a moment."

Bark got out of the carriage.

"I wish to leave before he wakes," said Raimundo. "I will go no farther with him."

"Leave him here?" queried Bark.

"I will not even speak to him again," added the second master. "Of course, I shall leave you to do as you please; though I should be glad to have you go with me, for you have proved yourself to be a plucky fellow and a gentleman. As it is impossible for me to endure Stout's company any longer, I shall have to leave you, if you stick to him."

"I shall not stick to him," protested Bark. "He is nothing but a hog, — one hundred pounds of pork."

Bark had decided to leave Bill as soon as he could, and now was his time. They took an omnibus for the *Fonda del Cid*. They had not been gone more than five minutes, before a porter woke Bill Stout, who found that he was alone. He understood it perfectly.

CHAPTER XVI.

BILL STOUT AS A TOURIST.

BILL STOUT indulged in some very severe reflections upon the conduct of his fellow-conspirator when he found that he was alone in the compartment where he had spent the night. The porter who woke him told him very respectfully (he was a first-class passenger), in good Spanish for a man in his position, that the train was to be run out of the station. Bill couldn't understand him, but he left the car.

"Where are the fellows that came with me?" he asked, turning to the porter; but the man shook his head, and smiled as blandly as though the runaway had given him a *peseta*.

Bill was not much troubled with bashfulness; and he walked about the station, accosting a dozen persons whom he met; but not one of them seemed to know a word of English.

"*No hablo Ingles*," was the uniform reply of all. One spoke to him in French; but, though Bill had studied this language, he had not gone far enough to be able to speak even a few words of it. He went into the street, and a crowd of carriage-drivers saluted him.

"Hotel," said he, satisfied by this time that it was of no use to talk English to anybody in Spain.

As this word is known to all languages, he got on so far very well.

"*Hotel Villa de Madrid!*" shouted one of the drivers.

Though Bill's knowledge of geography was very limited, he had heard of Madrid, and he identified this word in the speech of the man. He bowed to him to indicate that he was ready to go to the hotel he named. He was invited to take a seat in a *tartana*, a two-wheeled vehicle not much easier than a tip-cart, and driven to the hotel. Bill did not look like a very distinguished guest, for he wore the garb of a common sailor when he took off his overcoat. He had not even put on his best rig, as he did not go ashore in regular form. He spoke to the porter who received him at the door, in English, thinking it was quite proper for those about a hotel to speak all languages. But this man seemed to be no better linguist than the rest of the Spaniards; and he made no reply.

The guest was conducted to the hall where the landlord, or the manager of the hotel, addressed him in Spanish, and Bill replied in English.

"*Habla V. Frances?*" asked the manager.

"I don't *hablo* any thing but English," replied Bill, beginning to be disgusted with his ill-success in finding any one who could understand him.

"*Parlez-vous Français?*" persisted the manager.

"No. I don't *parlez-vous*."

"*Parlate voi Italiano?*"

"No: I tell you I don't speak any thing but English," growled Bill.

"*Sprechen Sie Deutsch?*"

"No; no Dutch."

The manager shrugged his shoulders, and evidently felt that he had done enough, having addressed the guest in four languages.

"Two fellows — no comee here?" continued Bill, trying his luck with pigeon English.

Of course the manager shook his head at this absurd lingo; and Bill was obliged to give up in despair. The manager called a servant, and sent him out; and the guest hoped that something might yet happen. He seated himself on a sofa, and waited for the waters to move.

"I want some breakfast," said Bill when he had waited half an hour; and as he spoke he pointed to his mouth, and worked his teeth, to illustrate his argument.

The manager took out his watch, and pointed to the " X " upon the dial, to indicate that the meal would be ready at that hour. A little later the servant came in with another man, who proved to be an English-speaking citizen of Valencia. He was a *valet de place*, or guide.

With his aid Bill ascertained that " two young fellows " had not been to the Hotel Villa de Madrid that morning. He also obtained a room, and some coffee and bread to last him till breakfast time. When he had taken his coffee, he went with the man to all the hotels in the place. It was nearly ten o'clock when he reached the *Fonda del Cid*. Two young gentlemen, one of them an officer, had just breakfasted at the hotel, and left for Grao, the port of Valencia, two miles distant, where they were to embark in a steamer which was to sail for Oran at ten. Bill had not the least idea where Oran was; and, when he asked his guide, he was astonished to learn that it was in Africa, a seaport of Algeria. Then he was madder than ever; for he would have been very glad to take a trip to Africa, and see something besides churches and palaces. He dwelt heavily upon the trick that Bark had played him. It was ten o'clock then, and it would not be possible to reach Grao before half-past ten. He could try it; the steamer might not sail as soon as advertised: they were often detained.

Bill did try it, but the steamer was two miles at sea when he reached the port. He engaged the guide for the day, after an effort to beat him down in his price of six *pesetas*. He went back to the hotel, and ate his breakfast. There was plenty of *Val de Peñas* wine on the table, and he drank all he wanted. Then he went to his room to take a nap before he went out to see the sights of the place. Instead of sleeping an hour as he intended, he did not wake till three o'clock in the afternoon. The wine had had its effect upon him. He found the guide waiting for him in the hall below. The man insisted that he should go to the cathedral; and when they had visited that it was dinner-time.

"How much do I owe you now?" asked Bill, when he came to settle with the guide.

"Six *pesetas*," replied the man. "That is the price I told you."

"But I have not had you but half a day: from eleven till three you did not do any thing for me," blustered Bill in his usual style.

"But I was ready to go with you, and waited all that time for you," pleaded the guide.

"Here is four *pesetas*, and that is one more than you have earned," added Bill, tendering him the silver.

The man refused to accept the sum; and they had quite a row about it. Finally the guide appealed to the manager of the hotel, who promptly decided that six *pesetas* was the amount due the man. Bill paid it under protest, but added that he wanted the guide the next day.

"I shall go with you no more," replied the man, as he put the money into his pocket. "I work for gentlemen only."

"I will pay you for all the time you go with me," protested Bill; but the guide was resolute, and left the hotel.

The next morning Bill used his best endeavors to obtain another guide; but for a time he was unable to make anybody comprehend what he wished. An Englishman who spoke Spanish, and was a guest at the hotel, helped him out at breakfast, and told the manager what the young man wanted.

"I will not send for a guide for him," replied the manager; and then he explained to the tourist in what manner Bill had treated his valet the day before, all of which the gentleman translated to him.

But we cannot follow Bill in all his struggles with the language, or in all his wanderings about Valencia. He paid his bill at the hotel *Villa de Madrid*, and went to another. On his way he bought a new suit of clothes, and discarded for the present his uniform, which attracted attention wherever he was. He went to the *Fonda del Cid* next; but he could not obtain a guide who spoke English: the only one they ever called in was engaged to an English party for a week. The manager spoke English, but he was seldom in the house. In some of the shops they spoke English; but Bill was almost as much alone as though he had been on a deserted island. The days wore heavy on his hands; and about all he could do was to drink *Val de Peñas*, and sleep it off. He wanted to leave Valencia, but knew not where to go. He desired to get out of Spain; and he had tried to get the run of the English steamers; but as he could not read the posters, or often find any one to read them for him, he had no success.

He was heartily tired of the place, and even more disgusted than he had been on board of the Tritonia. He desired to go to England, where he could speak the language of the country; but no vessel for England came along, so far as he could ascertain. One day an English gentleman arrived at the hotel; and Bill got up a talk with him, as he did with everybody who could speak his own language. He told him he wanted to get to England; and the tourist advised him to cross Spain and Portugal by rail, and take a steamer at Lisbon, where one sailed every week for Southampton or Liverpool, and sometimes two or three a week.

Bill adopted this suggestion, and in the afternoon started for Lisbon. He had been nearly a week in Valencia, and the change was very agreeable to him. He found a gentleman who spoke English, in the compartment with him; and he got along without any trouble till he reached Alcazar, where his travelling friend changed cars for Madrid. But, before he left the train, he told Bill that he was too late to connect for Lisbon, and that he would have to wait till half-past one in the afternoon. He could obtain plenty to eat in the station; but that ten hours of waiting at a miserable shed of a station was far worse than learning a lesson in navigation. He was on the high land, only ninety miles from Madrid, and it was cold in the night. There was no fire to warm him, and he had to walk to keep himself comfortable. He could not speak a word to any person; and, when any one spoke to him, he had learned to say, "*No hablo.*" He had picked up a few words of Spanish, so that he could get what he wanted to eat, though his variety was very limited.

In the afternoon he took the train for Ciudad Real, and arrived there at six o'clock. He was too tired to go any farther that night; indeed, he was almost sick. He found an omnibus at the station, and said "Hotel" to the driver. He felt better in the morning, and reached the railroad station at six o'clock. As at the hotel, he gave the ticket-seller a paper and pencil; and he wrote down in figures the price of a ticket to Badajos, in *reales*. He had changed his money into *Isabelinos*, and knew that each was one hundred *reales*. Bill had improved a good deal in knowledge since he was thrown on his own resources. He waited till the train arrived from Madrid. It was quite a long one; but the conductor seemed to know just where the vacant seats were, and led him to the last carriage, where he was assigned a place in a compartment in which four passengers occupied the corners, and seemed to be all asleep. The runaway took one of the middle seats. He only hoped, that, when the daylight came, he might hear some of his fellow-travellers speak English.

Unfortunately for him, they all spoke this language. The light in the top of the compartment had gone out, and the persons in the corners were buried in their overcoats, so that he could not see them after the conductor carried his lantern away.

The train started; and Bill, for the want of something better to do, went to sleep himself. His bed at the hotel had been occupied by a myriad of "*cosas de España*" before he got into it; and his slumbers had been much disturbed. He slept till the sun broke in through the window of the compartment. He heard his fellow-travellers conversing in English; and, when he was fairly awake, he was immediately conscious that a gentleman who sat in one of the opposite corners was studying his features. But, as soon as Bill opened his eyes, it was not necessary for him to study any longer. The gentleman in the corner was Mr. Lowington, principal of the academy squadron; and Bill's solitary wanderings had come to an end.

The principal knew every student in the fleet; but Bill's head had been half concealed, and his dress had been entirely changed, so that he did not fully identify him till he opened his eyes, and raised his head. The other persons in the compartment were Dr. Winstock, the captain, and the first lieutenant of the Prince.

"Good-morning, Stout," said Mr. Lowington, as soon as he was sure that the new-comer was one of the runaways from the Tritonia.

Of course Bill was taken all aback when he realized that he was on the train with the ship's company of the Prince. But the principal was good-natured, as he always was; and he smiled as he spoke. Bill had unwittingly run into the camp of the enemy; and that smile assured him that he was to be laughed at, in addition to whatever punishment might be inflicted upon him; and the laugh, to him, was the worst of it.

"Good-morning, sir," replied Bill sheepishly; and he had not the courage to be silent as he desired to be in that presence.

"Have you had a good time, Stout?" asked Mr. Lowington.

"Not very good," answered Bill; and by this time the eyes of the doctor and his two pupils, who had not noticed him before, were fixed upon the culprit.

"Where is Lingall?" inquired the principal. "Is he on the train with you?"

"No, sir: he and Raimundo ran away from me in Valencia."

"Raimundo!" exclaimed Mr. Lowington. "Was he with you?"

"Yes, sir; and they played me a mean trick," added Bill, who had not yet recovered from his indignation on account of his desertion, and was disposed to do his late associates all the harm he could.

"They ran away from you, as you did from the rest of us," laughed the principal, who knew Stout so well that he could not blame his companions for deserting him. "Do you happen to know where they have gone?"

"They left Valencia in a steamer at ten o'clock in the forenoon;" and Bill recited the particulars of his search for his late companions, feeling all the time that he was having some part of his revenge upon them for their meanness to him.

"But where was the steamer bound?" asked the principal.

"For Oban," replied Bill, getting it wrong, as he was very apt to do with geographical names.

"Oban; that's in Scotland. No steamer in Valencia could be bound to Oban," added Mr. Lowington.

"This place is not in Scotland: it is in Africa," Bill explained.

"He means Oran," suggested Dr. Winstock.

"That's the place."

Bill knew nothing in regard to the intended movements of Raimundo and Bark.

"How happened Raimundo to be with you?" asked the principal. "He left the Tritonia the night before we came from Barcelona."

"No, sir: he did not leave her at all. He was in the hold all the time."

As Bill was very willing to tell all he knew about his fellow-conspirator and the second master, — except that Bark and himself had tried to set the vessel on fire, — he related all the details of the escape, and the trip to Tarragona, including the affray with the boatman. He told the truth in the main, though he did not bring out the fact of his own cowardice, or dwell upon the cause of the quarrel between himself and his companions.

"And how happened you to be here, and on this train? Did you know we were on board of it?" inquired the principal.

"I did not know you were on this train; but I knew you were over this way somewhere."

"And you were going to look for us," laughed Mr.

Lowington, who believed that the fellow's ignorance had caused him to blunder into this locality at the wrong time.

"I was not looking for you, but for the Tritonias," replied Bill, who had come to the conclusion that penitence was his best dodge under the circumstances. "I was going over to Lisbon to give myself up to Mr. Pelham."

"Indeed! were you?"

"Yes, sir: I did not intend to run away; and it was only when Raimundo had a boat from the shore that I thought of such a thing. I have had hard luck; and I would rather do my duty on board than wander all about the country alone."

"Then it was Lingall that spoiled your fun?"

"Yes, sir; but I shall never want to run away again."

"That's what they all say. But, if you wished to get back, why didn't you go to Barcelona, where the Tritonia is? That would have been the shortest way for you."

"I didn't care about staying in the brig, with no one but Mr. Marline and Mr. Rimmer on board," answered Bill, who could think of no better excuse.

Bill thought he might get a chance to slip away at some point on the road, or at least when the party arrived at Lisbon. If there was a steamer in port bound to England, he might get on board of her.

"We will consider your case at another time," said the principal, as the train stopped at a station.

The principal and the surgeon, after sending Bill to the other end of the compartment, had a talk about

Raimundo, who had evidently gone to Africa to get out of the jurisdiction of Spain. After examining Bradshaw, they found the fugitives could take a steamer to Bona, in Algeria, and from there make their way to Italy or Egypt; and concluded they would do so.

CHAPTER XVII.

THROUGH THE HEART OF SPAIN.

BILL STOUT concluded that he was not a success as a tourist in Spain; but he was confident that he should succeed better in England. He resolved to be a good boy till the excursionists arrived in Lisbon, and not make any attempt to escape; for it was not likely that he could accomplish his purpose. Besides, he had no taste for any more travelling in Spain. In fact, he had a dread of being cast upon his own resources in the interior, where he could not speak the language.

"Do you know what country you are in?" asked Dr. Winstock, who sat opposite his pupils, as he had come to call them.

"I reckon you'd know if you had seen it as I have," interposed Bill Stout, who had a seat next to Murray, with a broad grin at the absurdity of the question. "It is Spain,— the meanest country on the face of the earth."

"So you think, Stout; but you have had a rather hard experience of it," replied the doctor. "We have had a very good time since we left Barcelona."

"I suppose you know the lingo; and that makes all the difference in the world," added Bill.

"When I spoke of country, I referred to a province," continued Dr. Winstock.

"This is La Mancha," answered Sheridan.

"The country of Don Quixote," added the doctor.

"I saw a statue of Cervantes at Madrid, and I heard one of the fellows say he was the author of 'Don Juan,'" laughed Murray.

"Cervantes wrote the first part at Valladolid, and it produced a tremendous sensation. I suppose you have read it."

"*I* never did," replied Bill Stout, who counted himself in as one of the party. "Is it a good story?"

"It is so considered by those who are competent judges."

"I read it years ago," added Sheridan.

"It is said to be a take-off on the knights of Spain," said Murray. "Is that so?"

"I don't think that was his sole idea in writing the book; or, if it was, he enlarged upon his plan. He was a literary man, with some reputation, before he wrote Don Quixote; and he probably selected the most popular subject he could find, and it grew upon him as he proceeded. Sancho Panza is a representative of homely common-sense, unaided by any imagination, while his master is full of it. He is used, in the first part of the story, to act as a contrast to the extravagant Don; and in this part of the work he does not use any of the proverbs which is the staple of the typical Spaniard's talk. The introduction of this feature of Sancho's talk was a new idea to the author."

"I suppose Cervantes was born and lived in **La Mancha**," said Murray.

"Not at all: he was born near Madrid, at Alcala de Henares. He was a soldier in the early years of his life. He fought in the battle of Lepanto, under Don John. At one time he was a sort of custom-house officer in Seville; but he got into debt, and was imprisoned for three months, during which time he is said to have been engaged in his great work. He was also a prisoner in Algiers five years; and ten times he risked his life in attempts to escape. He finally died in neglect, poverty, and want."

"Then this is where Don Quixote tilted at windmills," said Murray, looking out at the window; "and there is one of them."

"It is not in every province of Spain that the Don could have found a windmill to tilt at," added the doctor.

About eight o'clock the train stopped for breakfast, which the *avant-courier* had ordered.

"This is a vine and olive country," said the doctor, when the train was again in motion.

"Shall we have a chance to see how they make the oil and how they make wine?" asked Sheridan.

"You will have a chance to see how it is done; but you will not be able to see it done at this season of the year. There is an olive-orchard," continued the doctor, pointing out of the window.

"The trees look like willows; and I should think they were willows."

"They are not. These trees last a great number of years, — some say, hundreds."

"There are some which look as though they were planted by Noah after he left the ark. They are ugly-looking trees," added Murray.

"The people do not plant them for their beauty, but for the fruit they yield. You see they are in regular rows, like an apple-orchard at home. They start the trees from slips, which are cut off in January. The end of the slip is quartered with a knife, and a small stone put into the end to separate the parts, and the slip stuck into the ground. The earth is banked up around the plant, which has to be watered and tenderly cared for during the first two years of its growth. In ten years these trees yield some returns; but they are not at their best estate till they are thirty years old. The olives we eat"—

"I never eat them," interrupted Murray, shaking his head.

"It is an acquired taste; but those who do like them are usually very fond of them. The olive which comes in jars for table use is picked before it is quite ripe, but when full grown; and it is pickled for a week in a brine made of water, salt, garlic, and some other ingredients. The best come from the neighborhood of Seville."

"But I don't see how they make the oil out of the olive. It don't seem as though there is any grease in it," said Sheridan.

"The berry is picked for the manufacture of oil when it is ripe, and is then of a purple color. It is gathered in the autumn; and I have seen the peasants beating the trees with sticks, while the women and children were picking up the olives on the ground. The women drive the donkeys to the mill, bearing the berries in the panniers. The olives are crushed on a big stone hollowed out for the purpose, by passing a stone roller over them, which is moved by a mule. The pulp is then placed in a press not unlike that you have seen in a cider-mill. The oil flows out into a reservoir under the press, from which it is bailed into jars big enough to contain a man : these jars are sunk in the ground to keep them cool. The mass left in the press after the oil is extracted is used to feed the hogs, or for fuel."

"And is that the stuff they put in the casters?" asked Murray, with his nose turned up in disgust.

"That is certainly olive-oil," replied the doctor. "You look as though you did not like it."

"I do not : I should as soon think of eating lamp-oil."

"Every one to his taste, lieutenant ; but I have no doubt you have eaten a great deal of it since you came into Spain," laughed the doctor.

"Not if I knew it!"

"You did not know it; but you have had it on your beefsteaks and mutton-chops, as well as in the various made-dishes you have partaken of. Spanish oil is not so pure and good as the Italian. Lucca oil has the best reputation. A poorer quality of oil is made here, which is used in making soap."

"Castile soap?"

"Yes ; and all kinds of oils are used for soap."

"How do they fresco it?" asked Murray.

"Fresco it! They give it the marble look by putting coloring matter, mixed with oil, into the mass of soap before it is moulded into bars. What place is this?" said the doctor, as the train stopped.

"Almaden," replied Sheridan, reading the sign on the station.

"I thought so, for I spent a couple of days here. Do you know what it is famous for?"

"I don't think I ever heard the name of the place before," replied Sheridan.

"It contains the greatest mine of quicksilver in the world," added the doctor. "It was worked in the time of the Romans, and is still deemed inexhaustible. Four thousand men are employed here during the winter, for they cannot labor in the summer because the heat renders it too unhealthy. The men can work only six hours at a time; and many of them are salivated and paralyzed by the vapors of the mercury."

"Is this the same stuff the doctors use?" asked Murray.

"It is; but it is prepared especially for the purpose. These mines yield the government of Spain a revenue of nearly a million dollars a year."

The country through which the tourists passed was not highly cultivated, except near the towns. On the way they saw a man ploughing-in his grain, and the implement seemed to be a wooden one. But every thing in the agricultural line was of the most primitive kind. In another place they saw a farmer at work miles from his house, for there was no village within that distance. Though there is not a fence to be seen, every man knows his own boundary-lines. In going to his day's work, he may have to go several miles, taking his plough and other tools in a cart; and probably he wastes half his day in going to and from his work. But the Spanish peasant is an easy-going fellow, and he does not go very early, or stay very late. Often in the morning and in the middle of the afternoon our travellers saw them going to or coming from their work in this manner.

"Now we are out of La Mancha," said the doctor, half an hour after the train left Almaden.

"And what are we in now, sir?" asked Murray.

"We are in the province of Cordova, which is a part of Andalusia. But we only go through a corner of Cordova, and then we strike into Estremadura."

In the afternoon the country looked better, though the people and the houses seemed to be very poor. The country looked better; but it was only better than the region near Madrid, and, compared with France or Italy, it was desolation. The effects of the *mesta* were clearly visible.

"Medellin," said Murray, when he had spelled out the word on a station where the train stopped about half-past two.

"Do you know the place?" asked Dr. Winstock.

"Never heard of it."

"Yet it has some connection with the history of the New World. It is mentioned in Prescott's 'Conquest of Mexico.'"

"I have read that, but I do not remember this name."

"It is the birthplace of Hernando Cortes; and in Trujillo, a town forty miles north of us, was born another adventurer whose name figures on the glowing page of Prescott," added the doctor.

"That was Pizarro," said Sheridan. "I remember he was born at— what did you call the place, doctor?"

"Trujillo."

"But in Prescott it is spelled with an *x* where you put an *h*."

"It is the same thing in Spanish, whether you spell it with an *x* or a *j*. It is a strong aspirate, like *h*, but is pronounced with a rougher breathing sound. Loja and Loxa are the same word," explained the doctor. "So you will find Cordova spelled with a *b* instead of a *v;* but the letters have the same power in Spanish."

"What river is this on the right?" inquired Murray.

"That is the Guadiana."

"And where are its eyes, of which Professor Mapps spoke in his lecture?"

"We passed them in the night, and also went over the underground river," replied the doctor. "The region through which we are now passing was more densely peopled in the days when it was a part of the Roman empire than it is now. Without doubt the same is true of the period of the Moorish dominion. After America was discovered, and colonization began, vast numbers of emigrants went from Estremadura. In the time of Philip II. the country began to run down; and one of the reasons was the emigration to America. About four o'clock we shall arrive at Merida," added the doctor, looking at his watch.

"What is there at Merida?"

"There is a great deal for the antiquarian and the student of history. You must be on the lookout for it, for there are many things to be seen from the window of the car," continued the doctor. "It was the capital of Lusitania, and was called *Emerita Augusta,* from the first word of which title comes the present name. The river there is crossed by a Roman bridge twenty-five hundred and seventy-five feet long, twenty-five wide, and thirty-three above the stream. The city was surrounded by six leagues of walls, having eighty-four gates, and had a garrison of eighty thousand foot and ten thousand horsemen. The ruins of aqueducts, temples, forum, circus, and other structures, are still to be seen ; some of them, as I said, from the train."

Unfortunately the train passed the portion of the ruins of the ancient city to be seen from the window, so rapidly that only a glance at them could be obtained ; but perhaps most of the students saw all they desired of them. An hour and a half later the train arrived at Badajos, where they were to spend the night, and thence proceed to Lisbon the next morning. Each individual of the ship's company had been provided with a ticket ; and it was called for in the station before he was permitted to pass out of the building. As soon as they appeared in the open air, they were assailed by a small army of omnibus-drivers ; but fortunately, as the town was nearly two miles from the station, there were enough for all of them. These men actually fought together for the passengers, and behaved as badly as New York hackmen. Though all the vehicles at the station were loaded as full as they could be stowed, there was not room for more than half of the party.

The doctor and his pupils preferred to walk. In Madrid, the principal had received a letter from the *avant-courier*, informing him how many persons could be accommodated in each of the hotels ; and all the excursionists had been assigned to their quarters.

"We go to the *Fonda las Tres Naciones*," said the doctor as they left the station. " I went there when I was here before. Those drivers fought for me as they did to-day; and with some reason, for I was the only passenger. I selected one, and told him to take me to the *Fonda de las cuatro Naciones;* and he laughed as though I had made a good joke. I made it 'Four Nations' instead of 'Three.' Here is the bridge over the Guadiana, built by the same architect as the Escurial."

"What is there in this place to see?" asked Sheridan.

"Nothing at all; but it is an out-of-the-way old Spanish town seldom mentioned by tourists."

"I have not found it in a single book I have read, except the guide-books; and all these have to say about it is concerning the battles fought here," added Sheridan.

"Mr. Lowington has us stop here by my advice; and we are simply to spend the night here. You were on the train last night, and it would have been too much to add the long and tedious journey to Lisbon to that from Madrid without a night's rest. Besides, you should see what you can of Portugal by daylight; for we are to visit only Lisbon and some of the places near it."

The party entered the town, and climbed up the steep streets to the hotel. The place was certainly very primitive. It had been a Roman town, and did not seem to have changed much since the time of the Cæsars. A peculiarly Spanish supper was served at the Three Nations, which was the best hotel in the place, but poor enough at that. Those who were fond of garlic had enough of it. The room in which the captain and first lieutenant were lodged had no window, and the ceiling was composed of poles on which hay was placed; and the apartment above them may have been a stable, or at least a hay-loft. Some of the students took an evening walk about the town, but most of them "turned in" at eight o'clock.

The party were called at four o'clock in the morning; and after a light breakfast of coffee, eggs, and bread, they proceeded to the station. The train provided for them consisted of second-class carriages, at the head of which were several freight-cars. This is the regular day train, all of the first-class cars being used on the night train.

"Now you can see something of Badajos," said the doctor, as they walked down the hill. "It is a frontier town, and the capital of the province. It is more of a fortress than a city. Marshal Soult captured it in 1811; and it is said that it was taken only through the treachery of the commander of the Spaniards. The Duke of Wellington captured it in 1812. I suppose you have seen pictures by the Spanish artist Morales, for there are some in the *Museo* at Madrid. He was born here; and, when Philip II. stopped at Badajos on his way to Lisbon, he sent for the artist. The king remarked, 'You are very old, Morales.' — 'And very poor,' replied the painter; and Philip gave him a pension of three hundred ducats a year till he died. Manuel Godoy, the villanous minister of Charles IV., called the 'Prince of Peace,' was born also here."

The train started at six o'clock, while it was still dark. Badajos is five miles from the boundary-line of Portugal; and in about an hour the train stopped at Elvas. The Portuguese police were on hand in full force, as well as a squad of custom-house officers. The former asked each of the adult members of the party his name, age, nationality, occupation, and a score of other questions, and would have done the same with the students if the doctor had not protested; and the officers contented themselves with merely taking their names, on the assurance that they were all Americans, were students, and had passports. Every bag and valise was opened by the custom-house officers; and all the freight and baggage cars were locked and sealed, so that they should not be opened till they arrived at Lisbon. Elvas has been the seat of an extensive smuggling trade, and the officers take every precaution to break up the business.

The train was detained over an hour; and some of the students, after they had been "overhauled" as they called it, ran up into the town. Like Badajos, it is a strongly fortified place; but, unlike that, it has never been captured, though often besieged. The students caught a view of the ancient aqueduct, having three stories of arches.

The train started at last; and all day it jogged along at a snail's pace through Portugal. The scenery was about the same as in Spain, and with about the same variety one finds in New England. Dr. Winstock called the attention of his pupils to the cork-trees, and described the process of removing the bark, which forms the valuable article of commerce. They saw piles of it at the railroad stations, waiting to be shipped.

There were very few stations on the way, and hardly a town was seen before four in the afternoon, when the train crossed the Tagus. The students were almost in a state of rebellion at this time, because they had had nothing to eat since their early breakfast. They had come one hundred and ten miles in ten hours; and eleven miles an hour was slow locomotion on a railroad. The courier wrote that he had made an arrangement by which the train was to go to the junction with the road to Oporto in seven hours, which was not hurrying the locomotive very much; but the conductor said he had no orders to this effect.

"This is Entroncamiento," said the doctor, as the train stopped at a station. "We dine here."

"Glory!" replied Murray. "But we might starve if we had to pronounce that name before dinner."

The students astonished the keeper of the restaurant by the quantity of soup, chicken, and chops they devoured; but they all gave him the credit of providing an excellent dinner. The excursionists had to wait a long time for the train from Oporto, for it was more than an hour late; and they did not arrive at Lisbon till half-past nine. The doctor and his pupils were sent to the Hotel Braganza, after they had gone through another ordeal with the custom-house officers. Bill Stout was taken to the Hotel Central on the quay by the river. The runaway had been as tractable as one of the lambs, till he came to the hotel. While the party were waiting for the rooms to be assigned to them, and Mr. Lowington was very busy, he slipped out into the street. He walked along the river, looking out at the vessels anchored in the stream. He made out the outline of several steamers. While he was looking at them, a couple of sailors, "half seas over," passed him. They were talking in English, and Bill hailed them.

"Do you know whether there is a steamer in port bound to England?" he asked, after he had passed the time of night with them.

"Yes, my lad: there is the Princess Royal, and she sails for London early in the morning," replied the more sober of the two sailors. "Are you bound to London?"

"I am. Which is the Princess Royal?"

The man pointed the steamer out to him, and insisted that he should take a drink with them. Bill did not object. But he never took any thing stronger than wine, and his new friends insisted that he should join them with some brandy. He took very little; but then he felt obliged to treat his new friends in turn for their civility, and he repeated the dose. He then inquired where he could find a boat to take him on board of the steamer. They went out with him, and soon found a boat, in which he embarked. The boatman spoke a little English; and as soon as he was clear of the shore he asked which steamer his passenger wished to go to. By this time the brandy was beginning to have its effect upon Bill's head; but he answered the man by pointing to the one the sailor had indicated, as he supposed.

In a few moments the boat was alongside the steamer; and Bill's head was flying around like a top. He paid the boatman his price, and then with an uneasy step walked up the accommodation-ladder. A man was standing on the platform at the head of the ladder, who asked him what he wanted.

"I want to go to England," replied the runaway, tossing his bag over the rail upon the deck.

"This vessel don't go to England; you have boarded the wrong steamer," replied the man.

Bill hailed the boatman, who was pulling for the shore.

"Anchor watch!" called the man on the platform. "Bring a lantern here!"

"Here is one," said a young man, wearing an overcoat and a uniform cap, as he handed up a lantern to the first speaker.

"Hand me my bag, please, gen'l'men," said Bill.

At this moment the man on the platform held the lantern up to Bill's face.

"I thought I knew that voice," added Mr. Pelham, for it was he. "Don't give him the bag, Scott."

"That's my bag, and I want it," muttered Bill.

"I am afraid you have been drinking, Stout," continued the vice-principal, taking Bill by the collar, and conducting him down the steps to the deck of the American Prince.

"It is Stout, as sure as I live!" exclaimed Scott.

"No doubt of that, though he has changed his rig. Pass the word for Mr. Peaks."

Bill was not so far gone but that he understood the situation. He had boarded the American Prince, instead of the Princess Royal. The big boatswain of the steamer soon appeared, and laid his great paw on the culprit.

"Where did you come from, Stout?" asked the vice-principal.

"I came down with Mr. Lowington and the rest of them," answered Bill; and his tongue seemed to be twice too big for his mouth.

Mr. Pelham sent for Mr. Fluxion, and they got out of the tipsy runaway all they could. They learned that the ship's company of the Prince had just arrived. Bill Stout was caged; and the two vice-principals went on shore in the boat that was waiting for the "passenger for England." They found Mr. Lowington at the Hotel Central. He was engaged just then in looking up Bill Stout; and he was glad to know that he was in a safe place.

CHAPTER XVIII.

AFRICA AND REPENTANCE.

HAVING brought Bill Stout safely into port, we feel obliged to bestow some attention upon the other wanderers from the fold of discipline and good instruction. At the *Fonda del Cid*, where our brace of tourists went after taking such unceremonious leave of Bill Stout, was a party of English people who insisted upon having their breakfast at an hour that would permit them to use the forenoon in seeing the sights of Valencia; and thus it happened that this meal was ready for the fugitives at eight o'ciock.

"What day is this, Lingall?" asked Raimundo, as they came into the main hall of the hotel after breakfast.

"Wednesday," replied Bark.

"I thought so. Look at this bill," added the second master, pointing to a small poster, with the picture of a steamer at the head of it.

"I see it, but I can't read it."

"This steamer starts from Grao at ten this forenoon, for Oran. It is only half-past eight now."

"Starts from Grao? where is that?" asked Bark.

"Grao is the port of Valencia: it is not many miles from here."

"And where is the other place? I never heard of it."

"Oran is in Algeria. It cannot be more than three hundred miles from Valencia."

"But that will be going to Africa."

"It will be the best thing we can do if we mean to keep out of the way."

"I don't object: I am as willing to go to Africa as anywhere else."

"We can stay over there for a week or two, and then come back to Spain. We can hit the Tritonia at Cadiz or Lisbon."

"I don't think I want to hit her," replied Bark with a sheepish smile.

"I was speaking for myself; and I forgot that your case was not the same as my own," added Raimundo.

"I don't know what your case is; but, as you seem to be perfectly easy about it, I wish mine was no worse than I believe yours is."

"We will talk about that another time; for, if we are going to Oran, it is time we were on the way to the port," said Raimundo. "If you don't want to go to Africa, I won't urge it; but that will suit my case the best of any thing I can think of."

"It makes no difference to me where I go; and I am perfectly willing to go with you wherever you wish," replied Bark, who, from hating the second master, had come to have an intense admiration for him.

Bark Lingall believed that his companion had saved the lives of the whole party in the boat; and certainly he had managed the expedition with great skill. He was as brave as a lion, in spite of his gentleness. But perhaps his respect and regard for the young Spaniard had grown out of the contrast he could not help making between him and Bill Stout. He could not now understand how it was that he had got up such an intimacy with his late associate in mischief, or rather in crime. Burning the Tritonia was vastly worse than he had at first considered it. Its enormity had increased in his mind when he reflected that Raimundo, who must have had a very strong motive for his sudden disappearance, had preferred to reveal himself rather than have the beautiful craft destroyed. In a word, Bark had made some progress towards a genuine repentance for taking part in the conspiracy with Bill Stout.

Raimundo paid the bill, and they took a *tartana* for Grao. They learned from the driver that it was less than half an hour's ride. They first went to the office of the steamer, paid their passage, and secured their state-room.

"This is a good move for another reason," said Raimundo, as they started again.

"What's that?" asked Bark.

"I have been expecting to see Stout drop down upon us every moment since we went to the hotel."

"So have I; and I think, if it had been my case, I should have found you by this time, if I wanted to do so," added Bark.

"It is hardly time yet for him to get around; but he will find the *Fonda del Cid* in the course of the forenoon. You forget that Stout cannot speak a word of Spanish; and his want of the language will make it slow work for him to do any thing."

"I did not think of that."

"Do you feel all right about leaving him as we did?"

asked Raimundo. "For my part, I could not endure him. He insulted me without the least reason for doing so."

"He is the most unreasonable fellow I ever met in the whole course of my natural life. It was impossible to get along with him; and I am entirely satisfied with myself for leaving him," replied Bark. "He insulted you, as you say; and I gave him the alternative of apologizing to you, or of parting company with us. I believe I did the fair thing. A fellow cannot hug a hog for any great length of period."

"That's so; but didn't you know him before?"

"I knew him, of course; and he was always grumbling and discontented about something; but I never thought he was such a fellow as he turned out to be. I haven't known him but a couple of months or so."

"I should think you would have got at him while you were getting up something" — Raimundo did not say what — "with him."

"I was dissatisfied myself. The squadron did not prove to be what I anticipated," added Bark. "I had an idea that it was in for a general good time; that all we had to do was to go from place to place, and see the sights."

"But you knew it was a school."

"Certainly I did; but I never supposed the fellows had to study half as hard as they do. I thought the school was a sort of a fancy idea, to make it take with the parents of the boys. When I found how hard we had to work, I was disgusted with the whole thing. Then I fell in with Bill Stout and others; and, when we had talked the matter over a few times, it was even worse than I had supposed when I did all my own thinking on the subject. After we got together, we both became more and more discontented, till we were convinced that we were all slaves, and that it was really our duty to break the chains that bound us. This was all the kind of talk I ever had with Stout; and, as we sympathized on this matter, I never looked any farther into his character."

"We shall have time enough to talk over these things when we get on board the steamer," added Raimundo. "I have watched you and Stout a great deal on board of the Tritonia; and I confess that I was prejudiced against you. I didn't feel any better about it when I found you and Stout trying to destroy the vessel. But I must say now that you are a different sort of fellow from what I took you to be; and nobody ever grew any faster in another's estimation than you have in mine since that affair last night in the felucca. I believe your pluck and skill in hauling that cut-throat down saved the whole of us."

"I have been thinking all the time it was you that saved us," added Bark, intensely gratified at the praise of Raimundo.

"The battle would have been lost if it hadn't been for you; for I struck at the villain, and missed him. If you hadn't brought him down, his knife would have been into me in another instant. But here is the port."

The steamer was one of the "*Messageries Nationales*," though that name had been recently substituted for "Imperiales" because the emperor had been abolished. The tourists went on board in a shore-boat, and took possession of their state-room. They made their preparations for the voyage, and then went on deck. They found comfortable seats, and the weather was like spring.

"What is the name of this steamer?" asked Bark.

"The City of Brest."

"That was not the name on the handbill we saw; was it, Mr. Raimundo?"

"Yes, — *Ville de Brest.*"

"That was it," added Bark.

"Well, that is the French of City of Brest," laughed the second master. "Don't you speak French?"

"I know a little of it; and I know that a "*ville*" is a city; but I didn't understand it as you spoke the word."

"I learned all the French I know in the academy squadron; and I can get along very well with it. I have spent a whole evening where nothing but French was spoken by the party. Professor Badois never speaks a word of English to me."

"And you speak Italian and German besides, Mr. Raimundo."

"I can get along with them, as I can with French."

"That makes five languages you speak."

"I am not much in Italian," laughed the second master. "My uncle set me to learning it in New York; but I forgot most of it, and learned more while we were in Italy than I ever knew before."

"I wish I had some other lingo besides my own."

"You can have it by learning it."

"But I am not so good a scholar as you are, Mr. Raimundo."

"You don't know that; for, if I mistake not, you have never laid yourself out on study, as I had not when I first went on board of the Young America. But, to change the subject, you have called me Mr. Raimundo three times since we sat down here. I agree with Stout so far, that we had better drop all titles till I put on my uniform again."

"I have been so used to calling you Mr., that it comes most natural for me to do so," replied Bark.

"I think I shall change my name a little; at least, so far as to translate it into plain English. I have always kept my Spanish name, which is Enrique Raimundo. It is so entered on the ship's books; but I shall make it Henry Raymond for the present."

"And is that the English of the other name?"

"It is; and, when you call me any thing, let it be Henry."

"Very well, Henry," added Bark.

"That is the name I gave when I bought the tickets. I noticed that Stout called you Bark."

"My name is Barclay; and you can call me that, or Bark for short."

"Bark don't sound very respectful, and it reminds one of a dog."

"My bark is on the wave; and I do not object to the name. I was always called Bark before I went to sea, and it sounds more natural to me than any thing else would. My father always called me Barclay; and I believe he was the only one that did."

"All right, Bark: if you don't object, I need not. You hinted that you did not think you should go back to the Tritonia."

"It wouldn't be safe for me to do so," replied Bark anxiously.

"I have come to the conclusion that it is always the safest to do the right thing, whatever the consequences may be."

"What! stay in the brig the rest of the voyage!"

"Yes, if that is the penalty for doing the right thing," replied Henry, as he chooses to be called.

"Suppose you were in my place; that you had tried to set the vessel on fire, and had run away: what would you do?"

"You did not set the vessel on fire, or try to do it. It was Stout that did it," argued Raymond.

"But I was in the plot. I agreed to take part in it; and I hold myself to be just as deep in the mire as Bill Stout is in the mud," added Bark.

"I am glad to see that you are a man about it, and don't shirk off the blame on the other fellow."

"Though I did not get up the idea, I am as guilty as Bill; and I will not cast it all upon him."

"That's the right thing to say."

"But what would you do, if you were in my place?"

"Just as I said before. I should return to the Tritonia, and face the music, if I were sent home in a man-of-war, to be tried for my life for the deed."

"That's pretty rough medicine."

"Since I have been in the squadron, I have learned a new morality. I don't think it would be possible for me to commit a crime, especially such as burning a vessel; but, if I had done it, I should want to be hanged for it as soon as possible. I don't know that anybody else is like me; but I tell you just how I feel."

"But, if you were bad enough to do the deed, you could not feel as you do now," replied Bark, shaking his head.

"That may be; but I can only tell you how I feel now. I never did any thing that I called a crime, — I mean any thing that made me liable to be punished by the law, — but I was a very wild fellow in the way of mischief. I used to be playing tricks upon the fellows, on my schoolmasters, and others, and was always in a scrape. I was good for nothing till I came on board of the Young America. As soon as I got interested, I worked night and day to get my lessons. Of course I had to be very correct in my conduct, or I should have lost my rank. It required a struggle for me to do these things at first; but I was determined to be an officer. I was as severe with myself as though I had been a monk with the highest of aspirations. I was an officer in three months; and I have been one ever since, though I have never been higher than fourth lieutenant, for the reason that I am not good in mathematics. My strength is in the languages."

"But I should think you would get discouraged because you get no higher."

"Not at all. As the matter stands now with me, I should do the best I could if I had to take the lowest place in the ship."

"I don't understand that," added Bark, who had come to the conclusion that his companion was the strangest mortal on the face of the earth; but that was only because Bark dwelt on a lower moral plane.

"After I had done my duty zealously for a few months, I was happy only in doing it; and it gave me more pleasure than the reward that followed it. Like Ignatius Loyola, I became an enthusiastic believer in God, in a personal God, in Christ the Saviour, and in the Virgin Mary: blessed be the Mother of God, her Son, and the Father of all of us!" and Raymond crossed himself as devoutly as though he were engaged in his devotions.

Bark was absolutely thrilled by this narrative of the personal experience of his new-found friend; and he was utterly unable to say any thing.

"But God and duty seem almost the same to me," continued Raymond. "I am ready to die or to live, but not to live at the expense of right and duty. For the last six months I have believed myself liable to be assassinated at any time. I know not how much this has to do with my mental, moral, and religious condition; but I am as I have described myself to be. I should do my duty if I knew that I should be burned at the stake for it."

"What do you mean by assassinated?" asked Bark, startled by the statement.

"I mean exactly what I say. But I am going to tell you my story in full. I have related it to only one other student in the squadron; and, if we should be together again on board of the Tritonia, I must ask you to keep it to yourself," said Raymond.

"It has bothered me all along to understand how a fellow as high-toned as you are could allow yourself to be considered a runaway; for I suppose the officers look upon you as such."

"No doubt they do; but in good time I shall tell Mr. Lowington the whole story, and then he will be able to judge for himself."

By this time the steamer had started. Raymond told his story just as he had related it to Scott on board of the Tritonia. Bark was interested; and, when the recital was finished, the steamer was out of sight of land.

"I suppose you will not believe me when I say it; but I have kept out of my uncle's way more for his sake than my own," said Raymond in conclusion. "I will not tempt one of my own flesh and blood to commit a crime; and I feel that it would have been cowardice for me to run away from my ship for the mere sake of saving myself from harm. Besides, I think I could take care of myself in Barcelona."

"I have no doubt of that," replied Bark, whose admiration of his fellow-tourist was even increased by the narration to which he had just listened.

Certainly Raymond was a most remarkable young man. Bark felt as though he were in the presence of a superior being. He realized his own meanness and littleness, judged by the high standard of his companion. As both of them were tired, after the night on the train, they went to the state-room, and lay down in their berths. Raymond went to sleep; but Bark could not, for he was intensely excited by the conversation he had had with his new friend. He lay thinking of his own life and character, as compared with his companion's; and the conspiracy in which he had taken part absolutely filled him with horror. The inward peace and happiness which Raymond had realized from his devotion to duty strongly impressed him.

But we will not follow him through all the meanderings of his thought. It is enough to say that fellowship with Raymond had made a man of him, and he was fully determined to seek peace in doing his whole duty. He was prepared to do what his companion had counselled him to do, — to return to the Tritonia, and take the consequences of his evil-doing. When his friend awoke, he announced to him his decision. Raymond saw that he was sincere, and he did all he could to confirm and strengthen his good resolution.

"There is one thing about the matter that troubles me," said Bark, as they seated themselves on deck after dinner. "I am willing to own up, and take the penalty, whatever it may be; but, if I confess that I was engaged in a conspiracy to burn the Tritonia, I shall implicate others, — I shall have to blow on Bill Stout."

"Well, what right have you to do any thing else?" demanded Raymond earnestly. "Suppose Filipe had killed me last night, and had offered you a thousand dollars to conceal the crime: would it have been right for you to accept the offer?"

"Certainly not."

"You would be an accomplice if you had. You have no more right to cover up Stout's crime than you would have to conceal Filipe's. Besides, the principal ought to know that he has a fellow on board that is bad enough to burn the Tritonia. He may do it with some other fellow yet; and, if he should, you would share the guilt with him."

"You found out what we were doing," added Bark.

"And I felt that I ought not to leave the vessel without telling the steward," replied Raymond. "I certainly intended to inform the principal as soon as I had an opportunity. I believe in boy honor and all that sort of thing as much as you do; but I have no right to let the vessels of the squadron be burned."

The subject was discussed till dark, and Bark could not resist the arguments of his friend. He was resolved to do his whole duty.

It is not our purpose to follow the fugitives into Africa. They reached Oran the next day, and remained there two weeks, until a steamer left for Malaga, when they returned to Spain.

"That's the American Prince, as true as you live!" exclaimed Bark, as the vessel in which they sailed was approaching Malaga; and both of them had been observing her for an hour.

"She is on her way from Lisbon back to Barcelona; and she will not be in Malaga for a week or more," replied Raymond.

Before night they were in the hotel in Malaga.

CHAPTER XIX.

WHAT PORTUGAL HAS DONE IN THE WORLD.

MR. LOWINGTON and the two vice-principals had a hearty laugh over the misadventure of poor Bill Stout, and then discussed their plans for the future. The Prince had been in the river five days; and the Josephines and Tritonias were all ready to start for Badajos the next morning. It was Friday night; and if the party left the next morning they would be obliged to remain over Sunday at Badajos; or, if they travelled all the next night, they would arrive at Toledo on Sunday morning, and this was no place for them to be on that day. It was decided that they should remain on board of the Prince till Monday morning, and that the Princes should go on board the next morning to hear Professor's Mapps's lecture on Portugal.

"Have you heard any thing of Raimundo or Lingall?" asked the principal.

"Only what we got out of Stout," replied Mr. Pelham. "But he was too tipsy to tell a very straight story."

"I don't see how he got tipsy so quick; for he must have reached the Prince within fifteen or twenty minutes after he left this hotel," added Mr. Lowington. "However, he told me all he knew — at least, I suppose he did — about the others who ran away with him. It seems that Raimundo did not leave the Tritonia, and must have stowed himself away in the hold."

"But we searched the hold very thoroughly," said Mr. Pelham.

"Did you look under the dunnage?"

"No, sir: he could not have got under that."

"Probably he did, — made a hole in the ballast. He must have had some one to help him," suggested the principal.

"If any one assisted him it must have been Hugo; for, as he is a Spaniard, they were always very thick together."

"I have informed Don Francisco, the lawyer, that Raimundo had gone to Oran; and I suppose he will be on the lookout for him. I have also written to Manuel Raimundo in New York. He must get my letter in a day or two," continued the principal. "It is a very singular case; and I should as soon have thought of Sheridan running away as Raimundo."

"He must have had a strong reason for doing so," added the vice-principal of the Tritonia.

The next morning Mr. Pelham directed Peaks to bring his prisoner into the cabin. Bill Stout did not remember what he had said the night before; but he had prepared a story for the present occasion.

"Good-morning, Stout," the vice-principal began. "How do you feel after your spree?"

"Pretty well, sir; I did not drink but once, and I couldn't help it then," replied the culprit, beginning to reel off the explanation he had got up for the occasion.

"You couldn't help it? That's very odd."

"No, sir. I met a couple of sailors on shore, and asked them if they could tell me where the American Prince lay. They pointed the steamer out to me, and they insisted that I should take a drink with them. They wouldn't take No for an answer, and I couldn't get off," whined Bill; and he always whined when he was in a scrape.

"Doubtless you gave them No for an answer," laughed Mr. Pelham.

"I certainly did; for I never take any thing. They made me drink brandy; but I put very little into the glass, and, as I am not used to liquor, it made me very drunk."

"One horn would not have made you as tipsy as you were, Stout. I think you had better tell that story to the other marines."

"I am telling the truth, sir: I wouldn't lie about it."

"I think it is a bad plan to do so," added the vice-principal. "Then you were coming on board, were you?"

"Yes, sir: I wanted to see you, and own up."

"Oh! that was your plan, was it?" laughed Mr. Pelham, amused at the pickle into which the rascal was putting himself.

"Yes, sir: I came from Valencia on purpose to give myself up to you. I'm sorry I ran away. I got sick of it in a day or two."

"This was after Lingall left you, I suppose."

"Yes, sir; but I was sorry for it before he left. We were almost murdered in the felucca; and I had a hard time of it."

"And this made you penitent."

"Yes, sir. I shall never run away again as long as I live."

"I hope you will not. And you came all the way across Spain and Portugal to give yourself up to me," added Mr. Pelham. "You were so very anxious to surrender to me, that you were not content to stay a single night at the hotel with Mr. Lowington, who is my superior."

"I wanted to see you; and that's the reason I left the hotel, and came on board last night," protested the culprit.

"That's a very good story, Stout; but for your sake I am sorry it is only a story," said the vice-principal.

"It is the truth, sir. I hope to"—

"No, no; stop!" interposed Mr. Pelham. "Don't hope any thing, except to be a better fellow. Your story won't hold water. I was at the gangway when you came on board, and you told me that you wanted to go to England."

"I didn't know what I was saying," pleaded Bill, taken aback by this answer.

"Yes, you did: you were not as tipsy as you might have been; for, when I told you the steamer was not going to England, you called your boatman back. It is a plain case; and you can stay in the brig till the ship returns to Barcelona."

The lies did not help the case a particle; and somehow every thing seemed to go wrong with Bill Stout, but that was because he went wrong himself.

The boats were sent on ashore for the Princes; and when they arrived all hands were called to attend the lecture in the grand saloon.

"Young gentlemen, I am glad to meet you again," the professor began. "I have said all I need say about the geography of the peninsula. Some of you have been through Spain and Portugal, and have seen that the natural features of the two countries are about the same. The lack of industry and enterprise has had the same result in both. The people are alike in one respect, at least: each hates the other intensely. 'Strip a Spaniard of his virtues, and you have a Portuguese,' says the Spanish proverb; but I fancy one is as good as the other. There are plenty of minerals in the ground, plenty of excellent soil, and plenty of fish in the waters of Portugal; but none of the sources of wealth and prosperity are used as in England, France, and the United States. The principal productions are wheat, wine, olive-oil, cork, wool, and fruit. Of the forty million dollars' worth of agricultural products, twelve are in wine, ten in grain, and seven in wool. More than two-thirds of the exports are to England.

"The population of Portugal is about four millions. It has few large towns, only two having over fifty thousand inhabitants. Lisbon has two hundred and seventy-five thousand, and Oporto about ninety thousand. Coimbra, — which has the only university in the country, — Elvas, Evora, Braga, and Setubal, are important towns. The kingdom has six provinces; and we are now in Estremadura, as we were yesterday morning, though it is not the same one.

"The government is a constitutional monarchy, not very different from that of Spain. The present king is Luis II. The army consists of about eighteen thousand men; and the navy, of twenty-two steamers and twenty-five sailing vessels. The colonial possessions of Portugal have a population equal to the kingdom itself.

"The money of Portugal will bother you."

At this statement Sheridan and Murray looked at each other, and laughed.

"You seem to be pleased, Captain Sheridan," said the professor. "Perhaps you have had some experience with Portuguese money."

"Yes, sir: I went into a store to buy some photographs; and, when I asked the price of them, the man told me it was one thousand six hundred and forty *reis*. I concluded that I should be busted if I bought that dozen pictures."

"It takes about a million of those *reis* to make a dollar," added Murray.

"But, when I came to figure up the price, I found it was only a dollar and sixty-four cents," continued Sheridan.

"A naval officer who dined a party of his friends in this very city, when he found the bill was twenty-seven thousand five hundred *reis*, exclaimed that he was utterly ruined, for he should never be able to pay such a bill; but it was only twenty-seven dollars and a half. You count the *reis* at the rate of ten to a cent of our money,—a thousand to a dollar. About all the copper and silver money has a number on the coin that indicates its value in *reis*. For large sums, the count is given in *milreis*, which means a thousand *reis*. The gold most in use is the English sovereign, which passes for forty-five hundred *reis*. We will now give some attention to the history of the country.

"Portugal makes no great figure on the map of Europe. Looking at this narrow strip of territory, one would naturally suppose that its history would not fill a very large volume. But small states have had their history told in voluminous works; and Portugal happens to belong to this class. There are histories and chronicles of this country in the Portuguese, Spanish, Italian, French, English, and Latin languages, not to mention some Arabic works which I have not had time to examine," continued the professor, with a smile. "Some of these works consist of from ten to thirty volumes. Even the discoveries and conquests of this people in the East and West require quite a number of large volumes; for there was a time when Portugal filled a large place in the eye of the world, though that time was short, hardly reaching through the fifteenth and sixteenth centuries.

"But the history of this country does not begin at all till the eleventh century. There was, indeed, the old Roman province of Lusitania, which corresponded very nearly in size with modern Portugal, except that the latter extends farther north and not so far east. The ancient Lusitanians were a warlike people; and a hundred and fifty years before our era they gave the Romans a great deal of trouble to conquer them. Under Viriathus, the most famous of all the Lusitanians, they routed several Roman armies; and might have held their ground for many years longer, if their hero had not been treacherously murdered by his own countrymen.

"The lines of the old Roman provinces were not preserved after the barbarians, of whom I have spoken to you before, entered the peninsula in the fifth century. The Arabs occupied this province with the rest of the peninsula, after the defeat and death of King Roderick, or Don Rodrigo, the last of the Gothic kings of Spain; and held it till near the close of the eleventh century, a part of it somewhat later. In 1095 Alfonso VI., of Castile and Leon, bestowed a part of what is now Portugal upon his son-in-law, Henri of Burgundy, who had fought with Alfonso against the Moors, and seemed to have the ability to protect the country given him from the inroad of the Moslems. The region granted to Henri extended only from the Minho to the Tagus; and its capital was Coimbra, for Lisbon was then a Moorish city. The new ruler was called a count; and he had the privilege of conquering the country as far south as the Guadiana. His son Dom Alfonso defeated the Moors in a great battle near the Tagus, and was proclaimed king of Portugal on the battle-field. This was in the time of the crusades; but Spain and Portugal had infidels enough to fight at home, without going to the Holy Land, where hundreds of thousands were sent to die by other countries of Europe. Other additions were made to the country during the next century; but since the middle of the thirteenth century, when Sancho II. died, no increase has been made in the peninsula. The wealth and power of Portugal at a later period were derived from her colonies in America, Asia, and Africa.

"John I. — Dom João, in Portuguese — led an expedition against Ceuta, a Moorish stronghold just across the Strait of Gibraltar, and captured the place. After this began their wonderful series of discoveries, which brought the whole world to the knowledge of Europe. But the Portuguese were not the first to carry on commerce by sea. Though merchandise had been mainly transported by land in the East, there was some trade on the Mediterranean and Black Seas, and on the Indian Ocean. It does not appear that the Phœnicians, the Carthaginians, or the Greeks, ever sailed on the Baltic Sea; and, though the Romans explored some parts of it, they never went far enough to ascertain that it was bounded on all sides by land.

"The Eastern Empire of the middle ages, with its capital at Constantinople, carried on a much more extensive commerce than was ever known to the Romans in the days of their universal dominion. At first the goods brought from the East Indies were imported into Europe from Alexandria; but, when Egypt was conquered by the Arabs, a new route had to be found. Merchandise was conveyed up the Indus as far as that great river was navigable, then across the land to the Oxus, now the Amoo, flowing into the Sea of Aral, but then having a channel to the Caspian. From the mouth of this river it was carried over the Caspian Sea, and up the Volga, to about the point where there is now a railroad connecting this river with the Don. Then it was transported by land again to the Don, and taken in vessels by the Black Sea to Constantinople. The Suez Canal, opened this present year, makes an easy and expeditious route by water for steamers, connecting all the ports of Europe with those of India.

"During this period another commercial state was growing up. After the fall of the Roman empire, when the Huns under Attila were ravaging Italy, the inhabitants of Venetia fled for safety to the group of islands near the northern shore of the Adriatic, and laid the foundation of the illustrious city and state of Venice. The people of the city soon began to fit out small merchant fleets, which they sent to all parts of the Mediterranean, and particularly to Syria and Egypt, after spices and other products of Arabia and India. Soon after, the city of Genoa, on the other side of Italy, became a rival of Venice in this trade, and Florence and Pisa followed their example; but the Venetians, having some natural advantages, outstripped their rivals in the end, and became a great military and commercial power. The crusades, in which others wasted life and treasure, were a source of wealth to these Italian cities. During the twelfth and thirteenth centuries, the commerce of Europe was almost wholly confined to the Italians. The merchants of Italy scattered themselves in every kingdom; and the Lombards (for this was the name by which they were known) became the merchants and bankers everywhere. After a time, however, the commercial spirit began to develop itself, and to make progress in other parts of Europe; but, up to the fifteenth century, vessels were accustomed, in their voyages, to creep along the coast; and, though it was known that the magnetic needle points constantly to the North Pole, no use was made of this knowledge for purposes of navigation.

"In 1415 the commercial spirit had reached Portugal; and the Ceuta expedition was undertaken quite as much in the interest of trade as of religion, for the place was held by pirates who were daily disturbing Portuguese commerce. Immense treasures fell to the victors as the reward of their enterprise.

"Dom Henrique, or Henry, the son of King John, afterwards so famous in the history of his country, had a decided taste for study. He was an able mathematician, and made himself master of all the astronomy known to the Arabians, who were then the best mathematicians of Europe. Henry also studied the works of the ancients. At this period Ptolemy was the highest authority in geography; and he taught that the African Continent reached to the South Pole. But Henry had read the ancient accounts of the circumnavigation of Africa by the Phœnicians and others; and he believed, that, whether these voyages had or had not been made, good ships might sail around the southern point of the continent. If this could be done, the Portuguese would find a way to India by sea, and thus control the entire trade of the East.

"The prince had many obstacles to overcome. Vessels in that day were not built for the open sea; and every headland and far-stretching cape seemed to be an impossible barrier. There was a notion that near the equator was a burning zone, where the very waters of the ocean actually boiled under the intolerable heat of the sun. A superstition also prevailed, that whoever doubled Cape Bojador — on the coast of Africa, about a thousand miles south of Lisbon — would never return; and it was feared that the burning zone would change those who entered it into negroes, thus dooming them to wear the black marks of their temerity to the grave.

"The first voyage undertaken under the direction of Prince Henry was in 1419, and covered only five degrees of latitude. The expedition was driven out to sea. and landed at a small island north-east of Madeira, which they named Porto Santo. The next year three vessels were sent for a longer voyage. This fleet reached the dreaded cape, and discovered Madeira. On the next voyage they doubled Cape Bojador; and, having exploded the superstition, in the course of a few years they advanced four hundred leagues farther, and discovered the Senegal River. Here they found men with woolly hair and skins as black as ebony; and they began to dread a nearer approach to the equator.

"When they returned, their countrymen with one voice attempted to dissuade Prince Henry from any further attempts; but he would hear of no delay. He applied to Pope Eugene IV.; and, representing that his chief object was the pious wish to spread a knowledge of the Christian faith among the idolatrous people of Africa, he obtained a bull conferring on the people of Portugal the exclusive right to all the countries they had discovered, or might discover, between Cape Nun — about three hundred miles north of Cape Bojador — and India. Such a donation may appear ridiculous enough to us; but it was never doubted then that the pope had ample right to bestow such a gift; and for a long time all the powers of Europe considered the right of the Portuguese to be good, and acknowledged their title to almost the whole of Africa. About this time Prince Henry died, and little progress was made in discovery for some years. But the Portuguese had begun to push boldly out to sea, and had lost all dread of the burning zone.

"In the reign of John II., from 1481 to 1495, discoveries were pushed with greater vigor than ever before. The Cape de Verde Islands were colonized; and the Portuguese ships, which had advanced to the coast of Guinea, began to return with cargoes of gold-dust, ivory, gums, and other valuable products. It was during the reign of this monarch that Columbus visited Lisbon, and offered his services to Portugal; and it appears that the king was inclined to listen to the plans of the great navigator, but he was dissuaded from doing so by his own courtiers.

"The revenue derived at this time from the African coast became so important that John feared the vessels of other nations might be attracted to it. To prevent this, the voyages there were represented as being in the highest degree dangerous, and even impossible except in the peculiar vessels used by the Portuguese. The monarchs of Castile had some idea of what was going on, and were very eager to learn more; and in one case came very near succeeding. A Portuguese captain and two pilots, in the hope of a rich reward, set out for Castile to dispose of the desired information; but they were pursued by the king's agents. When overtaken, they refused to return; but two of them were killed on the spot, and the other brought back to Evora and quartered. The attempt of a rich Spaniard, the Duke of Medina Sidonia, to build vessels in English ports for the African trade, turned out no better. King John reminded the English king, Edward IV., of the ancient alliance between the two crowns; and so these preparations were prohibited.

"In 1497 a Portuguese fleet under Vasco de Gama doubled the Cape of Good Hope, or the Cape of Storms as they called it then; and soon the voyagers began to hear the Arabian tongue spoken on the other shore of the continent, and found that they had nearly circumnavigated Africa. At length, with the aid of Mohammedan pilots, they passed the mouths of the Arabian and Persian Gulfs, and, stretching along the western coast of India, arrived, after a cruise of thirteen months, at Calicut, on the shore of Malabar, less than three hundred miles from the southern point of the peninsula.

"The Court of Lisbon now appointed a viceroy to rule over new countries discovered. Expeditions followed each other in rapid succession; and, in less than half a century more, the Portuguese were masters of the entire trade of the Indian Ocean. Their flag floated triumphantly along the shores of Africa from Morocco to Abyssinia, and on the Asiatic coast from Arabia to Siam; not to mention the vast regions of Brazil, which this nation began to colonize about the same time. These conquests were not made without opposition; but the Portuguese were as remarkable for their valor as for their enterprise, in those days; and, for a time, their prowess was too much for their enemies in Africa, in India, and even in Europe. The Venetians, who had lost the trade between India and Europe, were of course their enemies; and the Sultan of Egypt was hostile when he found that he was about to lose the profitable trade that passed through Alexandria. These two powers joined hands; and the Venetians sent from Italy to the head of the Red Sea, at an immense expense, the materials for building a fleet to meet and destroy the Portuguese vessels on their passage to India. But, as soon as this fleet was ready for active operations, it was attacked and destroyed by the Portuguese navy.

"Thus the Portuguese were masters of an empire on which the sun never set. It reached the height of its glory in the reign of John III., from 1521 to 1557. He was succeeded by his son Dom Sebastian, who made several expeditions against the Moors in Africa. In the last of these, he was utterly routed, his army destroyed, and he perished on the battle-field. This disaster seemed to initiate the decline of Portugal; and it continued to run down till it was only the shadow of its former greatness.

"Concerning Dom Sebastian, a very remarkable superstition prevails, even at the present time, in Portugal, to the effect that he will return, resume the crown, and restore the realm to its former greatness. For nearly two hundred years this belief has existed, and was almost universal at one time, not among the ignorant only, but in all classes of society. It was claimed that he was not killed in the battle, though his body was recognized by his page, and that he will come back as the temporal Messiah of Portugal. Several persons have appeared who have claimed to be the prince, the most remarkable of whom turned up at Venice twenty years after the prince's presumed death. He told a very straight story; but the Senate of Venice banished him, and he was afterwards imprisoned in Naples and Florence for insisting upon the truth of his statements. He finally died in Castile; and many believed that he was not an impostor. Several times have been fixed for his coming; but it is not likely that he will be able to put in an appearance, on account of the two hundred years that have elapsed since he was in the flesh.

"As Sebastian did not come back from Africa, his uncle Henry assumed the crown; and at his death, as he had no direct heirs, Philip II., the Prince of Parma, and the Duchess of Braganza, claimed the throne, as did several others; but Philip settled the question by sending the Duke of Alva into Portugal, and taking forcible possession of the kingdom. In 1580, therefore, the whole of the vast dominions I have described were annexed to the Spanish empire. This connection lasted for sixty years; and the Portuguese call it "the sixty years' captivity." During this time the people were never satisfied with their government, and in 1640 got up a revolution, and placed the Duke of Braganza on the throne, under the title of John IV. This was the beginning of the house of Braganza, which has held the throne up to the present time.

"Even in the seventeenth century Portugal had fallen from her high estate. She had lost part of her possessions and all her prestige; and from that time till the present she has had no great weight in European politics. Some of her colonial territories returned to the original owners, while others were taken by the Dutch, the English, and the Spaniards. For two centuries the most remarkable events in her history have been misfortunes. In 1755 an earthquake destroyed half the city of Lisbon, and buried thirty thousand people under its ruins. It came in two shocks, the second of which left the city a pile of ruins. Thousands of men and women fled from the falling walls to the quays on the river. Suddenly the ground under them sank with all the crowd upon it; and not one of the bodies ever came up. At the same time all the boats and vessels, loaded down with fugitives from the ruin, were sucked in by a fearful whirlpool; and not a vestige of them returned to the surface.

"Fifty-five years later came the French Revolution; in the results of which Portugal was involved. In 1807 she entered into an alliance with Great Britain; and Napoleon decided to wipe off the kingdom from the map of Europe. A French army was sent to Lisbon; and at its approach the Court left for Brazil, where it remained for several years. An English army arrived at Oporto the next year; and with these events began the peninsular war. The struggle lasted till 1812, and many great battles were fought in this kingdom. The country was desolated by the strife, and the sufferings of the people were extremely severe. Subscriptions were raised for them in England and elsewhere; and Sir Walter Scott wrote 'The Vision of Don Roderick' in aid of the sufferers.

"In 1821 Brazil declared her independence; but it was not acknowledged by Portugal till 1825. After fourteen years of absence, the Court — John VI. was king, having succeeded to the throne while in Brazil — returned to Portugal. During this period the home kingdom was practically a colony of Brazil; and the people were dissatisfied with the arrangement. A constitution was made, and the king accepted it. He had left his son as regent of Brazil, and he was proclaimed emperor of that country as Pedro I. He was the father of the present emperor, Pedro II.

"John VI. died in 1826. His legitimate successor

was Pedro of Brazil; but he gave the crown to his daughter Maria. Before she could get possession of it, Dom Miguel, a younger son of John VI., usurped the throne. As he did not pay much deference to the constitution, the people revolted; and civil war raged for several years. Pedro, having abdicated the crown of Brazil in favor of his son, came to Portugal in 1832, to look after the interests of his daughter. He was made regent, — Maria da Gloria was only thirteen years old, — and with the help of England, cleaned out the Miguelists two years later. The little queen was declared of age at fifteen, and took the oath to support the constitution. She died in 1853; and her son, Pedro V., became king when he was fifteen. But he lived only eight years after his accession, and was followed by his brother, Luis I., the present king. There have been several insurrections since the Miguelists were disposed of, but none since 1851. The royal family have secured the affections of the people; for the sons of Maria have proved to be wise and sensible men. The finances are in bad condition; for the expense of the government exceeds the income every year. Now you have heard, and you may go and see for yourselves."

CHBPTER XX.

LISBON AND ITS SURROUNDINGS.

THE room in the Hotel Braganza occupied by Sheridan and Murray was an excellent one, so far as the situation was concerned; for it commanded a beautiful view of the Tagus and the surrounding country.

"I should think this hotel had been a fort some time," said Sheridan, when they rose in the morning. "Those windows look like port-holes for cannon."

"It is the house of Braganza, and ought to be a royal hotel; but it is not very elegantly furnished. There are no towels here. Where is the bell?"

"I noticed that there was one outside of each room on this floor. Here is the bell-pull. It is an original way to fix the bells," added Sheridan. "The bell-boys must come up three flights of stairs in order to hear them ring."

"But, if the waiter don't speak English, what will you ask for?" laughed Murray.

"I have a book of four languages that I picked up in Madrid, — French, Spanish, Italian, and Portuguese," said the captain, as he took the volume from his bag. "Here it is. '*Une serviette*,' — that's a napkin, but it will do as well, — '*um guardinapo.*'"

The bell was rung, and a chambermaid answered it. The word brought the towels, but Sheridan pointed to the wash-stand; and the pantomime would have answered just as well as speech, for the woman could see what was wanting. When they were dressed, Dr. Winstock came to the door, and invited them to visit the top of the house, which commanded a view even more extensive than the window.

"The Tagus runs about east and west here," said he. "It is about a mile wide, but widens out into a broad bay opposite the city. There is no finer harbor in the world. The old part of the city, between the castle and the river, was not destroyed by the earthquake. Between us and the castle is a small region of straight streets; and this is the part that was destroyed. On the river below us are the marine arsenal and the custom-house, with the *Praça do Commercio* between them."

"The what?" asked Murray.

"*Praça* is the Portuguese for 'square;' 'Commercial Square' in English will cover it. This one has several names; and the English, who are in great force in Lisbon, call it Black Horse Square. There is very little to see in Lisbon. Orders have come up for all hands to be on the quay at nine o'clock, to go on board the Prince for the lecture; and we must breakfast first."

After the lecture the Princes went on shore again. The doctor with his pupils took a carriage, and proceeded to "do" the city. Their first point was the square they had seen from the housetop. On one side of it was an arch supporting a clock-tower. In the centre was an equestrian statue of Joseph I., erected by the inhabitants out of gratitude to the king and the Marquis of Pombal for their efforts to rebuild the city after the great earthquake. On the pedestal is an effigy of the marquis, who was the king's minister, as powerful as he was unpopular. The populace cut his head out of the statue when the king died, but it was restored fifty years later."

"This street," said the doctor, indicating the one over which the ornamental arch was extended, "is the *Rua Augusta.*"

"I think the Commercial is as fine a square as I have seen in Europe," added Sheridan.

"Most people agree with you. Now, if we pass through the *Rua Augusta*, we shall come to the *Praca do Rocio*, which is also a beautiful square. There are three other streets running parallel with this; on one side is Gold, and on the other Silver Street."

"They build their houses very high for an earthquaky country," said Murray.

"And this is the very spot which was sunk. I suppose they don't expect to have another convulsion."

The carriage proceeded into the square, and then to another, only a couple of blocks from it, in which was the fruit-market. It was lined with trees, with a fountain in the centre. All around it were men and women selling fruit and other commodities. It was a lively scene. In this square they saw a Portuguese cart of the model that was probably used by the Moors. The wheels do not revolve on the axle, but the axle turns with the wheels, as in a child's tin wagon, and creak and groan fearfully as they do so.

As they passed through the Campo Santa Anna, the doctor pointed out the *Circo dos Touros*, or bull-ring.

"But a bull-fight here is a tame affair compared with those in Spain," he explained. "They do not kill the bull, nor are any horses gored to death; for the horns of the animal are tipped with large wooden balls. It is a rather lively affair, and will answer very well if you have not seen the real thing. It is said that there are seven hills in Lisbon, as in Rome; but this is a vanity of many other cities. There are many hills in Lisbon, however; and there seems to be a church or a convent on every one of them. This is the *Passio Publico;* and it is crowded with people on a warm evening," continued the doctor, as they came to a long and narrow park. "It is the *prado* of Lisbon.

"I shall ask you to visit only one church in this city, unless you desire to see more; and this is the one," said the doctor, as the carriage stopped at a plain building. "This is St. Roque. It is said that Dom John V., when he visited this church, was greatly mortified at the mean appearance of the chapel of his patron saint. He ordered one to be prepared in Rome, of the richest materials. When it was done, mass was said in it by the pope, Benedict XIV.; and then it was taken to pieces, and sent to Lisbon, where it was again set up as you will find it."

The party entered the church, and the attendant gave each of them a printed sheet on which was a description of the chapel. It proved to be a rather small recess; but the mosaics of the baptism of Christ in the Jordan by John, and other scriptural designs, are of the highest order of merit. The floor, ceiling, and sides are of the same costly work, the richest marbles and gems being used. The chapel contains eight columns of lapis-lazuli. The whole of this is said to have cost fourteen million *crusados*, over eight million dollars; but others say only one million *crusados*, and probably the last sum is nearer the truth.

The next day was Sunday; and in the morning the United States steamer Franklin — the largest in the service — came into the river. There was a Portuguese frigate off the marine arsenal; and what with saluting the flag of Portugal, and the return-salute, saluting Mr. Lewis the American minister, and saluting Mr. Diamond the American consul, when each visited the ship, the guns of the great vessel were blazing away about all the forenoon. But the students were proud of the ship; and they did not object to any amount of gun-firing, even on Sunday. In the afternoon, some of them went to the cathedral, which was formerly a mosque, and to some of the other churches. All hands attended service on board of the American Prince at eleven.

The next morning the Josephines and Tritonias started on their tour through the peninsula to Barcelona; and the ship's company went on board of the steamer. Regular discipline was restored; but the business of sight-seeing was continued for two days more. The doctor conducted his little party to the palace of the *Necessidades*.

"What a name for a palace!" exclaimed Murray. "I suppose that jaw-breaker means 'necessities.'"

"That is just what it means. Circumstances often give names to palaces and other things; and it was so in this case. A weaver brought an image of the Blessed Virgin from a place on the west coast, from which he fled to escape the plague. With money he begged of the pious, he built a small chapel for the image, near this spot. Like so many of these virgins, it wrought the most wonderful miracles, healing the sick, restoring the lame, and opening the eyes of the blind; and many people came to it in their 'necessities,' for relief. Dom John V. believed in it, and built a handsome church, with a convent attached to it, for the blessed image. It had restored his health once, and he built this palace near it, that it might be handy for his 'necessities.' During the long sickness preceding his death, he had it brought to the palace with royal honors, and kept it there in state, taking it with him wherever he went.

"This square is the *Fraca Alcantara*," continued the doctor, when they came from the palace. "There are plenty of fountains in the city, nearly every public square being supplied with one. When I was here before, there were more water-carriers than now; and they were all men of Gallicia, as in Madrid. Three thousand of them used to be employed in supplying the inhabitants with water; but now it is probably conveyed into most of the houses in pipes. You can tell these men from the native Portuguese, because they carry their burden, whatever it may be, on their shoulders instead of their heads. A proverb here is to the effect that God made the Portuguese first, and then the Gallego to wait upon him. Most of the male servants in houses come from Gallicia. They are largely the porters and laborers, for the natives are too proud to carry burdens: it is too near like the work of a mule or a donkey. It is said, that when the French approached Coimbra in the peninsular war, and the people deserted the city, the men would not carry their valuables with them, so great was their prejudice against bundles; and every thing was lost except what the women could take with them. They could not disgrace themselves to save their property."

"No wonder the country is poor," added Sheridan.

"Now we will cross the bridge, and ride through Buenos Ayres, where many of the wealthy people live, and some of the ambassadors," continued the doctor.

They had a pleasant ride, passing the English cemetery in which Henry Fielding and Dr. Doddridge were buried. On the return, they passed the principal cemetery of the city. It is called the *Prazeres*, which means "pleasures;" a name it obtained by accident, and not because it was considered appropriate.

The following day was set apart for an excursion to Cintra and Mafra, and a sufficient number of omnibuses were sent to a point on the north-west road; for the students were to walk over the aqueduct in order to see that wonderful work. The party ascended some stone steps to a large hall which contains the reservoir. It is near the *Praca do Rato*, and not far from the centre of the city. The party then entered the arched gallery, eight feet high and five feet wide, through which the water-ways are led. In the middle is a paved pathway for foot-passengers. On either side of it is a channel in the masonry, nine inches wide and a foot deep in the centre, rounded at the bottom. It looked like a small affair for the supply of a great city. The aqueduct is carried on a range of arches over the valley of the Alcantara, which is the name of the little stream that flows into the Tagus near the *Necessidades*. The highest of these arches are two hundred and sixty-three feet above the river. A causeway was built on each side of it, forming a bridge to the villages in the suburbs; but its use was discontinued because so many people committed suicide by throwing themselves from the dizzy height, or were possibly murdered by robbers. This aqueduct was erected by Dom John V., and it is the pride of the city. The water comes from springs six miles away.

"Why did we have those water-jars in the hotel if they have spring-water?" asked Sheridan, as they walked along the gallery.

"They think the water is better kept in those jars," replied Dr. Winstock; "and I believe they are right; at least, they would be if they would keep the ants out of them."

On the other side of the valley the excursionists loaded themselves into the omnibuses, and were soon on their way to Cintra, which is fourteen miles from Lisbon. It is a sort of Versailles, Potsdam, or Windsor, where the court resides during a part of the year, and where all the wealthy and fashionable people spend their summers. It is a beautiful drive, with many pleasant villages, palaces, country-seats, groves, and gardens by the way.

"Here we are," said the doctor to his young companions, when the carriage in which they had come stopped before Victor's Hotel. "Southey said this was the most blessed spot in the habitable world. Byron sang with equal enthusiasm; and the words of these poets have made the place famous in England. Our American guide-book does not even mention it."

Cintra is a town of forty-five hundred inhabitants. It is built on the southern end of the Estrella Mountains, at an elevation of from eighteen hundred to three thousand feet. It is only a few miles from the seashore, and the Atlantic may be seen from its hills. The party of the doctor first went to the royal palace. It was the Alhambra of the Moorish monarchs, and has been a favorite residence of the Christian kings. Dom Sebastian held his last court here when he left for Africa. The students wandered through its numerous apartments, laughed at its magpie saloon, and thought of the kings who had dwelt within its walls. They were more pleased with the gardens, though it was winter; for there was a great deal in them that was curious and interesting.

The Pena Convent was the next attraction. All convents have been suppressed in Portugal, as in Spain; but the Gothic building has been repaired, and it looks more like a castle than a religious house. Its garden and grounds must be magnificent in the proper season. The view from the highest point presents an almost boundless panorama of country, river, and ocean. The Moorish castle that commands the town was examined; and the next thing was the Cork Convent. It is an edifice built in and on the rock, and contains twenty cells, each of which is lined with cork to keep out the dampness of the rock on which it is founded. These cells are dungeons five feet square, with doors so low that even the shortest of the students had to stoop to enter them.

A country-house in Portugal is a *quinta;* and that
of Dom John de Castro, the great navigator and the
viceroy of the Indies, is called *Penha Verda,* and is
still in the hands of his descendants. The gardens
are very pretty; and the first orange-trees set out in
Europe were on this estate.' In the garden is the
chapel built by him on his return from the Indies, in
1542, and the rock with six trees on it, which was the
only reward he desired for the conquest of the Island
of Diu, in Hindostan. He died in the arms of St.
Francis Xavier, in 1548, protesting that he had spent
every thing he had in supplying the wants of his com-
rades in arms. He declared that he had not a change
of linen, or money enough to buy him a chicken for his
dinner. Most of the enormous wealth of the Indies
had passed through his hands; and he had not stolen
a *vintem* of it. What an example for modern office-
holders! When he was dead, only one *vintem* — about
two cents — was found in his coffers. His descendants
were prohibited from deriving any profit from the culti-
vation of this property.

The rest of the time was given to wandering about
among the estates of the wealthy men, including some
of the foreign ministers, who have *quintas* in Cintra.

After a lunch, the excursionists proceeded to Mafra,
about ten miles from Cintra. This place contains an
enormous pile of buildings on the plan of the Escurial, and rather larger, if any thing. It was erected by
John V. to carry out his vow to change the poorest
monastery into the most magnificent one when Heaven
would give him a son. It contains eight hundred and
sixty-six apartments; but the only one of interest to

the students was the audience-chamber, preserved as it was when the palace was inhabited by Dom John.

It was late in the evening when the Princes returned to Lisbon; and they were rather glad to learn that the ship was to sail for Barcelona after breakfast the next morning.

"I am rather sorry that we do not go to Oporto," said the doctor, when the captain informed him of the order. "It is an old city set on a hillside; but it would not interest the students any more than Lisbon has."

"By the way, doctor, we have not seen any port wine," added Sheridan.

"It is not a great sight to look at the casks that contain port wine. In Porto, not Oporto in Portugal, it is not the black, logwood decoction which passes under the name of port in the United States, though it is darker than ordinary wines. It gets its color and flavor from the peculiarity of the grapes that grow in the vicinity of Porto."

The officers were tired enough to turn in. Early the next morning the fires were roaring in the furnaces of the Prince; at a later hour the pipe of the boatswain was heard; and at half-past eight the steamer was standing down the river. As the students had not come to Lisbon from the sea, they all gathered on the deck and in the rigging to see the surroundings.

"That building on the height is the palace of Ajuda, where the present king ordinarily resides," said the surgeon, when the captain pointed it out to one of the officers. "A temporary wooden house was built on that hill for the royal family after the earthquake. It is very large for this little kingdom, but is only one-third of the size it was intended to be. It was erected by John VI.; or, rather, it was begun by him, for it is not finished."

"You can see the buildings on the Cintra hills," added Murray.

"Yes; and you can see them better from the ocean."

"That is Belem Castle," said Sheridan, as the ship approached the mouth of the river. "I saw a picture of it in an illustrated paper at home."

"It is called the Tower of Belem; and there is a palace with the same name on the shore. This is half Gothic and half Moorish. It is round, and the style is unique. What it was built for, no one knows. I suppose you are not aware how Columbus ascertained that there was a Western Continent," added the doctor, smiling.

"I know what the books say,—that he reasoned it out in his own mind," replied the captain.

"You see that town on the north: it is Cascaes, in which Sanchez, the renowned pilot, was born," continued the doctor. "In 1486 Sanchez was blown off in a storm; and, before he could bring up, he was carried to an unknown land somewhere in North America. On his way back he stopped at Madeira, where he was the guest of Columbus. Somehow the log-book of the pilot fell into the hands of the great navigator, and from it he learned that there was an American Continent."

"Do you believe that story?" asked Sheridan seriously.

"I do not. There are too many difficulties in the way of it; but it was told me by a Portuguese pilot."

When the ship had passed the bar, the pilot was discharged, and the course laid to the south. Just at dark she was in sight of Cape St. Vincent. The doctor related the story of its name, which was given to it because the body of St. Vincent, martyred in Rome, found its way to this cape, where it was watched over for a long period by crows. The ship that conveyed it to Lisbon was followed by these birds; and tame crows were afterwards kept in the cathedral, where the remains were deposited, in memory of the miraculous care of these birds. Three great naval victories have been won by the English Navy off this cape. Rodney defeated the Spanish fleet in 1780; Nelson, with fifteen small vessels, beat twenty-seven Spanish men-of-war, in 1797; and Sir Charles Napier, in 1833, with six vessels, only one of them a frigate, defeated ten Portuguese ships, thus putting an end to the Miguel war, and placing Maria I. on the throne of Portugal. The next day the Prince passed Cape Trafalgar, where, in 1805, Nelson gained his great naval victory over the combined fleets of France and Spain.

On Sunday morning the Prince arrived at Barcelona.

CHAPTER XXI.

A SAFE HARBOR.

"WE are in Malaga now; and we have to decide what to do next," said Raymond, when they were shown to their room in the hotel.

"I supposed you would wait till the squadron arrived," replied Bark.

"I do not intend to wait. We have talked so much about your affairs that we have said nothing about mine," added Raymond. "My circumstances are very different from yours. I feel that I have been right all the time; and I expect that I shall be fully justified in the end for what I have done in violation of the discipline of the vessel to which I belong."

"I know that my case is very different from yours; but I do not want to part company with you," said Bark, with an anxious look on his face.

"I don't know that it is necessary for us to part. Though I think it is your duty to join your ship as soon as convenient, I shall keep out of the way till she is ready to sail from Spain. The fleet will certainly visit Cadiz, whether it goes to sea from there or not. For this reason, I must work my way to Cadiz."

"And must I stay here till the squadron arrives?"

"Let us look it over."

"I cannot speak Spanish; and I shall be like a cat in a strange garret, unless I employ a guide."

"The right thing for you to do is to return to your ship."

"Go back to Barcelona?"

"I should advise you to do that if I were not afraid the fleet would leave before you could get there. The Prince will arrive within three days; and, if the Josephines and Tritonias have returned, the vessels may sail at once. It is a long, tedious, and expensive journey by rail; and you could not get there in this time by any steamer, for they all stop at the ports on the way. I don't know where the fleet will put in on its way south; and you might miss it. On the whole, I think you had better stay with me."

"I think so myself," replied Bark, pleased with the decision.

"Because you want to think so, perhaps," laughed Raymond. "We must be careful that our wishes don't override our judgment."

"But you decided it for me."

"I think we have settled it right," added Raymond. "I want to see something of my native land; and I shall go to the Alhambra and Seville on the way to Cadiz. In your case it will make only a difference of two or three days, whether you join the Tritonia here or in Cadiz."

This course was decided upon in the end; and, after a day in Malaga, they started for Granada. At the expiration of ten days, they had completed the tour marked out by Raymond, and were in Cadiz, waiting for the arrival of the squadron. At the end of a week it had not come. Another week, and still it did not appear. Raymond looked over the ship-news in all the papers he could find in the club-house; but the last news he could obtain was that the Prince and her consorts had arrived at Carthagena. In vain he looked for any thing more. The next port would certainly be Malaga, unless the fleet put into Almeria, which was not probable. It was now the middle of January.

"I don't understand it," said Raymond. "The vessels ought to have been here before this time."

"Perhaps they have gone over into Africa to look after us," suggested Bark.

"That is not possible: Mr. Lowington never goes to hunt up or hunt down runaways; but he may have gone over there to let the students see something of Africa," replied Raymond. "I don't think he has gone over to Africa at all."

"Where is he, then?"

"That's a conundrum, and I can't guess it."

Raymond continued to watch the papers till the first of February; but still there were no tidings of the fleet. He had a list of the vessels that had passed Tarifa, and of those which had arrived at Algiers, Oran, and Nemours; but they did not contain the name of the Prince. Then he looked for ships at Alexandria, thinking the principal might have concluded to take the students to Egypt; but he found nothing to support such a possibility.

"I don't think I shall stay here any longer," said Raymond. "We have been here a month."

"Where will you go?" asked Bark.

"I believe we had better take a steamer, and follow the coast up to Carthagena, where we had the last news of the fleet," replied Raymond. "When we get there we can ascertain for what port she sailed."

"Why not go on board of one of the steamers that come down the coast from Barcelona, and inquire of the officers if they have seen the squadron?" suggested Bark, who was always full of suggestions.

"That's a capital idea!" exclaimed Raymond. "I wonder we did not think of that idea before."

Then they had to wait a week for a steamer that had come down the coast; but one of the line from Oran had been in port, and they ascertained that the fleet was not in the port of Malaga. Raymond went to the captain of the steamer from Barcelona, and was informed that the squadron was at Carthagena, and had been there for over a month.

"That accounts for it all," said Raymond, as they returned to the boat in which they had boarded the steamer. "But I can't imagine why the fleet is staying all this time in the harbor of Carthagena."

"Perhaps the Prince has broken some of her machinery, and they have stopped to repair damages," suggested Bark.

"That may be; but they could hardly be a month mending a break. They could build a new engine in that time almost."

"Well, we know where the fleet is; and the next question is, What are we to do about it?" added Bark, as they landed on the quay.

They returned to the Hotel de Cadiz, where they boarded, and went to their room to consider the situation with the new light just obtained.

"Your course is plain enough, Bark," said Raymond. "Mine is not so plain."

"You think I ought to return to the Tritonia; don't you?" added Bark.

"That is my view."

"But suppose the fleet should sail before I get to Carthagena?"

"You must take your chance of that."

"But you will not go back with me?"

"No: it would not be safe for me to do that. It will be better for my uncle in Barcelona not to know where I am."

"But what shall I say to Mr. Lowington, or Mr. Pelham, when I am asked where you are?" inquired Bark. "I suppose it is still to be part of my programme not to lie."

"Undoubtedly; and I hope you will stick to it as long as you live."

"I intend to do so; and you might as well go with me as to have me tell them where you are."

"That is true, Bark; and, when you get on board of the Tritonia, tell all you know about me, and say that you left me in Cadiz."

"You might as well go with me."

"I think not."

"Then that *alguacil* will be after you in less than a week," said Bark.

"But he will not find me; for I shall not be in Cadiz when he arrives," laughed the Spaniard.

"Where are you going?" asked Bark curiously.

"If I don't tell you, you will not know."

"I see," added Bark. "You do not intend to stay in Cadiz."

"Of course not."

"But you may miss the squadron when it goes to sea."

"If I do, I cannot help it; and in that case I may go to New York, or I may go to the West Indies in the Lopez steamers. I have not made up my mind what I shall do."

Raymond wrote a long letter to Scott, and gave it to his companion to deliver to him. In a few days a steamer came along that was going to stop at Carthagena. Bark went on board of her; and, after a hard parting, he sailed away in her to join the Tritonia, after an absence of two months.

On the following day Raymond went to Gibraltar in the Spanish steamer, and remained there a full month, watching the papers for news of the fleet. At the end of this time he found the arrival of the squadron at Malaga. A few days later he saw that the Prince had passed Tarifa, and then that she had arrived at Cadiz. But, while he is watching the movements of the steamer, we will follow her to Barcelona, where she went nearly three months before.

When the Prince reached her destination, the overland party had not returned, and were not expected for two or three days. An excursion to Monserrat was organized by Dr. Winstock, who declared that it would be ridiculous to leave Barcelona, when they had time on their hands, without visiting one of the most remarkable sights in Spain. The party had to take a train at seven o'clock in the morning; and then it was ten before they reached their destination.

Monserrat is a lofty mountain, and takes its name

from a Spanish word that means a "saw," because the sharp peaks which cover the elevation resemble the teeth of that implement. At the *posada* in the village Dr. Winstock related the legend of the place.

"This is one of the most celebrated shrines in Spain," he began. "Sixty thousand pilgrims used to visit it every year; but now the various chapels and monastery buildings are mostly in ruins. In 880 mysterious lights were seen over a part of the mountain. The bishop came up to see what they were, and discovered a small image of the Virgin in one of the numerous grottos that are found in the mountain. This little statue was the work of St. Luke, of course, and was brought to Spain by St. Peter himself. The Bishop of Barcelona hid it in this cave when the Moors invaded Catalonia. Bishop Gondemar, who found it, attempted to carry it to Manresa; but it became so heavy that he did not succeed. This was a miraculous intimation from the image that it did not wish to go any farther. The obliging bishop built a chapel on the spot, and the image was shrined at its altar. He also appointed a hermit to watch over it.

"Now, the Devil came to live in one of the caverns for the purpose of leading this anchorite astray. The Count of Barcelona had a beautiful daughter whose name was Riquilda; and the Devil 'possessed' her. She told her father that the evil spirit would not leave her till ordered to do so by Guarin, the pious custodian of the image. The count left her in his care. The hermit was wickedly inclined by the influence of the Devil, and finally killed the maiden, cutting off her head, and burying the body. Guarin was immediately sorry for what he had done, and, fleeing from his evil neighbor, went to Rome. The pope absolved him with the penance that he should return to Monserrat on his hands and knees, and continue to walk like a beast, as he was morally, and never to look up to heaven which he had insulted, and never to speak a word. He became a wild beast in the forest; and Count Wildred captured the strange animal, and conveyed him to his palace, where he doubtless became a lion. One day the creature was brought in to be exhibited to the count's guests at a banquet. A child cried out to him, 'Arise, Juan Guarin! thy sins are forgiven!' Then he arose in the form of the hermit; and the count pardoned him, having the grace to follow the example set him.

"But the end was not yet; for, when the count and Guarin went to search for the body, Riquilda appeared to them alive and well, though she had been buried eight years, but with a red ring around her neck, like a silk thread, rather ornamental than otherwise. The count founded a nunnery at once; and his daughter was made the lady superior, while Guarin became the *mayor-domo* of the establishment. In time the nuns were removed, and monks took their places; and the miracles performed by the image attracted thousands to its shrines. The treasury of this Virgin was immense at one time, being valued at two hundred thousand ducats; but most of it was carried away by the French. The scenery, you see, is wild and grand, and I think is more enjoyable than the relics and the grottos."

For hours the students wandered about the wild

locality. They saw the wonderful image; and those who had any taste for art thought that St. Luke, if he made the little statue, had not done himself any great credit. They visited the thirteen hermitages, and explored the grottos till they had had enough of this sort of thing. An hour after dark they were on board of the Prince. In two days more the Josephines and Tritonias arrived; and on Wednesday the squadron sailed for the South.

During his stay in port, the principal had seen Don Francisco, and told him all he knew in regard to the fugitive. The lawyer was satisfied that Mr. Lowington had done nothing to keep the young Don out of the way of his guardian; and neither of them could suggest any means to recover possession of him. As yet no letter from Don Manuel in New York had been received.

Favored by a good wind, the squadron arrived at Valencia in thirty hours. After a night's sleep, all hands were landed at the port of the city, which the reader knows is Grao. The professor of geography and history, while the party were waiting for the vehicles that were to convey them to the city, gave the students a description of Valencia. It is an ancient city, founded by the Phœnicians, inhabited by the Romans for five centuries, captured by the Moors and held by them about the same time, though the Cid took the town, and held it for five years. At his death, in 1099, the Moors came down upon the city; and the body of the Cid was placed on his horse, and marched out of the city. The Moslems opened for it; and the Castilians passed through their army in safety, the enemy not daring to attack them. It was not such a victory for the Spaniards as some of the chronicles describe; for the Christians had to abandon the place. It was taken from the Moors in 1238, and became a part of Aragon, to be united with the other provinces of Spain by the union of Ferdinand and Isabella. The Moriscoes — the Moors who had been allowed to remain in Spain after the capture of Granada — made a great city of it, building its palaces and bridges; but they were driven out of the peninsula by Philip II. They had cultivated its vicinity, and made a paradise of the province; and their departure was almost a death-blow to the prosperity of the city.

Though the modern kings of Spain have not spared its memorials of the past, it is still an interesting city. It has a population of nearly one hundred and fifty thousand, making it the fourth city of Spain. It is one of the most industrious cities of the peninsula; and its manufactures of silk and velvet are quite extensive. The city contains nothing very different from other Spanish towns. The students wandered over the most of it, looking into a few of the churches, nearly every one of which has a wonder-working image of the Virgin, or of St. Vincent, who is the patron saint of Valencia.

The next day the squadron sailed, and put into Alicante after a twenty-four hours' run; the wind being so light that the steamer had to tow her consorts nearly the whole distance. The students went on shore; but the old legend, "Nothing to see," was passed around among them. Alicante is an old Spanish town, composed of white houses, standing at the foot of a high hill crowned with an old fortress. The lines, walls, covered ways, and batteries, seem to cover one side of the elevation. Those who cared to do it climbed to the top of the hill, and were rewarded with a fine view of the sea and the country.

"When the Cid had captured Valencia," said Dr. Winstock to his pupils, as they stood on the summit of the hill, " he conducted Ximine, his wife, to the top of a tower, and showed her the country he had conquered. It was called the *Huerta*, which means a large orchard. The land had been irrigated by the industrious and enterprising Moors, and bore fruit in luxurious abundance. The *vega*, or plain, which we see, is scarcely less fertile; and the region around us is perhaps the most productive in Spain. Twelve miles south is Elche, which is filled with palm-plantations. We see an occasional palm and fig tree here."

Mr. Lowington did not favor excursions into the country when it could be avoided; but the doctor insisted that the students ought to visit Elche, and the point was yielded. They made the excursion in four separate parties; for comfortable carriages could not be obtained to take them all at once. The road was dry and dusty at first, and the soil poor; but the aspect of the country soon changed. Palms began to appear along the way, and soon the landscape seemed to be covered with them.

"There is something to see here, at any rate," said Sheridan, as the party approached the town.

"I thought you would enjoy it," replied the doctor. "This is the East transplanted in Spain."

"These palms are fifty feet high," added Murray, measuring them with his eye.

"Some of them are sixty; but fifty is about the average. Now we are in the palm-forest, which is said to contain forty thousand trees. This region is irrigated by the waters of the Vinalopo River, which are held back by a causeway stretched across the valley above. These plantations are very profitable."

"But all palms are not like these," said Murray. "My uncle has seen palms over a hundred feet high."

"There are nearly a hundred kinds of palm, bearing different sorts of fruit. These are date-palms; and one of them bears from one to two hundred pounds of dates."

"And they sell at from ten to fifteen cents a pound at home," added Sheridan.

"But for not more than one or two cents a pound here," continued the doctor. "I suppose you have learned about sex in plants, which is a modern discovery; but it is most strikingly illustrated in these date-palms. Only the female tree bears fruit. The male palm bears a flower whose pollen was shaken over the female trees by the Moors long before any thing was known about sex in plants; and the practice is continued by their successors. But the male palm yields a profit in addition to supplying the orchard with pollen. Its leaves are dried, and made into fans, crowns, and wreaths, and sold for use on Palm Sunday. This town gets seventy thousand dollars for its dates, and ten thousand for its palm-leaves."

"When are the dates picked?" asked Sheridan.

"In November. The men climb the trees by the aid of ropes passed around the trunk and the body. I will ask one of them to ascend a tree for your benefit."

The excursionists reached the village, which is in the middle of the forest of palms. It was very Oriental in its appearance. The people were swarthy, and wore a peculiar costume, in which were some remnants of the Moorish fashion. The church has its image of the Virgin, who dresses very richly, and owns a date-plantation which pays the expenses of her wardrobe.

The students were so delighted with the excursion that they made a rollicking time of it on the way back to Alicante, and astonished the peasants by their lively demonstrations. The road was no road at all, but merely a path across the country, and was very rough in places. The cottages of the vicinity were thatched with palm-leaves in some instances. At the door of many of them was a hamper of dates, from which any one could help himself, and leave a *cuarto* in payment for the feast. It is not watched by the owner, for the Spaniard here is an honest man. The students frequently availed themselves of these hampers when the doctor had explained to them the custom of the country; but he exhorted them to be as honest as the natives.

The squadron remained at anchor in the port of Alicante four days; and, when the students of the first party had told their story, the trip to Elche was the most popular excursion since they left Italy.

"Which is the best port on the east coast of Spain, doctor?" asked the principal, as they sat on the deck of the Prince while the third party had gone to Elche.

"I shall answer you as the admiral did Philip II., — Carthagena," replied the doctor.

"I find that the students are tired of sight-seeing,

and the lessons have been much neglected of late," continued the principal. "I think we all need a rest. I have about made up my mind to lie up for three months in some good harbor, recruit the students, and push along their studies."

"I think that is an excellent plan. April will be a better month to see the rest of Spain than the middle of winter."

The plan was fully discussed and adopted; and on the following day the squadron sailed for Carthagena, and having a stiff breeze was at anchor in its capacious harbor at sunset. The students were not sorry to take the rest; for the constant change of place for the last six months had rendered a different programme acceptable. There was nothing in the town to see; and the harbor was enclosed with hills, almost landlocked, and as smooth as a millpond.

CHAPTER XXII.

THE FRUITS OF REPENTANCE.

THE mail for the squadron — forwarded by the principal's banker in Barcelona — had been following the fleet down the coast for a week, but was received soon after it anchored at Carthagena. Among the letters was one from Don Manuel, Raymond's uncle in New York. He was astonished that his nephew had ventured into Spain, when he had been cautioned not to do so. He was glad he had left his vessel, and hoped the principal would do nothing to bring him back. It was extremely important that his nephew should not be restored to his uncle in Barcelona, for reasons which Henry would explain if necessary. If the fugitive was, by any mischance, captured by Don Alejandro or his agents, Don Manuel wished to be informed of the fact at once by cable; and it would be his duty to hasten to Spain without delay.

Mr. Lowington was greatly astonished at this letter, and handed it to Dr. Winstock. It seemed to indicate that a satisfactory explanation could be given of the singular conduct of the second master of the Tritonia, and that he would be able to justify his course.

"That is not the kind of letter I expected to receive," said the principal, when the surgeon had read it.

"There is evidently some family quarrel which Don Manuel does not wish to disclose to others," replied the doctor.

"But Don Manuel ought to have informed me that he did not wish to have his nephew taken into Spain."

"We can't tell about that till we know all the facts in the case. I have no doubt that the uncle in Barcelona is the legal guardian of Enrique Raimundo," continued the doctor.

"Then how did the boy come into the possession of Don Manuel?"

"I don't know; but he seems to be actuated by very strong motives, for he is coming to Spain if the young man falls into the hands of his legal guardian. I don't understand it; but I am satisfied that it is a case for the lawyers to work upon."

"I think not; for Don Manuel seems to believe that the safety of his nephew can only be secured by keeping him out of Spain; in other words, that he has no case which he is willing to take into a Spanish court."

"Perhaps you are right; but it looks to me like a fortune for the lawyers to pick upon; though I must say that Don Francisco is one of the most gentlemanly and obliging attorneys I ever met, and seems to ask for nothing that is not perfectly fair."

They could not solve the problem; and it was no use to discuss it. The principal had done all he could to recover the second master of the Tritonia, or rather to assist the detective who was in search of him. The last news of him, brought by Bill Stout, was that the fugitive had gone to Africa. The *alguacil* had gone to Africa, but Raimundo had left before he arrived. He was unable to obtain any clew to him, for Raymond looked like Spaniards in general; and in the dress he had put on in Valencia he did not look like Raymond in the uniform of an officer. While the fugitive was sunning himself in Gibraltar, the pursuer was looking for him in Italy and Egypt. The principal was confident he had gone to the East, for runaways would not expose themselves to capture till their money was all gone. Besides, some of the officers of the Tritonia said that Raymond had often expressed a desire to visit Egypt and the Holy Land.

The affairs of the squadron went along smoothly for six weeks. The students were studious, now that they had nothing to distract their attention. Bill Stout staid in the brig till he promised to learn his lessons, and then was let out. He did not like the brig after the trap in the floor was screwed down so that he could not raise it. Ben Pardee and Lon Gibbs fell out with him; first, because he had run away without them, and, second, because he was a disagreeable and unreasonable fellow. Bill did study his lessons in order to keep out of the brig; but he was behind every class in the vessel, and his ignorance was so dense that the professors were disgusted with him. It was about six weeks after the squadron took up its quarters in the harbor of Carthagena, that a shore-boat came up to the gangway, and Bark Lingall stepped upon the deck of the Tritonia. Of course his heart beat violently; but he came back like the Prodigal Son. He was wiser and better than when he left, and he was ready to submit cheerfully to the penalty of his offence; and he expected to be committed to the brig as soon as he showed himself to the principal.

It was nearly dark when the prodigal boarded the Tritonia, and Scott was in charge of the anchor watch which had been set for the night. He looked at Bark as he came up the side; and, though the fugitive had changed his dress, he recognized him at once.

"Lingall!" exclaimed Scott. "You haven't made a mistake as Stout did; have you?"

"I don't know what mistake Stout made, except the mistake of running away; and I made that one with him," replied Bark.

"Stout came on board of the Prince at Lisbon, thinking she was a steamer bound to England," laughed Scott.

"I could not mistake the Tritonia for a steamer, even if I wanted to go to England."

"Where did you leave Raimundo?" asked the officer anxiously.

"Here is a letter from him for you; and that will explain it all. I wish to see the vice-principal," continued Bark.

Mr. Pelham was summoned, and he gave a good-natured greeting to the returned fugitive, not doubting that he had spent all his money in riotous living, and had come back because he could not travel any more without funds.

"Money all gone, Lingall?" asked the vice-principal, who, like his superior, believed that satire was an effective means of discipline at times.

"No, sir: I have over fifty pounds left," replied Bark, more respectfully than he had formerly been in the habit of speaking, even to the principal.

"What did you come back for, then?" demanded Mr. Pelham.

"Because I am sorry for what I have done, and ask to be forgiven," answered Bark, taking off his hat, and fixing his gaze upon the deck, while his bosom was swelling with emotion.

The vice-principal was touched by his manner. He had stood in the same position before the principal five years before; and he indulged in no more light words. He took the prodigal down into his cabin, so that whatever passed between them might have no witnesses.

"Do you come back voluntarily, Lingall?" asked the vice-principal in gentle tones.

"I do, sir: I left Cadiz three days ago. I had been waiting there a month for the squadron to arrive We did not know where it was, for the last we could learn of it was its arrival in Carthagena."

"You say we: were you not alone?"

"No, sir: Raymond was with me."

"Who is Raymond?"

"Raimundo: he has translated his name into English, and now prefers to be called by that name."

"And you left him in Cadiz?"

"Yes, sir."

"Is he there now?"

"I don't know, sir; but I think not. He did not tell me where he was going, and I did not wish to know."

"I see," added Mr. Pelham. "I hope he will not be taken by those who are after him."

Bark looked up, utterly astonished at this last remark; for he supposed the sympathies of the officers were with Don Francisco, as they had been at the time he left the Tritonia. As Mr. Pelham was in the confidence of the principal in regard to the affair of the second master, he had been permitted to read the letter from Don Manuel; and this fact will explain the remark.

"Raymond does not know from what port the squadron will sail for the islands; but he wants to return to his ship as soon as he can," added Bark.

As Raymond's case seemed to be of more interest than his own, Bark told all he knew about his late companion; but no one was any wiser in regard to his present hiding-place.

"Where have you been all this time?" asked the vice-principal, when his curiosity was fully satisfied concerning Raymond.

"I have been a good deal worse than you think I have; and I wish that running away was the worst thing I had on my conscience," replied Bark, in answer to this question.

"I am sorry to hear you say that; but, whatever you have done, it is better to make a clean breast of it," added Mr. Pelham.

"That is what I am going to do, sir," replied Bark; and he prefaced his confession with what had passed between Raymond and himself when he decided upon his course of action.

He related the substance of his conversations with

Bill Stout at the beginning of the conspiracy, and then proceeded to inform the vice-principal what had occurred while they were in the brig together, including the setting of the fire in the hold.

"Do you mean to say that Stout intended to burn the vessel?" demanded Mr. Pelham, astonished and shocked at the revelation.

"He and I so intended; and we actually started the fire three or four times," answered Bark, detailing all the particulars.

"You are very tender of Stout — the villain!" exclaimed the vice-principal. "It appears that he proposed the plan, and set the fire, while you assented to the act."

"I don't wish to make it out that I am not just as guilty as Stout."

"I understand you perfectly," added Mr. Pelham. "The villain pretended to be penitent when he came back, and told lies enough to sink the ship, if they had had any weight with me. Mr. Marline reported to me that there had been fire in the old stuff in the hold. I thought there was some mistake about it; but it is all plain enough now."

Bark proceeded with his narrative of the escape, which had been before related by Bill Stout; but the two stories differed in some respects, especially in respect to the conduct of Bill in the affray with the Catalonian in the felucca. He told about his wanderings and waitings with Raymond, which explained why he had not come back before.

"Stout said that you and he pulled the boatman down when Raimundo missed him with the tiller," said Mr. Pelham.

"I mean to tell the truth, if I know how; but Bill did not lift his finger to do any thing, not even after Raymond and I had the fellow down," replied Bark. "Raymond called him a coward on the spot; and I wish he were here to tell you so, for I know you would believe him."

"And I believe you, Lingall."

At this moment there was a knock at the state-room door.

"Come in," said the principal; and Scott opened the door at this summons.

"I have a letter from Mr. Raimundo, sir, in which he has a great deal to say about Lingall," said the lieutenant. "I thought you might wish to know what he says before you settle this case. I will leave it with you, sir; for there is nothing private in it."

"Thank you, Mr. Scott," replied the vice-principal, as he took the letter.

He opened and read the letter. It related entirely to the affairs of Lingall, and was an earnest plea for his forgiveness. It recited all the incidents of the cruise in the felucca, and the particulars of Bark's reformation. The writer added that he hoped to be able to join his ship soon; and should do so, if he could, when she was out of Spanish waters.

"Now, Lingall, you may go on board of the Prince with me," said Mr. Pelham, when he had finished reading the letter.

A boat was manned, and they were pulled to the steamer. The whole story was gone over again; and Mr. Lowington read the letter of Raymond. The principal and Mr. Pelham had a long consultation alone; and then Bark was ordered to return to his duty, without so much as a reprimand. Bark was bewildered at this unexpected clemency. He was satisfied that it was Raymond's letter that saved him, because it assured the principal of the thorough reformation of the culprit. The vice-principal told him afterwards, that it was as much his own confession of the conspiracy, which was not even suspected on board, as it was the letter, that produced the leniency in the minds of the authorities. The boat that brought Mr. Pelham and Bark back to the Tritonia immediately conveyed Bill Stout, in charge of Peaks, to the Prince, where he was committed to the brig, without any explanation of the charge against him.

Bill did not know what to make of this sharp discipline; and he felt very much like a martyr, for he believed he had been "a good boy," as he called the chaplain's lambs. He had time to think about it when the bars separated him from the rest of his shipmates. The news that Bark Lingall had returned was circulated through the Tritonia before he left the vessel. He could only explain his present situation by the supposition that Bark had told about the conspiracy to burn the vessel. This must be the reason why he was caged in the Prince rather than in the Tritonia.

For three days the stewards brought him his food; and for an hour, each forenoon, the big boatswain walked him up and down the deck to give him his exercise; but it was in vain that he asked them what he was caged for. As none of these officials knew, none of them could tell him. On the fourth day of his confinement, a meeting of the faculty was held for consultation in regard to the affairs of the squadron. This was the high court of the academy, and consisted of the principal, the vice-principals, the chaplain, the surgeon, and the professors, — fourteen in all. Though the authority of the principal was supreme, he preferred to have this council to advise him in important matters.

When the faculty had assembled, Peaks brought Bill Stout into the cabin, and placed him at the end of the long table at which the members were seated. He was awed and impressed by the situation. The principal stated that the culprit was charged with attempting to set fire to the Tritonia, and asked what he had to say for himself. Bill made haste to deny the charge with all his might; but he might as well have denied his own existence. Raymond's letter describing what he saw in the hold was read, but the parts relating to Bark were omitted. Bill supposed the letter was the only evidence against him, and the writer had spared Bark because he was a friend. Bill declared that Raymond hated him, and had made up this story to injure him. He had been trying to do his duty, and no complaint had been made against him since the fleet had been at anchor.

The chaplain thought a student ought not to be condemned on the evidence of one who had run away from his vessel. As Bill would not be satisfied, it became necessary to call Bark Lingall. The reformed seaman gave his evidence in the form of a confession; and, when he had finished his story, no one doubted his sincerity, or the truth of his statement. By a unanimous vote of the faculty, approved by the principal,

Bill Stout was dismissed from the academy as one whom it was not safe to have on board any of the vessels, and as one whose character was too bad to allow him to associate with the students. A letter to his father was written; and he was sent home in charge of the carpenter of the Josephine, who was about to return to New York on account of the illness of his son.

The particulars of this affair were kept from the students; for the principal did not wish to have them know that any one had attempted to burn one of the vessels, lest it might tempt some other pupil to seek a dismissal by the same means. Bill Stout was glad to be sent away, even in disgrace.

Early in March Mr. Lowington received a letter from Don Francisco, asking if any thing had been heard from Raymond, and informing him that his client Don Alejandro was dangerously sick. The principal, since he had received the letter from Don Manuel, had declined to assist in the search for the absentee, though he had not communicated his views to the lawyer. The detective had not returned from his tour in the East, and was doubtless willing to continue the search as long as he was paid for it. The principal was "a square man;" and he informed Don Francisco that his views on the subject had changed, and that he hoped the fugitive would not be captured. Ten days after this letter was answered came Don Francisco himself. He went on board of the Prince; and, in spite of the reply of the principal, he was as cordial and courteous as ever.

"I suppose you have received my letter, declining to

do any thing more to secure the return of the absentee," Mr. Lowington began, when they were seated in the grand saloon.

"I have received it," replied Don Francisco; "but now all the circumstances of the case are changed, and I am confident that you will do all you can to find the young man. Your letter came to me on the day before the funeral of my client."

"Then Don Alejandro is dead!" exclaimed the principal, startled by the intelligence.

"He died in the greatest agony and remorse," added the lawyer. "He was sick four weeks, and suffered the most intense pain till death relieved him. He confessed to me, when I went to make his will, that he had intended to get his nephew out of the way in some manner, before the boy was of an age to inherit his father's property. Don Manuel had charged him with this purpose before he left Spain, and had repeated the charge in his letters. He confessed because he wanted his brother's forgiveness, as well as that of the Church. He wished me to see that justice was done to his nephew. When I wrote you that last letter, my client desired to see the young man, and to implore his forgiveness for the injury he had done him as a child, and for that he had meditated."

"This is a very singular story," said Mr. Lowington. "You did not give me the reason for which Don Alejandro wished to see his nephew."

"I did not know it myself. What I have related transpired since I wrote that letter. The case is one of the remarkable ones; but I have known a few just like it," continued the lawyer. "My client was told by the physicians that he could not recover. Such an announcement to a Christian who has committed a crime — and to meditate it is the same thing in the eye of the Church, though not of the law — could not but change the whole current of his thoughts. I know that it caused my client more suffering than his bodily ailments, severe as the latter were. The terrors of the world to come haunted him; and he believed, that, if he did not do justice to that young man before he died, he would suffer for his crime through all the ages of eternity; and I believe so too. I think he confessed the crime to me, after he had done so to the priest, because he believed his son, who had been in his confidence, would carry out his wicked purpose after his father was gone; for this son would inherit the estate as the next heir under the will of the grandfather."

"I can understand how things appear to a man as wicked as your client was, when death stares him in the face," added Mr. Lowington.

"Now the young man is wanted. He is not of age, but he ought to have a voice in the selection of his guardian."

"I don't know where he is under the altered circumstances, any more than I did before," replied the principal; "but I am willing to make an effort to find him. Is he in any danger from the son of your late client?"

"None at all: the son denies that he ever had any knowledge of the business; and, since the confession of the father, the son would not dare to do any thing wrong. Besides, my client put all the property in my hands before he died."

The next thing was to find Raymond. He might see the announcement of the death of his uncle in the newspapers; but, if he did not, he would be sure to keep out of the way till the squadron was ready to sail for the "isles of the sea." Mr. Lowington sent for Bark Lingall, who had by this time established his character as one of the best-behaved and most earnest students in his vessel. The principal rehearsed the events that made it desirable to find Raymond.

"Do you think you could find him, Lingall?" asked Mr. Lowington.

"I think I might if I could speak Spanish," replied Bark modestly.

"You and Scott are the only students who know his history; and he would allow you to approach him, while he would keep out of the way of any other person connected with the squadron. We shall sail for Malaga to-morrow; and you shall have a courier to do your talking for you," continued the principal.

Bark was pleased with the mission. He was furnished with a letter from Don Francisco; and, as he had some idea of what Raymond's plans were, he was hopeful of success. The squadron sailed the next day, and arrived at Malaga in thirty hours.

CHAPTER XXIII.

GRANADA AND THE ALHAMBRA.

WHEN the academy fleet arrived at Malaga, the principal decided to follow the plan he had adopted at Barcelona, though on a smaller scale, and send the Josephines and Tritonias to Cadiz, while the Princes proceeded by rail to the same place, seeing Granada, Cordova, and Seville on the way. As soon as the transfer could be made, the steamer sailed with its company of tourists; and her regular crew were domiciled at the Hotel de la Alameda, in Malaga.

"Here we are again," said Sheridan, as the party of the doctor came together again at the hotel.

"I feel more like looking at a cathedral than I did when we were sight-seeing in December," added Murray.

"You have not many more cathedrals to see," replied the doctor. "There is one here; but, as this is Saturday, we will visit it to-morrow. Suppose we take a walk on the Alameda, as this handsome square is called."

It is a beautiful bit of a park, with a fountain at each end; but it was so haunted with beggars that the tourists could not enjoy it. It was fresh and green, and bright with the flowers of early spring.

"What an abomination these beggars are!" exclaimed Sheridan, as a pair of them, one with his eyes apparently eaten out with sores, leaning on the shoulder of another seemingly well enough, saluted them with the usual petition. "It makes me sick to look at them."

Murray gave the speaker two *reales;* but they would not go till the others had contributed. A little farther along they came to a blind man, who had stationed himself by a bridge, and held out his hand in silence.

"That man deserves to be encouraged for holding his tongue," said the captain, as he dropped a *peseta* into the extended hand. "Most of them yell and tease so that one don't feel like giving."

The blind beggar called down the blessing of the Virgin upon the donor, in a gentle and devout tone. But he seemed to be an exception to all the other mendicants in Malaga. As the captain said, many of them were most disgusting sights; and they pointed out their ailments as though they were proud of them.

"This is a commercial city, and there is not much to see in it," said the doctor, as they returned to the hotel. "Its history is but a repetition of that of nearly all the cities of Spain. It was a place of great trade in the time of the Moors: it is the fifth city of Spain, ranking next to Valencia. You saw the United States flag on quite a number of vessels in the port; and it has a large trade with our country. Wine, raisins, oranges, lemons, and grapes are the principal exports."

The next day most of the students visited the cathedral, where they heard mass, which was attended by a battalion of soldiers, with a band which took part in the service. Early on Monday morning the tourists started for Granada, taking the train at quarter past six o'clock. The ride was exceedingly interesting; for the country between Malaga and Cordova is very fertile, though a small portion of it is a region abounding in the wildest scenery. The first part of the journey was in the midst of orange-orchards and vineyards.

"What is that sort of an inclined plane?" asked Sheridan, pointing to a stone structure like one side of the roof of a small house. "I have noticed a great many of them here and near Alicante."

"You observe that they all slope to the south," replied the doctor. "They are used in drying raisins. This is a grape as well as an orange country. Raisins are dried grapes; and, when you eat your plum-pudding in the future, you will be likely to think of the country around Malaga, for the nicest of them come from here."

"This is a wild country," said Murray, after they had been nearly two hours on the train.

"We pass through the western end of the Sierra Nevada range. Notice this steep rock," added the doctor, as they passed a lofty precipice. "It is 'Lovers' Rock.'"

"Of course it is," laughed Murray; "and they jumped down that cliff; and there is not a precipice in the world that isn't a lovers' leap."

"I think you are right. In this case it was a Spanish knight, and a Moorish maiden whose father didn't like the match."

The travellers left the train at Bobadilla, and proceeded by rail to Archidona. Between this place and

Loxa the railroad was not then built; and the distance — about sixteen miles — had to be accomplished by diligence. Half a dozen of these lumbering vehicles were in readiness, with their miscellaneous teams of horses and mules all hitched on in long strings. This part of the journey was likely to be a lark to the students; and they piled into and upon the carriages with great good-nature. The doctor and his pupils secured seats on the outside.

"This is the *coupé* in Spain, but it is the *banquette* in Switzerland," said he, when they were seated. "It is called the dickey in England."

"But the box for three passengers, with windows in the front of the diligence, is always the *coupé*," added Sheridan.

"Not in Spain: that is called the *berlina* here. The middle compartment, holding four or six, is *el interior;* and *la rotundo*, in the rear, like an omnibus, holds six. The last is used by the common people because it is the cheapest."

"But this seat is not long enough for four," protested Murray, when the conductor directed another officer to mount the *coupé*.

"Come up, commodore: I think we can make room for you," added Sheridan.

"This is a long team," said Commodore Cantwell, when they were seated, — "ten mules and horses."

"I have travelled with sixteen," added the doctor.

On a seat wide enough for two, under the windows of the *berlina*, the driver took his place. His reins were a couple of ropes reaching to the outside ends of the bits of the wheel-horses. He was more properly the brakeman, since he had little to do with the team, except to yell at the animals. On the nigh horse or mule, as he happened to be, rode a young man who conducted the procession. He is called the *delantero*. The *zagal* is a fellow who runs at the side of the animals, and whips them up with a long stick. The *mayoral* is the conductor, who is sometimes the driver; but in this case he seemed to have the charge of all the diligences.

"Oja! oja!" (o-ha) yelled the driver. The *zagal* began to hammer the brutes most unmercifully, and the team started at a lively pace.

"That's too bad!" exclaimed Sheridan, when he saw the *zagal* pounding the mules over the backbone with his club, which was big enough to serve for a bean-pole.

"I agree with you, captain, but we can't help ourselves," added the doctor. "That villain will keep it up till we get to the end of our journey."

The *dilijencia* passed out of the town, and went through a wild country with no signs of any inhabitants. The road was as bad as a road could be, and was nothing but a track beaten over the fields, passing over rocks and through gullies and pools of water. Carts, drawn by long strings of mules or donkeys, driven by a peasant with a gun over his shoulder, were occasionally met; but the road was very lonely. Half way to Loxa they came to a river, over which was a narrow bridge for pedestrians; but the *dilijencia* had to ford the stream.

At this point the horses and mules were changed; and some of the students went over the bridge, and walked till they were overtaken by the coaches. At three o'clock they drove into Loxa. The streets of the town are very steep and very narrow; and the *zagal* had to crowd the team over to the opposite side, in order to get the vehicle around the corners. The students on the outside could have jumped into the windows of the houses on either side, and people on the ground often had to dodge into the doorways, to keep from being run over. From this place the party proceeded to Granada by railroad. Crossing a part of this city, which is a filthy hole, the party went to the Hotel Washington Irving, and the Hotel Siete Suelos, both of which are at the very gate of the Alhambra.

The doctor and his friends were quartered at the former hotel, which is a very good one, but more expensive than the *Siete Suelos* on the other side of the street. They are both in the gardens of the Alhambra, the avenues of which are studded with noble elms, the gift of the Duke of Wellington.

"And this is the Alhambra," said Capt. Sheridan, as the trio came out for a walk, after dinner.

"What is the meaning of the name of that hotel?"

"*Hotel de los Siete Suelos*, — the hotel of the seven stories, or floors."

"But it hasn't more than four or five."

"Haven't you read Irving's Alhambra? He mentions a tower with this name, in which was the gate where Boabdil left the Alhambra for the last time. It was walled up at the request of the Moor."

The party walked about the gardens till it was dark. The next morning, before the ship's company were ready, the doctor and the three highest officers entered the walled enclosure.

"This is the Tower of Justice," said the doctor, as they paused at the entrance. "It is so called because the Moorish kings administered the law to the people here. You see the hand and the key carved over the door. If you ask the grandson of Mateo Ximenes, who is a guide here, what it means, he will tell you the Moors believed that, when this hand reached down and took the key, the Alhambra might be captured; but not till then. Then he will tell you that they were mistaken; and give glory to the Spaniards. The key was the Moslem symbol for wisdom and knowledge; and the hand, of the five great commandments of their religion."

The party entered the tower, in which is an altar, and passed into the square of the cisterns. Charles V. began to build a huge palace on one side of it; but the fear of earthquakes induced him to desist. He destroyed a portion of the Moorish palace to make room for it. The visitors entered an office where they registered their names, paid a couple of *pesetas*, and received a plan of the palace. The first names in the book are those of Washington Irving and his Russian companion.

"This is the Court of the Myrtles," said the doctor, as they entered the first and largest court of the palace. "It is also called 'the Court of Blessing,' because the Moors believed water was a blessing; and this pond contains a good deal of it."

"My guide-book does not call it by either of these names," said Commodore Cantwell, who had Harper's Guide in his hand. "It says here it is 'the *Patio de la Alberca*,' or fish-pond."

"And so says Mr. Ford, who is the best authority on Spain. We must not try to reconcile the differences in guide-books. We had better call it after the myrtles that surround the tank, and let it go at that. This court is the largest of the palace, though it is only one hundred and forty by seventy-five feet. But the Alhambra is noted for its beauty, and not for its size. We will now pass into the Court of the Lions," continued the doctor, leading the way. "This is the most celebrated, as it is the most beautiful, part of the palace."

"I have seen many pictures of it, but I supposed it was ten times as large as it is," said Sheridan.

"It is about one hundred and twenty by seventy feet. There are one hundred and twenty-four columns around the court. Now we must stop and look at the wonderful architecture and exquisite workmanship. Look at these graceful arches, and examine that sort of lacework in the ceilings and walls."

While they were thus occupied, the ship's company came into the court, and the principal called them together to hear Professor Mapps on the history of the Alhambra.

"In 1238 Ibnu-l-Ahamar founded the kingdom of Granada, and he built the Alhambra for his palace and fortress. In Arabic it was *Kasr-Alhamra*, or Red Castle; and from this comes the present name. The Vermilion Tower was a part of the original fortress. Under this monarch, whose title was Mohammed I., Granada became very prosperous and powerful. When the Christians captured Valencia, the Moors fled to Granada, and fifty thousand were added to the population of the kingdom; and it is estimated that a million more came when Seville and Cordova were conquered by the Castilians. The work of this king was continued by his successors; and the Alhambra was finished in 1333 by Yosuf I. He built the Gate of Judgment, Justice, or Law, as it is variously called, and the principal parts of the palace around you. The city was in its glory then, and is said to have had half a million inhabitants. But family quarrels came into the house of the monarch, here in the Alhambra; and this was the beginning of the decline of the Moorish power.

"Abul-Hassan had two wives. One of them was Ayesha; and the other was a very beautiful Christian lady called Zoraya, or the Morning Star. Ayesha was exceedingly jealous of the other; and fearing that the son of the Morning Star, instead of her own, might succeed to the crown, she organized a powerful faction. On Zoraya's side were the Beni-Serraj, whom the Spaniards called the Abencerrages. They were the descendants of a vizier of the King of Cordova, — Abou-Serraj. Abou-Abdallah was the eldest son of Ayesha; and in 1482 he dethroned his father. The name of this prince became Boabdil with the Spaniards; and so he is called in Mr. Irving's works. As soon as he came into power, his mother, and the Zegris who had assisted her, persuaded him to retaliate upon the Abencerrages for the support they had given to Zoraya. Under a deceitful plea, he gathered them together in this palace, where the Zegris were waiting for them. One by one they were called into one of these courts, and treacherously murdered. Thus was Granada deprived of its bravest defenders; and the Moors were filled with indignation and contempt for their king. While they were quarrelling among themselves, Ferdinand and Isabella advanced upon Granada. They had captured all the towns and strong fortresses; and there was nothing more to stay their progress. For nine months the sovereigns besieged the city before it fell. It was a sad day for the Moors when the victors marched into the town. There is a great deal of poetry and romance connected with this palace and the Moslems who were driven out of it. You should read Mr. Lockhart's translation of the poems on these subjects, and the works of Prescott and Irving."

When the professor had completed his account, the doctor's party passed in to the right, entering one of the apartments which surround the court on three of its sides.

"That's as mean a lot of lions as I ever saw," said Murray, who had lingered at the fountain which gives its name to the court.

"The sculpture of the lions is certainly very poor; but we can't have every thing," replied the doctor. "This is the Hall of the Abencerrages; and it gets its name from the story Mr. Mapps has just told you. Some say these nobles were slain in this room; and others, that they were beheaded near the fountain in the court, where the guides point out a dark spot as the stain of blood. You must closely examine the work in this little room if you wish to appreciate it."

They returned to the Court of the Lions, and, crossing it, entered the Hall of the Two Sisters. The students expected to hear some romance told of these two ladies; but they proved to be two vast slabs in the floor. This room and that of the Abencerrages were probably the sleeping apartments of the monarch's family; and several small chambers, used for baths and other purposes, are connected with them. On each side of them are raised platforms for the couches. At the farther end of the court is the council-hall of justice. It is long and narrow, seventy-five by sixteen feet; and is very elaborately ornamented.

At the northern end of the Court of Myrtles, is the Hall of Ambassadors, which occupies the ground floor of the Tower of Comares. It is the largest apartment of the palace, seventy-five by thirty-seven feet. This was the throne-room, or hall of audience, of the monarchs. The doctor again insisted that his pupils should scrutinize the work; and he called their attention to the horseshoe arches and various other forms and shapes, to the curious niches and alcoves, to the delicate coloring in the ceilings and on the walls, and to the interlacing designs, in the portions of the palace they visited.

They had now seen the principal apartments on the ground floor; and they ascended to the towers, the open galleries of which are a peculiarity in the construction of the edifice. They were shown the rooms occupied by Washington Irving when he "succeeded to Boabdil," and became an inhabitant of the Alhambra; but the Alhambra is a thing to be seen, and not described. They visited the Royal Chapel, the fortress, and for two days they were busy as bees, though one day was enough to satisfy most of the students.

On the third day of their sojourn at the Alhambra,

the doctor's party visited the Generalife. The name means "The Garden of the Architect," who was probably an employee of the king; but the palace was purchased and used as a pleasure-house by one of the kings. The sword of Boabdil is shown here. The gardens, which are about all the visitor sees, are more quaint than beautiful. The walks are hedged in with box, and the cypress-trees are trimmed in square blocks, as in the gardens of Versailles. Passing through these, the visitor ascends a tower on a hill, which commands a magnificent view of Granada and the surrounding country.

The abundance of water in and around the Alhambra attracts the attention of the tourist. The walks have a stream trickling down the hill on each side. It comes from the snow-crowned Sierra Nevadas; and, the warmer the weather, the faster do the ice and snow melt, and the greater is the flow of the water. In the Alhambra and in the Generalife these streams of water are to be met at almost every point.

One day was given to the city of Granada, though the visitor cares but little for any thing but the Alhambra. Without mentioning what may be seen in the cathedral in detail, there is one sight there which is almost worth the pilgrimage to the city; and that is the tomb of Ferdinand and Isabella. Dr. Winstock ordered a carriage for the purpose of taking his charge to the church.

When the team appeared at the door of the hotel, the students were very much amused at its singular character; for it was a very handsome carriage, but it was drawn by mules. The harness was quite elaborate and elegant; yet to be drawn by these miserable mules seemed to some of the party to be almost a disgrace. But the doctor said that they had been highly honored, since they had been supplied with what was doubtless the finest turnout to be had. These mules were very large and handsome for their kind, and cost more money than the finest horses. After this explanation, they were satisfied to ride behind a pair of mules.

There are plenty of pictures and sculptures in the cathedral; but the party hastened to the royal chapel built by order of the sovereigns, which became their burial-place. The mausoleum is magnificent beyond description. It consists of two alabaster sepulchres in the centre of the chapel, on one of which are the forms of Ferdinand and Isabella, and on the other those of Crazy Jane and Philip, the parents of Charles V. But the lion of the place, to the students, was the vault below the chapel, to which they were conducted, down a narrow staircase of stone, by the attendant. On a low dais in the middle of the tomb were two very ordinary coffins, not differing from those in use in New England, except that they were strapped with iron bands.

"This one, marked 'F,' contains the remains of Ferdinand," said the doctor, in a low tone. "The other has an 'I' upon it, and holds all that time has left of the mortal part of Isabella, whose patronage enabled Columbus to discover the New World."

"Is it possible that the remains of Ferdinand and Isabella are in those coffins?" exclaimed Sheridan.

"There is not a doubt of the fact. Eight years ago the late queen of Spain visited Granada, and caused mass to be said for the souls of these sovereigns at the same altar used by them at the taking of the city. Some of the guides will tell you that these coffins were opened at this time, and the remains of the king and queen were found to be in an excellent state of preservation. I don't know whether the statement is true or not."

"Here are two other coffins just like them," said Murray, as he turned to a sort of shelf that extended across the sides of the vault.

"They contain the remains of Crazy Jane and Philip her husband, both of whose effigies are introduced in the sculpture on the monuments in the chapel above," replied the doctor. "The coffin of Philip is the very one that she carried about everywhere she went, and so often embraced in the transports of her grief. She is at rest now."

Deeply impressed by what they had seen in the vault, which made the distant past more real to the young men, they returned to the chapel above. In the sacristy they saw the sword of Ferdinand, a very plain weapon, and his sceptre; but more interesting were the crown of silver gilt worn by Isabella, her prayer-book, and the chasuble, or priest's vestment, embroidered by her.

The party next visited the Carthusian Monastery, just out of the city, which contains some exquisite marble-work and curious old frescos. On their return to the Alhambra, they gave some attention to the gypsies, who are a prominent feature of Granada, where they are colonized in greater numbers than at any other place in Spain, though they also abound in the vicinity of Seville. They live by themselves, on the side of a hill, outside of the city. The tourists crossed the Darro, which flows at the foot of the hill on which the Alhambra and Generalife stand. They found the gypsies lolling about in the sun, hardly disturbed by the advent of the visitors. They seem to lead a vagabond life at home as well as abroad. They were of an olive complexion, very dirty, and very indolent. Some of the young girls were pretty, but most of the women were as disagreeable as possible. The men work at various trades; but the reputation of all of them for honesty is bad. They do not live in houses, but in caverns in the rocks of which the hill is composed. They are not natural caverns, but are excavated for dwellings.

The doctor led the party into one of them. It was lighted only by the door; but there was a hole in the top for the escape of the smoke. There was a bed in a corner, under which reposed three pigs, while a lot of hens were picking up crumbs thrown to them by a couple of half-naked children. It was the proper habitation of the pigs, rather than the human beings. The onslaughts of the beggars were so savage that the visitors were compelled to beat a hasty retreat. The women teased the surgeon to enter their grottos in order to get the fee.

In the evening some British officers from "Gib," as they always call the great fortress, had a gypsy dance at the *Siete Suelos*. The doctor and his pupils were invited to attend. There were two men dressed in full Spanish costume, and three girls, also in costume, one of whom was quite pretty. One of the men was the captain of the gypsies, and played the guitar with marvellous skill, an exhibition of which he gave the party. There was nothing graceful about the dancing: it was simply peculiar, with a curious jerking of the hips. At times the dancers indulged in a wild song. When the show was finished, the gypsy girls made an energetic demonstration on the audience for money, and must have collected a considerable sum from the officers, for they used all the arts of the coquette.

Just at dark a small funeral procession passed the hotel. It was preceded by half a dozen men bearing great candles lighted. The coffin was borne on the shoulders of four more, and was highly ornamented. The funeral party were singing or chanting, but so irreverently that the whole affair seemed more like a frolic than a funeral.

"That is a gay-looking coffin," said Murray to Mariano Ramos, the best guide and courier in Spain, who had been in the employ of the principal since the squadron arrived at Malaga.

"That is all for show," laughed Mariano. "The men will bring it back with them."

"Don't they bury the dead man in it?"

"No: that would make it too expensive for poor folks. They tumble the dead into a rough box, or bury him without any thing."

The next morning the excursionists started for Cordova, and arrived late at night, going by the same route they had taken to Granada as far as Bobadilla.

CHAPTER XXIV.

AN ADVENTURE ON THE ROAD.

IN, twelve hours after she started, the American Prince was in the harbor of Cadiz. Bark Lingall was on board; and Jacob Lobo, who spoke five languages, had been engaged at the Hotel de la Alameda as his companion. Mr. Pelham sent them ashore as soon as the anchor went over the bow.

"Do you expect to find the Count de Escarabajosa in Cadiz?" asked the interpreter, as they landed.

"Of course not: I told you he would not be here," replied Bark. "I may find out where he went to from here, and I may not. I left him at the Hotel de Cadiz; and we will go there first."

"I can tell you where he went without asking a question," added Lobo, to whom Bark had told the whole story of Raymond.

"I can guess at it, as you do; but I want information if I can obtain it," replied Bark.

"You would certainly have been caught if you hadn't thrown the detective off the track by going over to Oran."

"We went to Oran for that purpose."

"The count has got out of Spanish territory, and he

will keep out of it for the present. Our next move will be to go to Gibraltar. He is safe there."

"I think we shall find him there."

The landlord of the hotel recognized Bark, who had been a guest in his house for several weeks. Raymond had not told him where he was going when he left. He had gone from the hotel on foot, carrying his bag in his hand.

"Where do you think he went?" asked Bark.

"My opinion at the time was that he went to Gibraltar; for a steamer sailed for Algeciras that day, and there was none for any other port," replied the landlord.

"But he might have left by the train," suggested Bark.

"He went away in the middle of the day, and the steamer left at noon."

"He did not leave by train," added the guide.

"I don't think he did," said Bark. "Now, when does the next steamer leave for Gibraltar?"

"You will find the bills of the steamers hanging in the hall," replied the landlord.

One of these indicated that a Spanish steamer would sail at noon the next day.

"Perhaps she will, and perhaps she will not," said Lobo.

"But she is advertised to leave to-morrow," added Bark.

"Very likely before night you may find another bill, postponing the departure till the next day: they do such things here."

"What shall we do?"

"Wait till a steamer sails," replied Lobo, shrugging his shoulders.

"Is there any other way to get there?" asked Bark, troubled by the uncertainty.

"Some other steamer may come along: we will go to the office of the French line, and inquire when one is expected," replied Jacob.

They ascertained that the French steamer did not touch at Gibraltar; and there was no other way than to depend upon the Spanish line. As Jacob Lobo had feared, the sailing of the boat advertised was put off till the next day.

"You can go by land, if you are not afraid of the brigands," said the interpreter.

"Brigands?"

"Within a year a party of English people were robbed by brigands, on the way from Malaga to Ronda; but that is the only instance I ever heard of. The country between here and Malaga used to be filled with smugglers; and there are some of that trade now. When their business was dull, they used to take to the road at times."

"How long would it take to go by the road?" asked Bark, who was very enthusiastic in the discharge of his duty, and unwilling to lose a single day.

"That depends upon how fast you ride," laughed Lobo. "It is about sixty miles, and you might make it in a day, if you were a good horseman."

"But I am not: I was never on a horse above three times in my life."

"Then you should take two days for the journey."

"If we should start to-morrow morning, we should not get there as soon as the steamer that leaves the following day."

"That steamer may not go for three or four days yet: it will depend upon whether she gets a cargo, or not."

Bark was vexed and perplexed, and did not know what to do. He went down to the quay where they had landed, and found the boats from the ship, bringing off the Josephines and the Tritonias. He applied to Mr. Pelham for advice; and, after consulting Mr. Fluxion, it was decided that he should wait for a steamer, if he had to wait a week; for there was no such desperate hurry that he need to risk an encounter with brigands in order to save a day or two. So the services of Bark and Jacob Lobo were economized as guides, for both of them knew the city. Two days later the Spanish steamer actually sailed; and in seven hours Bark and his courier were in Algeciras, whence they crossed the bay in a boat to Gibraltar.

We left Raymond in Gibraltar, watching the newspapers for tidings of the American Prince; and he had learned of her arrival at Cadiz, where she had been for three days when Bark arrived at the Rock. He had heard nothing of the death of his uncle in Barcelona, and had no suspicion of the change of the circumstances we have described. He was not willing to risk himself in Cadiz while the Prince was there. As her consorts had not gone to Cadiz with her, he was satisfied that the steamer was to return to Malaga.

After he obtained the news, and had satisfied himself that the Princes were going overland to Cadiz, he went to his chamber at the King's Arms, where he attempted to reason out the future movements of the squadron. He had concluded, weeks before, that the fleet would not go to Lisbon, since all hands had visited that city; and now it appeared that Cadiz would be avoided for a second time, for the same reason. The Prince would wait there till her own ship's company arrived, and then go back to Malaga. The Josephines and Tritonias would do the place, and then return to Malaga overland. It looked to Raymond like a very plain case; and he was confident that the fleet would come to Gibraltar next.

He was entirely satisfied that his conclusion was a correct one. The squadron would certainly visit the Rock, for the principal could not think of such a thing as passing by a fortress so wonderful. Raymond was out of the way of arrest, if the detective should trace him to this place; and he could join his ship when she came. If the principal still wanted to send him to Barcelona, he would tell his whole story; and, if this did not save him, he would trust to his chances to escape. He sat at the window, thinking about the matter. It was just before sunset, and the air was delicious. He could look into the square in front of the hotel, and he was not a little startled to see the uniform of the squadron on a person approaching the hotel. He looked till he recognized Bark as the one who wore it.

But who was the man with him? This question troubled him. The man was a stranger to him; for the fugitives had not employed a guide in Malaga, and therefore Jacob Lobo was all unknown to him. Neither the Prince nor her consorts were in Gibraltar; and it was plain enough to the Spaniard that Bark and his companion had come in the steamer he had seen going into Algeciras two hours before. They had come from

Cadiz, and they could have no other errand in Gibraltar than to find him. Had Bark become a traitor? or, what was more likely, had he been required by the principal to conduct this man in search of him? Had Mr. Lowington ascertained that he was at the Rock? It was almost impossible, for he had met no one who knew him.

He saw Bark and his doubtful companion enter the Club-House Hotel, and he understood their business there. He had not seen the *alguacil*, or detective, who had come on board of the Tritonia for him; but he jumped at the conclusion that this was the man. The principal had afforded him every facility for finding the object of his search; and now it appeared that he had sent Bark with him, to identify his expected prisoner. Raymond decided on the moment not to wait for the detective to see him. He rang the bell, and sent for his bill: he paid it, and departed before Bark could reach the hotel. He scorned to ask the landlord or waiters to tell any lies on his account. He hastened down to the bay; and at the landing he found the very boat that had brought Bark and his companion over from Algeciras, just hoisting her sails to return. The boatman was glad enough to get a passenger back, and thus double the earnings of the trip. It is about five miles across the bay; and, with a fresh breeze from the south-east, the distance was made in an hour.

On the way, Raymond learned that the boat had brought over two passengers; and, from the boatman's description of them, he was convinced that they were Bark and his companion. He questioned the skipper in regard to them; but the man had no idea who or what they were. The passengers talked in English all the way over, and he could not understand a word they said. It was not prudent for the fugitive to stay over night in Algeciras; and, procuring a couple of mules and a guide, he went to San Roque, where he passed the night. He found a fair hotel at this place; and he decided to remain there till the next day.

He had time to think now; and he concluded that Bark and his suspicious companion would depart from the Rock when they found he was not there. But he did not lose sight of the fact that he was in Spain again. What would his pursuers do when they found that he had left the hotel? They would see his name on the books, and the landlord would tell them he had just left. There were plenty of boatmen at the landing, who had seen him embark in the boat for Algeciras. Raymond did not like these suggestions as they came up in his mind. They would cross the bay, and find the boatman, who would be able to describe him, as he had them. Then, when they had failed to find him at the *fondas*, they would visit the stables. It was easy enough to trace him.

At first he thought of journeying on horseback to Xeres, and there taking the train to the north, and into Portugal; but he abandoned the thought when he considered that he was liable to meet the students at any point on the railroad. Finally he decided to start for Ronda, an interior city, forty miles from the Rock. At eight o'clock in the morning, he was in the saddle. He had retained the mules that brought him from Algeciras. José, his guide, was one of the retired brigands, of whom there are so many in this region.

As it was too soon for him to be pursued, he did not hurry, and stopped at Barca de Cuenca to dine.

After dinner he resumed his journey. José was a surly, ugly fellow, and Raymond was not disposed to converse with him. This silence made the miles very long; but the scenery was wild and grand, and the traveller enjoyed it. After he had ridden about five miles he came to a country which was all hills and rocks. The path was very crooked; and it required many angles to overcome steeps, and avoid chasms. Suddenly, as he passed a rock which formed a corner in the path, he was confronted by three men, all armed to the teeth, with muskets, pistols, and knives. José was provided with the same arsenal of weapons; but he did not offer to use any of them.

The leading brigand was a good-natured ruffian, and he smiled as pleasantly as though his calling was perfectly legitimate. He simply held out his hand, and said, "*Por Dios*," which is the way that beggars generally do their business.

"*Perdon usted por Dios hermano*," replied Raymond, shaking his head.

This is the usual way to refuse a beggar: "Excuse us for God's sake, brother." Raymond did not yet understand whether the three men intended to beg or rob; but he soon ascertained that the leader had only adopted this facetious way of doing what is commonly done with the challenge, "Your money or your life!" It was of no avail to resist, even if he had been armed. Most of his gold was concealed in a money-belt worn next to his skin, while he carried half a dozen Isabelinos in his purse, which he handed to the gentlemanly brigand.

"*Gracias, señorito!*" replied the leader. "Your watch, if you please."

Raymond gave it up, and hoped they would be satisfied. Instead of this, they made him a prisoner, leading his mule to a cave in the hills, where they bound him hand and foot. José waited for his mule, and then, with great resignation, began his return journey.

CHAPTER XXV.

CORDOVA, SEVILLE, AND CADIZ.

CORDOVA is a gloomy and desolate city with about forty thousand inhabitants. It was once the capital of the kingdom of Cordova, and had two hundred thousand people within its walls; and some say a million, though the former number is doubtless nearer the truth. The grass grows in its streets now, and it looks like a deserted city, as it is. There is only one thing to see in Cordova, and that is the mosque. As soon as the party had been to breakfast, they hastened to visit it.

"We will first take a view of the outside," said the doctor to his pupils when they had reached the mosque. "This square in front of it is the Court of Oranges; you observe a few palms and cypresses, as well as orange-trees. The fountain in the centre was built by the Moors nearly a thousand years ago."

"But I don't see any thing so very grand about the mosque, if that great barn-like building is the one," said Murray. "It looks more like a barrack than a mosque. We have been in the mosque business some, and they can't palm that thing off upon us as a real mosque. We have seen the genuine thing in Constantinople."

"I grant that the outside is not very attractive," added the doctor. "But in the days of the Moors, when the mosque was in its glory, the roof was covered with domes and cupolas. In spite of what you say, Murray, this was the finest, as it is one of the largest mosques in the world. It covers an area of six hundred and forty-two by four hundred and sixty-two feet. It was completed in the year 796; and the work was done in ten years. It was built to outdo all the other mosques of the world except that at Jerusalem. Now we will go in."

The party entered the mosque, and were amazed, as everybody is who has not been prepared for the sight, by the wilderness of columns. There are about a thousand of them; and they formerly numbered twelve hundred. Each of them is composed of a single stone, and no two of them seem to be of the same order of architecture. They come from different parts of the globe; and therefore the marbles are of various kinds and colors, from pure white to blood red. These pillars form twenty-nine naves, or avenues, one way, and nineteen the other. The roof is only forty feet high, and the columns are only a fraction of this height. They have no pedestal, and support a sort of double arch, the upper one plain, and the lower a horseshoe; indeed, this last looks like a huge horseshoe stretching across below the loftier arch.

For an hour the party wandered about in the forest of pillars, pausing at the *Mih-ràb*, or sanctuary of the mosque, where was kept the copy of the Koran made by Othman, the founder of the dynasty of that name. It is still beautiful, but little of its former magnificence remains; for the pulpit it contained is said to have cost the equivalent of five millions of dollars.

"St. Ferdinand conquered Cordova in 1236; and then the mosque was turned into a Christian church without any great change," said Dr. Winstock, as they approached the choir in the centre of the mosque. "The victors had the good sense and the good taste to leave the building pretty much as they found it. But three hundred years later the chapter of the church built this choir, which almost ruins the interior effect as we gaze upon it. The fine perspective is lost. Sixty columns were removed to make room for the choir. When Charles V. visited Cordova, and saw the mischief the chapter had wrought, he was very angry, and severely reproached the authors of it."

The tourists looked into the high chapel, and glanced at the forty-four others which surround the mosque. Then they walked to the bridge over the Guadalquiver. Arabian writers say it was built by Octavius Cæsar, but it was entirely reconstructed by the Moors. An old Moorish mill was pointed out; and the party returned to the mosque to spend the rest of their time in studying its marvellous workmanship. Early in the afternoon the excursionists left for Seville, and arrived in three hours. The journey was through a pleasant country, affording them an occasional view of the Guadalquiver.

"To my mind," said Dr. Winstock, as the party passed out of the *Hotel de Londres* to the *Plaza Nueva*, which is a small park in front of the City Hall, — "to my mind Seville is the pleasantest city in Spain. I have always been in love with it since I came here the

first time; and I have spent four months here altogether. The air is perfectly delicious; and, though it often rains, I do not remember a single rainy day. The streets are clean, the houses are neat and pretty, the people are polite, the ladies are beautiful, — which is a consideration to a bachelor like myself, — and, if I had to spend a year in any city of Europe, Seville would be the place."

"What is there to see here?" asked Murray. "I should like a list of the sights to put in a letter I shall write to-day."

"The principal thing is the cathedral; then the *Giralda*, the *Alcazar*, the tobacco-factory, the Palace of San Telmo, the *Casa de Pilatos*."

"That will do, doctor. I can't put those things in my letter," interposed Murray.

"You may say 'Pilate's house' for the last; and add the *Calle de las Sierpes*, which is the most frequented street of the city."

"But I can't spell the words."

"It is not in good taste to translate the name of a street; but it means 'the street of the serpents.' But I think you had better wait till you have seen the sights, before you attempt to describe them in your letter."

"I will look them up in the guide-book, when I write."

"This is the *Calle de las Sierpes*," continued the doctor, as they entered a narrow street leading from the *Plaza de la Constitucion* — nearly every Spanish city has one with this name — in the rear of the City Hall. "This is the business street of the town, and it is generally crowded with people. Here are the retail stores, the cafés, the post-office, and the principal theatre."

The students were interested in this street, it was so full of life. The ends of it were barred so that no carriages could enter it; and the whole pavement was a sidewalk, as O'Hara would have expressed it. Passing the theatre, they followed a continuation of the same street.

"Do you notice the name of this street?" said the doctor, as he pointed to the sign on a corner. "It is the *Calle del Amor de Dios*. It is so near like the Latin that you can tell what it means."

"But it seems hardly possible that a street should have such a name, — the 'Street of the Love of God,'" added Sheridan.

"That is just what it is; and it was given by reverent men. There is also in this city the *Calle de Gesu*, or Jesus Street; and the names of the Virgin and the saints are applied in the same way."

Passing through this street, the party came to the *Alameda de Hercules*.

"The city has about the same history as most others in the South of Spain, — Romans, Goths, Vandals, Moors, Christians," said the doctor. "But some of the romancists ascribe its origin to Hercules; and this *alameda* is named after him. Now we will take a closer view of one of the houses. You observe that they differ from those of our cities. They are built on the Moorish plan. What we call the front door is left open all day. It leads into a vestibule; and on the right and left are the entrances to the apartments. Let us go in."

"Is this a private house?" asked Sheridan, who seemed to have some doubts about proceeding any farther; but then the doctor astonished him by ringing the bell, which was promptly answered by a voice inquiring who was there.

"*Gentes de paz*" (peaceful people), replied the surgeon; and this is the usual way to answer the question in Spain.

It presently appeared that Dr. Winstock was acquainted with the gentleman who lived in the house; and he received a cordial welcome from him. The young gentlemen were introduced to him, though he did not speak English; and they were shown the house.

In the vestibule, directly opposite the front door, was a pair of iron gates of open ornamental work, set in an archway. A person standing in the street can look through this gateway into the *patio*, or court of the mansion. It was paved with marble, with a fountain in the middle. It was surrounded with plants and flowers; and here the family sit with their guests in summer, to enjoy the coolness of the place. Thanking the host, and promising to call in the evening, the surgeon left with his pupils, — his "*pupilos*," as he described them to the gentleman.

After lunch the sight-seers went to the *Giralda*, which is now the campanile or bell-tower of the cathedral. It was built by the Moors in 1296 as a muezzin tower, or place where the priest calls the faithful to prayers, and was part of the mosque that stood on this spot. It is square, and built of red brick, and is crowned with a lofty spire. The whole height is three hundred and fifty feet. To the top of this tower the party ascended, and obtained a fine view of the city and its surroundings, — so fine that they remained on their lofty perch for three hours. They could look down into the bull-ring, and trace the Guadalquiver for many miles through the flat country. The doctor pointed out all the prominent objects of interest; and when they came down they had a very good idea of Seville and its vicinity.

The next day, as Murray expressed it, they "commenced work on the cathedral." It is the handsomest church in Spain, and some say in the world. It is the enlargement of an old church made in the fifteenth century. On the outside it looks like a miscellaneous pile of buildings, with here and there a semicircular chapel projecting into the area, and richly ornamented with various devices. It is in the oblong form, three hundred and seventy by two hundred and seventy feet, not including the projecting chapels.

"Now we will enter by the west side," said the doctor, when they had surveyed the exterior of the vast pile. "The *Giralda* is on the other side. By the way, did I tell you what this word meant?"

"You did not; but I supposed it was some saint," replied Sheridan.

"Not at all. It comes from the Spanish verb *girar*, which means to turn or whirl; and from this comes *Giralda*, a weathercock. The name is accidental, coming probably from the vane on the top of it at some former period," continued the doctor as they entered the cathedral. "The central nave is about one hundred and twenty-five feet high; and here you get an idea of the grandeur of the edifice. Here is the burial-place of the son of Columbus. This slab in the pavement contains his epitaph: —

FERNANDO COLON.

A Castilla y á Leon
Nuevo mundo dio Colon.

"*Hablo Español!*" exclaimed Murray. "And I know what that means, — 'To Castile and Leon Columbus gave a new world.'"

"It is in all the school-books, and you ought to know it," added Sheridan. "Colon means Columbus; but what was his full name in Spanish?"

"Cristobal Colon. This son was quite an eminent man, and gave his library to the chapter of this church. Seville was the birthplace and the residence of Murillo; and you will find many of his pictures in the churches and other buildings."

The party went into the royal chapel. The under part of the altar is formed by the silver and glass casket which contains the remains of St. Ferdinand, nearly perfect. It is exhibited three days in the year; and then the body lies dressed in royal robes, with the crown on the head. The doctor pointed out the windows of stained glass, of which there are ninety-three. Nearly the whole day was spent in the church by those of the students who had the taste to appreciate its beautiful works of art. The next morning was devoted to the *Alcazar*. It was the palace of the Moorish sovereigns when Seville became the capital of an independent kingdom. After the city was captured, St. Ferdinand took up his quarters within it. Don Pedro the

Cruel repaired and rebuilt portions of it, and made it his residence; and it was occupied by the subsequent sovereigns as long as Seville was the capital of Spain. Though the structure as it now stands was mainly erected by Christian kings, its Arabian style is explained by the fact that Moorish architects were employed in the various additions and repairs.

It is very like the Alhambra, but inferior to it as a whole. It contains apartments similar to those the students had seen at Granada, and therefore was not as interesting as it would otherwise have been. The gardens of the palace were more to their taste. They are filled with orange-trees and a variety of tropical plants. The avenues are lined with box, and the garden contains several small ponds. The walks near the palace are underlaid with pipes perforated with little holes, so that, when the water is let on, a continuous line of fountains cools the air; and it is customary to duck the visitors mildly as a sort of surprise.

The tobacco-factory is the next sight, and is located opposite the gardens of the *Alcazar*. It is an immense building used for the manufacture of cigars, cigarillos, and smoking-tobacco. The article is a monopoly in the hands of the Government; and many of the larger cities have similar establishments, but none so large as the one at Seville. At the time of which we write, six thousand women were employed in making cigars, and putting up papers of tobacco. Visitors go through the works more to observe the operatives than to see the process of making cigars; and the students were no exception to the rule. Most of the females were old and ugly, though many were young. Among them were not a few gypsies, who could be distinguished by their olive complexion.

These women all have to be searched before they leave the building, to prevent them from stealing the tobacco. Women are employed for this duty, who become so expert in doing it that the operation is performed in a very short time.

On the river, near the factory, is the palace of San Telmo, the residence of the Duke de Montpensier, son of Louis Philippe, who married the sister of the late queen of Spain. It is a very unique structure, with an elaborate portico in the centre of the front, rising one story above the top of the palace, and surmounted with a clock. It has a score of carved columns, and as many statues. The rest of the building is quite plain, which greatly increases the effect of the complicated portico. The picture-gallery and the museums of art in the palace are opened to the tourist, and they richly repay the visit. Among the curiosities is the guitar used by Isabella I., the sword of Pedro the Cruel, and that of Fernando Gonzales. The building was erected for a naval school, and was used as such for a hundred and fifty years. It was presented by the queen to her sister in 1849.

Leaving the palace, the party walked along the quays by the river, till they came to the *Toro del Oro*, or tower of gold. It was originally part of a Moorish fortress; but now stands alone on the quay, and is occupied as a steamboat-office. The Moors used it as a treasure-house, and so did Pedro the Cruel. In the time of Columbus it was a place of deposit for the gold brought over by the fleets from the New World, and landed here. It is said that more than eight million ducats were often stored here.

Near this tower, is the hospital of *La Caridad*, or charity. It was founded by a young nobleman who had reformed his dissipated life, and passed the remainder of it in deeds of piety in this institution. It is a house of refuge for the poor and the aged. It contains two beautiful *patios*, with the usual plants, flowers, and fountains. The institution is something on the plan of the Brotherhood of Pity in Florence; and the young gentlemen of the city render service in it in turn. The founder was an intimate friend of Murillo, which accounts for the number of the great artist's pictures to be found in the establishment. Its little church contains several of them. A singular painting by another artist attracted the attention of some of the students as a sensation in art. It represents a dead prelate in full robes, lying in the tomb. The body has begun to decay; and the worms are feasting upon it, crawling in and out at the eyes, nose, and mouth. It is a most disgusting picture, though it may have its moral.

A day was given to the museum which contains many of Murillo's pictures, and next to that at Madrid is the finest in Spain. The *Casa de Pilatos* was visited on the last day the excursionists were in Seville at this time, though it happened that they came to the city a second time. It belongs to the Duke of Medina Celi, though he seldom occupies it. It is not the house of Pilate, but only an imitation of it. It was built in the sixteenth century, by the ancestors of the duke, some of whom had visited the Holy Land. The *Patio* is large and is paved with white marble, with a checkered border and other ornaments. In the centre is a fountain, and in each corner is a colossal statue of a goddess. Around it are two stories of galleries, with fine arches and columns. The palace contains a beautiful chapel, in which is a pillar made in imitation of that to which Christ was bound when he was scourged. On the marble staircase the guides point out a cock, which is said to be in the place of the one that crowed when Peter denied his Master; but of course this is sheer tomfoolery, and it was lawful game for Murray, who was the joker of the officers' party.

On another day the doctor and his pupils walked over the bridge to the suburb of Triana, where the gypsies lived. They were hardly more civilized than those seen at Granada. Then, as the order was not given for the departure, they began to see some of the sights a second time; and many of them will bear repeated visits. During a second examination of the *Alcazar*, Dr. Winstock told them many stories of Pedro the Cruel, of Don Fadrique, of Blanche of Bourbon, and of Maria de Padilla, which we have not the space to repeat, but which are more interesting than most of the novels of the day. After the ship's company had been in Seville five days, the order was given to leave at quarter before six; and the party arrived at Cadiz at ten.

This city is located nearly on the point of a tongue of land which encloses a considerable bay; and, when the train had twenty miles farther to go, the students could see the multitude of lights that glittered like stars along the line of the town. Cadiz is a commercial place, was colonized by the Phœnicians, and they supposed it to be about at the end of the earth. They believed that the high bluff at Gibraltar, which was called Calpe, and Abyla at Ceuta in Africa, were part of the same hill, rent asunder by Hercules; and they erected a column on each height, which are known as the Pillars of Hercules. Cadiz was held by the Romans and the Moors in turn, and captured by the Spaniards in 1262. After the discovery of America, it shared with Seville the prosperity which followed that event; and the gold and merchandise were brought to these ports. Its vast wealth caused it to be often attacked by the pirates of Algiers and Morocco; the English have twice captured it, and twice failed to do so; and it was the civil and military headquarters of the Spaniards during the peninsular war. When the American colonies of Spain became independent, it lost much of its valuable commerce, and has not been what it was in the last century since the French Revolution.

The boats of the American Prince, in charge of the forward officers and a squad of firemen and stewards, were on the beach near the railroad station; and the ship's company slept on board that night. The next day was devoted to Cadiz. The cathedral is a modern edifice and a beautiful church, though the tourist who had been to Toledo and Seville does not care to give much of his time to it. In the Capuchin Monastery, to which the doctor took his pupils, is the last picture painted by Murillo. It is the Marriage of St. Catharine, and is painted on the wall over the high altar of the chapel. Before it was quite finished, Murillo fell from the scaffold, was fatally injured, and died soon after. The picture was finished by one of his pupils, at his request.

There are no other sights to be seen in Cadiz; but the students were very much pleased with the place. Its public buildings are large and massive; its white dwellings are pretty; and its squares and walks on the seashore are very pleasant. By the kindness of the banker, the club-house was opened to the party.

"I am rather sorry we do not go to Xeres," said the doctor, when they were seated in the reading-room. "I supposed we should stop there on our way from Seville. I wished to take you into the great wine-vaults. I think you know what the place is noted for."

"*Vino del Xeres*," replied Murray, — "Sherry wine."

"It is made exclusively in this place; and its peculiarity comes from the kind of grapes and method of manufacture. The business here is in the hands of English, French, and German people, who far surpass the Spaniards in the making of wine. The immense cellars and store-houses where the wine is kept are well worth seeing, though they are not encouraging to men with temperance principles. The place has forty thousand inhabitants, and is the *Xeres de la Frontera*, where Don Roderick was overwhelmed by the Moors, and the Gothic rule in Spain was ended."

"Seville is a larger place than Cadiz, isn't it?" asked Sheridan.

"More than twice as large. Seville is the third city of Spain, having one hundred and fifty-two thousand inhabitants; while Cadiz is the ninth, with only seventy-two thousand."

The party returned to the steamer; and the next morning she sailed for Malaga, where the Josephines and Tritonias had arrived before them. The fleet immediately departed for Gibraltar, and in five hours was at anchor off the Rock.

CHAPTER XXVI.

THE CAPTURE OF THE BEGGARS.

WHEN Bark Lingall and Jacob Lobo arrived at Gibraltar, they went to the Club-House Hotel to inquire for the fugitive. He was not there; but they spent half an hour questioning the landlord and others about the hall, in regard to the town and its hotels and boarding-houses. Then they went to the King's Arms; and, in the course of another half-hour, they learned that Henry Raymond had left this hotel within an hour. Where had he gone? The landlord could not tell. No steamer had left that day; he might have left by crossing the Neutral Ground, or he might have gone over to Algeciras in a boat.

"I wonder why he cleared out so suddenly," said Bark, very much annoyed at the situation.

"I suppose he was frightened at something," replied Jacob. "Very likely he saw you when we went into the Club-House."

"But he wouldn't run away from me. He and I are the best of friends."

"But circumstances alter cases," laughed the interpreter. "He may have supposed you had gone over to the enemy, and had come here to entrap him in some way."

"It may be; but I hardly believe it," mused Bark.

Jacob Lobo had no suspicion that he had been the cause of Raymond's hurried departure; and he did not suggest the true solution of the problem. But the fugitive was gone; and all they had to do was to look him up. They were zealous in the mission with which they were charged, and lost not a moment in prosecuting the search. But they had almost gained the battle in obtaining a clew to the fugitive. Lobo declared that it would be easy enough to trace him out of the town, for he must have gone by the Neutral Ground, which is the strip of land separating the Rock from the mainland, or crossed to Algeciras in a boat. They were on their way to the landing-port, when the evening gun was fired.

"That's as far as we can go to-night," said Lobo, coming to a sudden halt.

"Why? what's the matter now?" asked Bark.

"That's the gun, and the gate will be closed in a few minutes," replied Lobo. "They wouldn't open it to oblige the King of Spain, if he happened along here about this time."

It was no use to argue the matter in the face of fact; and they spent the rest of the day in making inquiries about the town. They went to the drivers of cabs, and to those who kept horses and mules to let. They questioned men and women located near the gate. No one had seen such a person as was described. They went to the King's Arms for the night; and as soon as the gate was opened in the morning they hastened to the landing-port to make inquiries among the boatmen. They found one with whom they had spoken when they landed the day before. He wanted a job, as all of them do. He had seen a young man answering to the description given; and he had gone over to Algeciras in the very boat that brought them over. Would they like to go over to Algeciras? They would, immediately after breakfast; for they had left their bags, and had not paid their bill at the hotel.

The wind was light, and it took them two hours to cross the bay. With but little difficulty they found the stable at which the fugitive had obtained his mules, and learned that the name of the guide was José Barca. The keeper of the *fonda* volunteered the information that José was a brigand and a rascal; but the stable-keeper, who had furnished the guide, insisted that the landlord spoke ill of José because he had not obtained the job for his own man.

"About all these guides are ex-brigands and smugglers," said Lobo.

"But the landlord of the *fonda* looks like a more honest man than the stable-keeper," added Bark. "I think I should prefer to trust him."

"I believe you are right, Mr. Lingall; but either of them would cheat you if he got the chance," laughed Lobo; but, being a courier himself, it was for his interest to cry down the men with whom travellers have to deal, in order to enhance the value of his own calling.

The landlord would furnish mules and a guide; and in an hour the animals were ready for a start. It was not known where Raymond had gone: he had taken the mules for San Roque, but with the understanding that he could go as far as he pleased with them. The name of the landlord's guide was Julio Piedra. He was armed to the teeth, as Raymond's guide had been. He was a good-natured, talkative fellow; and the fugitive would certainly have done better, so far as the agreeableness of his companion was concerned, if he had patronized the landlord instead of the stable-keeper.

When the party arrived at the hotel in San Roque, their store of information was increased by the knowledge that Raymond had started that morning for Ronda. The pursuit looked very hopeful now, and the travellers resumed their journey.

"We are not making more than three or four knots an hour on this tack," said Bark, when they had ridden a short distance.

"Three miles an hour is all you can average on mules through this country," replied Lobo.

"Can't we offer the guide a bonus to hurry up?"

"You can't stand it to ride any faster; and, as it is, you will be very sore when you get out of bed to-morrow morning."

"I can stand any thing in this chase," added Bark confidently.

"What good will it do to hurry?" persisted Lobo. "It is one o'clock now; and Raymond has five hours the start of us. It will be impossible to overtake him to-day. The mules can go about so far; and at six o'clock we shall reach the place where Raymond stopped to dine. That will be Barca de Cuenca; and that will be the place for us to stop over night."

"Over night! I don't want to stop anywhere till we come up with Raymond," replied Bark.

"You won't say that when you get to Barca," laughed

Lobo. "You will be tired enough to go to bed without your supper. Besides, the mules will want rest, if you do not; for the distance will be twenty miles from Algeciras. Raymond stopped over night at San Roque."

"But where shall we catch up with him?"

"Not till we get to Ronda, as things now stand."

"I don't like the idea of dragging after him in this lazy way," protested Bark.

"What do you wish to do?" demanded Lobo, who had been over this road twenty times or more, and knew all about the business.

"I don't believe in stopping anywhere over night," replied Bark with enthusiasm.

"Very well, Mr. Lingall," added Lobo, laughing. "If when you get to Barca, and have had your supper, you wish to go any farther, I will see what can be done. I can make a trade with Julio to go on with these mules, or we can hire others."

"You say that Raymond left at noon the place where we shall be at supper-time: where will he be at that time?" asked Bark.

"He will go on to Barca de Cortes, which is twelve miles farther; unless he takes it into his head, as you do, that he will travel in the night."

"I am in favor of going on to that place where he sleeps."

"You are in favor of it now; but, take my word for it, you will not be in favor of it when you get to Barca de Cuenca," laughed Lobo.

"It will be only four hours more; and I can stand that, if I am tired, as I have no doubt I shall be. In fact, I am tired now, for I am not used to riding on horseback, or muleback either."

Before six o'clock they reached Barca de Cuenca; and Bark was certainly very tired. The motion of the mule made him uncomfortable, and he had walked a good part of the distance. But, in spite of his weariness, he was still in favor of proceeding that night to the place where it was supposed the fugitive lodged. It would save going about twenty miles in all; and he thought he should come out of the journey better in the end if he were relieved of riding this distance. Julio was willing to take out his mules again after they had rested two hours, for a consideration.

While they were making these arrangements in the court of the *venta*, or inn, a man mounted on one mule, and leading another, entered the yard. He was dressed and armed in the same style as Julio. At this moment the landlord called the party to supper. Bark was democratic in his ideas; and he insisted that the guide should take a seat at the table with Lobo and himself. Julio was a little backward, but he finally took the seat assigned to him. He said something in Spanish to the interpreter as soon as he had taken his chair, which seemed to excite the greatest astonishment on the part of the latter. Lobo plied him with a running fire of questions, which Julio answered as fast as they were put. Bark judged, that, as neither of them touched the food which was on their plates, the subject of the conversation must be exceedingly interesting.

"What is it, Lobo?" he asked, when he had listened, as long as his patience held out, to the exciting talk he could not understand.

"Did you notice the man that rode into the yard on a mule, leading another?" said Lobo.

"I did: he was dressed like Julio," replied Bark.

"That was José Barca, who came from Algeciras as Raymond's guide."

"But what has he done with Raymond?" demanded Bark, now as much excited as his companions.

"We don't know. Julio has quarrelled with José, and refuses to speak to him; and he says José would not answer him if he did."

"Do you suppose any thing has gone wrong with Raymond?" asked Bark anxiously.

"I don't know; but it looks bad to see this fellow coming back at this time."

"Well, can't you see José, and ask him what has become of Raymond?"

"Certainly I can; but whether he will tell me is another thing."

"Of course he will tell you: why shouldn't he?"

"Circumstances alter cases. If Raymond has dismissed him in order to continue his journey in some other way, José will tell all he knows about it."

"Do you suppose that is what he has done?"

"I am afraid not," answered Lobo seriously.

"What has become of him, then?" asked Bark, almost borne down by anxiety for his friend.

"There is only one other thing that can have happened to him; and that is, that he has been set upon by brigands, and made a prisoner for the sake of the ransom. If this is the case, José will not be so likely to tell what he knows about the matter."

"Brigands!" exclaimed Bark, startled at the word.

"A party of English people were captured last year; but I have not heard of any being on the road this year," added Lobo. "But they won't hurt him if he is quiet, and don't attempt to resist."

After supper Lobo had a talk with José. He did not know what had become of the young gentleman. Three beggars had met them on the road, and Raymond had gone away with them. They wanted to show him a cave in the mountains, and he accompanied them. José had waited two hours for him, and then had gone to look for him, but could not find him.

"Where was this?" demanded Lobo.

"Less than two leagues from here," replied José.

Lobo translated this story to Bark, and declared that every word of it was a lie.

"Raymond went from this *venta* five hours ago; and it must have taken six or seven hours for all that José describes to take place," added Lobo. "But we must pretend to believe the story, and not say a word."

Bark could not say a word except to the interpreter, who had a talk with Julio next; and the guide presently disappeared. Lobo had formed his plan, and put it into execution.

"The route by which we have come is not by the great road from San Roque to Ronda, but a shorter one by which two leagues are saved," said Lobo, explaining his operations to Bark. "All the guides take this route. About a league across the country, is a considerable town, which is the headquarters of the civil guard, sent here last year after the English party was captured, to guard the roads. This is an extra force; and I have sent Julio over to bring a squad of them to this place. José will spend the night here, and start for home to-morrow morning. I want some of the civil guard before he goes; and they will be here in the course of a couple of hours. Julio is glad enough of a chance to get José into trouble."

"But do you believe José has done any thing wrong, even if Raymond has been captured by brigands?" asked Bark.

"Very likely he is to have a share of the plunder and the ransom; and I think you will find him ready to negotiate for the ransom now."

This proved to be the case; for in the course of an hour José broached the subject to Lobo. He thought, if the friends of the young man would pay liberally for the trouble of looking him up, he might possibly be found. He did not know what had become of him; but he would undertake to find him. He was a poor man, and he could not afford to spend his time in the search for nothing. Lobo encouraged him to talk as much as he could, and mentioned several sums of money. They were too small. The beggars had probably lured the young man into the mountains; and he did not believe they would let him go without a reward. He thought that the beggars would be satisfied with fifty thousand *reales*.

While they were talking about the price, Julio returned with an officer and ten soldiers, who at once took José into custody. It seemed that he had been mixed up in some other irregular transaction, and the officers knew their man. Lobo stated the substance of his conversation with José, who protested his innocence in the strongest terms. It was evident that he preferred to deal with the friends of Raymond, rather than the civil guard.

The officer of the guard examined the guide very closely; and his story was quite different from that he had told Lobo, though he still insisted that the men whom they had encountered were beggars. The officer was very prompt in action. José was required to conduct the party to the spot where the young man had been captured. Bark and Lobo mounted their mules again, and Julio led the way as before.

"Can any thing be done in the night?" asked Bark.

"The officer says the night is the best time to hunt up these gentlemen of the road," replied Lobo. "They often make fires, and cook their victuals, for the soldiers do not like to follow them in the dark."

When the procession had been in motion an hour and a quarter, José indicated that it had reached the place where the beggars — as he still persisted in calling them — had stopped the traveller. For some reason or other, he told the truth, halting the soldiers at the rock which made a corner in the road. He also indicated the place where the beggars had taken to the hills. The officer of the civil guard disposed of his force for a careful but silent search of the region near the road. Many of the soldiers were familiar with the locality; for they had examined it in order to become acquainted with the haunts of brigands. The members were widely scattered, so as to cover as much territory as possible. Bark and Lobo were required to remain with the officer.

Not a sound could be heard while the soldiers were creeping stealthily about among the rocks, and visiting the various caverns they had discovered in their former survey. In less than half an hour, several of the guard returned together, reporting a fire they had all seen at about the same time. One of them described the place as being not more than ten minutes' walk from the road; and he knew all about the cave in which the fire was built.

"The mouth of the cave is covered with mats; but they do not conceal the light of the fire," continued the soldier; and Lobo translated his description to Bark. "The smoke goes out at a hole in the farther end of the cave; and, when the brigands are attacked in front, they will try to escape by this opening in the rear."

"We will provide for that," replied the officer.

He sent out some of the men to call in the rest of the party; and, at a safe distance from the fire, they used a whistle for this purpose. In a short time all the soldiers were collected in the road, at the nearest point to the cave. The lieutenant sent five of his men to the rear of the cave, and four to the front, leaving José in charge of one of them.

"Tell him not to let his men fire into the cave," said Bark to the interpreter. "I am afraid they will shoot Raymond."

"I will speak to him; but I do not think there will be any firing," replied Lobo. "When the beggars find they are in any danger, they will try to get out at the hole in the rear; and the lieutenant will bag them as they come out."

The officer directed the men in front not to fire at all, unless the brigands came out of the cave; and not then, if they could capture them without. Bark and Lobo accompanied the party to the rear, which started before the others. They went by a long roundabout way, creeping like cats the whole distance. They found the hole, and could see the light of the fire through the aperture.

The beggars appeared to be having a jolly good time in the cavern, for they were singing and joking; and Lobo said they were drinking the health of the prisoner while he was listening at the aperture. The lieutenant thought that one of their number had been to a town, a league from the place, to procure wine and provisions with the money they had taken from Raymond; for they could smell the garlic in the stew that was doubtless cooking on the fire. And this explained the lateness of the hour at which they were having their repast.

Bark looked into the hole. It appeared to be formed of two immense bowlders, which had been thrown together so as to form an angular space under them. The aperture was quite small at the rear end, and the bottom of the cave sloped sharply down to the part where the beggars were. Raymond could not be seen; but Bark heard his voice, as he spoke in cheerful tones, indicating that he had no great fears for the future. But, while Bark was looking into the den, the soldiers in front of the cave set up a tremendous yell, as they had been instructed to do; and the brigands sprang to their feet.

The rear opening into the cave was partly concealed by the rocks and trees: and probably the brigands supposed the cave was unknown to the soldiers. The officer pulled Bark away from the hole, and placed himself where he could see into it.

"*Arrida! Alto ahi!*" (Up! Up there!) shouted one of the brigands; and in a moment Raymond appeared at the opening, with his hands tied behind him, urged forward by the leader of the beggars.

They evidently intended to make sure of their prisoner, and were driving him out of the cave before them. The moment the first beggar appeared, he was seized by a couple of the soldiers; and in like manner four others were captured, for their number had been increased since Raymond was captured. Bark was overjoyed when he found that his friend was safe. He cut the rope that bound his hands behind him, and then actually hugged him.

"Who are you?" demanded Raymond; for it was too dark, coming from the bright light of the fire, for him to identify the person who was so demonstrative.

"Why, don't you know me, Henry?" asked Bark, wringing the hand of his friend.

"What! Is it Bark?" demanded Raymond, overwhelmed with astonishment to find his late associate at this place.

"Of course it is Bark."

"What are you doing here?"

"I came after you; and I think, under the circumstances, it is rather fortunate I did come," added Bark.

"God bless you, Bark! for you have saved me from these vagabonds, who might have kept me for months, so that I could not join my ship."

That was all the harm the fugitive seemed to think would come of his capture. The soldiers had led the brigands down into the cavern, and the young men followed them. The fire was still burning briskly, and the pot over it was boiling merrily. Everybody was happy except the brigands; and the leader of these did not appear to be much disturbed by the accident that had happened to him.

"*Por Dios*," said Raymond, extending his hand to this latter worthy.

"*Perdon usted por Dios hermano*," replied the leader, shrugging his shoulders.

Raymond informed the lieutenant that this was the manner the interview on the road had commenced. The officer ordered the ruffians to be searched; and the purse and watch of Raymond were found upon the chief beggar. They were restored to the owner, with the request that he would see if the money was all in the purse.

"I was not fool enough to give the beggar all I had," answered Raymond. "I have a large sum of money in my belt, which was not disturbed."

The good-natured leader of the beggars opened his eyes at this statement.

"There were six *Isabelinos* in the purse, and now there are but five," added Raymond.

"We spent one of them for food and wine," said the gentle beggar. "We had nothing to eat for two days, till we got some bread we bought with this money. We were going to have a good supper before we started for the mountains; but you have spoiled it."

The officer was good-natured enough to let them eat their supper, as it was ready by this time. But Raymond and Bark did not care to wait, and started for the *venta*, where they intended to pass the night. Julio walked, and Raymond rode his mule.

"I congratulate the Count de Escarabajosa on his escape," said Lobo, as they mounted the mules.

"I thank you; but where did you get that title, which I will thank you never to apply to me again?" replied Raymond rather coldly.

"I beg your pardon; but I meant no offence," said Lobo, rather startled by the coldness and dignity of Raymond.

"He is a good friend; and if it hadn't been for him I never should have found you, Henry," interposed Bark.

"I do not understand where he learned about that title, and I do not know who he is," added Raymond. "If you say he is a friend, Bark, I am satisfied."

"He is, and a good friend. But why did you leave Gibraltar so suddenly?" asked Bark, thinking it best to change the subject.

"I left because I saw you and your companion go into the Club-House Hotel; and I knew that you would come to the King's Arms next," replied Raymond.

"You left because you saw me!" exclaimed Bark, astonished at this statement. "Why, I was sent after you because the principal thought you would not dodge out of sight if you saw Scott or me."

"I did not dodge out of sight because I saw you, but because I saw you had a companion I did not know: I came to the conclusion that your friend was the detective sent after me."

Bark explained who and what Lobo was; and Raymond apologized to the interpreter for his coldness. Before the party reached the *venta*, the messenger of the principal had explained the situation as it was changed by the death of Don Alejandro. Raymond was happy in being justified for his past conduct, and glad that his uncle had died confessing his sins and at peace with the Church.

The fugitive and his friend were asleep when the soldiers arrived with the prisoners. In the morning Raymond read the letter of Don Francisco, and immediately wrote a reply to it, requesting him to take charge of his affairs in Barcelona; and to ask the advice of his uncle in New York. Bark wrote to the principal a full account of his adventures in search of Raymond. These letters were mailed at Ronda, where the prisoners were taken, and where Raymond had to go as a witness. The testimony was abundant to convict them all; but Spanish courts were so slow, that Bark and Raymond were detained in Ronda for two weeks, though Lobo was sent back to Malaga at once.

The three brigands were sentenced to a long imprisonment; the two men who were found in the cave with them to a shorter term, as accomplices; but nothing was proved against José. Raymond made a handsome present to each of the soldiers, and to Julio, for the service they had rendered him; and, though his gratitude to Bark could not be expressed in this way, it was earnest and sincere. Julio and José were still in Ronda with their mules; and it was decided to return to Gibraltar as they had come. During their stay in this mountain city, the two students had seen the sights of the place; and they departed with a lively appreciation of this wild locality.

In two days they arrived at Gibraltar, to find that the fleet had been there, and left. Both of them were astonished at this information, which was given them at the King's Arms, where they had both been guests before. They had been confident that the squadron would take her final departure for the "Isles of the Sea" from this port.

"Left!" exclaimed both of them in the same breath.

"The three vessels sailed three days ago," replied the landlord.

"Where have they gone?" asked Raymond, who had depended upon meeting his friends on board of the Tritonia that evening.

"That I couldn't tell you."

They walked about the town, making inquiries in regard to the fleet; but no one knew where it had gone. The custom-house was closed for the day; and they were obliged to sleep without knowing whether or not the vessels were on their way across the ocean, or gone to some port in Spain.

CHAPTER XXVII.

THE BULL-FIGHT AT SEVILLE.

"NOW we are under the meteor flag of old England," said Clyde Blacklock, the fourth lieutenant of the Prince, after the squadron had come to anchor off the Rock.

"Do you call that the meteor flag of England?" laughed Murray, as he pointed to the stars and stripes at the peak of the steamer.

"We are in British waters anyhow," replied Clyde.

"That's so; but the flag you are under just now is the glorious flag of the United States of America — long may it wave!"

"They are both glorious flags," said Dr. Winstock; "and both nations ought to be proud of what they have done for the human race."

"And Johnny Bull is the father of Brother Jonathan," added Clyde.

"There is the sunset gun," said the doctor, as the report pealed across the water, and a cloud of smoke rose from one of the numerous batteries on the shore. "The gates of the town are closed now, and no one is allowed to enter or leave after this hour."

The surgeon continued to point out various buildings

and batteries, rather to prevent the students from engaging in an international wrangle, to which a few were somewhat inclined, than for any other reason, though he was always employed in imparting information to them.

The next morning, as soon as the arrangements were completed, the several ships' companies landed at the same time, and marched in procession to the top of the hill, where the students were formed in a hollow square to hear what Professor Mapps had to say about the Rock. The view was magnificent, for the hill is fourteen hundred and thirty feet above the sea level.

"Young gentlemen, I know that the view from this height is grand and beautiful," the professor began, "and I cannot blame you for wishing to enjoy it at once; but I wish you to give your attention to the history of the Rock for a few minutes, and then I shall ask Dr. Winstock, who is more familiar with the place than I am, to point out to you in detail the various objects under your eye."

In addition to the twenty non-commissioned officers who had been detailed to act as guides for the party, quite a number of superior officers, and not a few ladies, formed a part of the professor's audience. The latter had been attracted by curiosity to follow the students; and the majors, captains, and lieutenants were already on speaking-terms with the principal, the vice-principals, and the professors, though no formal introductions had taken place; and, before the day was over, all hands had established a very pleasant relation with the officers of the garrison and their families.

"When the Phœnicians came to the Rock and to

Cadiz, they believed they had reached the end of the world; and here they erected one of the two Pillars of Hercules, which have already been mentioned to you. The Berbers were the original inhabitants of the Barbary States; and Tarìk, a leader of this people, captured the place. He gave his own name to his conquest, calling it Ghebal-Tarìk, or the Hill of Tarìk. This was in 711; but Guzman the Good, the first of the Dukes of Medina Sidonia, recovered it in 1309. Soon after, the Spanish governor of the Rock stole the money appropriated for its defence, employing it in a land speculation at Xeres; and the place surrendered to the Moors. In 1462 another Duke of Medina Sidonia drove out the Moslems; and Spain held the Rock till 1704. In this year, during the war of the Spanish succession, the fortress was attacked by the combined forces of the English and the Dutch. The Spanish garrison consisted of only one hundred and fifty men; but it killed or disabled nearly twice this number of the assailants before the Rock was surrendered, which shows that it was a very strong place even then; and its defences have been doubled since that time. The Spaniards have made repeated attempts to recover possession of the fortress, but without success; and it has been settled that it is entirely impregnable."

The English officers applauded this last statement; and Dr. Winstock, stepping upon the rock which served the professor for a rostrum, proceeded to point out the objects on interest in sight.

"You have two grand divisions before you," said the surgeon. "On the other side of the strait is Africa, with its rough steeps. The nest of white houses you see at the head of the deep bay is Ceuta; and the hill is the Mount Abyla of the ancients, on which the other Pillar of Hercules was planted. Turning to the west, the broad Atlantic is before you. Below is the beautiful Bay of Gibraltar, with Algeciras on the opposite side. The village north of us is San Roque; and the lofty snow-capped mountains in the north-east are the Sierra Nevadas, which you saw from Granada. Now look at what is nearer to us. The strait is from twelve to fifteen miles wide. Perhaps you saw some of the monkeys that inhabit the Rock on your way up the hill. Though there are plenty of them on the other side of the strait, they are not found in a wild state in any part of Europe except on this Rock. How they got here, is the conundrum; and some credulous people insist that there is a tunnel under the strait by which they came over.

"Below you is Europa Point; or, rather, three capes with this name. You see the beautiful gardens near the Point; and in the hands of the English people the whole Rock blossoms like the rose, while, if any other people had it, it would be a desolate waste. Stretching out into the bay, near the dockyard, is the new mole, which is seven hundred feet long. The one near the landing-port is eleven hundred feet; but it shelters only the small craft. The low, sandy strip of ground that bounds the Rock on the north is the Neutral Ground, where the sentinels of the two countries are always on duty. This strip of land is diked, so that it can be inundated and rendered impassable to an army in a few moments."

The doctor finished his remarks, but we have not

reported all that he said; nor have we space for the speeches of a couple of the English officers who were invited to address the students, though they gave much information in regard to the fortress and garrison life at the Rock. The crowd was divided into small parties, and spent the rest of the day in exploring the fortifications with the guides. As usual, the doctor had the captain and first lieutenant under his special charge.

"The east and south sides of the Rock, as you observed when we came into the bay from Malaga," said he, "are almost perpendicular; and at first sight it would seem to be absurd to fortify a steep which no one could possibly ascend. But an enemy would find a way to get up if it were not for the guns that cover this part of the Rock. The north end is also too steep to climb. The west side, where we came up by the zigzag path, has a gentler slope; and this is protected by batteries in every direction."

"I can see the guns of the batteries; but I do not see any on the north and east sides of the Rock," said Sheridan.

"The edges of the Rock on all sides are tunnelled: and these galleries form a series of casemates, with embrasures, or port-holes, every thirty or forty yards, through which the great guns are pointed. These galleries are in tiers, or stories, and there are miles of them. They were made just before the French Revolution began, nearly a hundred years after the English got possession."

"They must have cost a pile of money," suggested Murray.

"Yes; and it costs a pile of money to support them,"

added the doctor. "Five thousand troops are kept here in time of peace. Some British statesmen have advocated the policy of giving or selling the Rock to Spain; for it has been a standing grievance to this power to have England own a part of the peninsula. But in other than a military view the Rock is valuable to England. Whatever wars may be in progress on the face of the earth, her naval and commercial vessels can always find shelter in the port of Gibraltar."

"But I don't see how it could prevent ships of war from entering the Mediterranean Sea," added Sheridan.

"I doubt whether it could ever do that except by sheltering a fleet to do the fighting; for no gun in existence could send a shot ten or twelve miles," replied the doctor.

By this time the party had reached the entrance of the galleries, and they went in to view what the surgeon had described. The students were amazed at the extent of the tunnels, and the vast quantities of shot and shell piled up in every part of the works; at the great guns, and the appliances for handling them. They walked till they were tired out; and then the party descended to the town for a lunch.

"This isn't much of a city," said Murray, as they walked through its narrow and crooked streets to Commercial Square, where the hotels are located.

"I believe the people do not brag of it, though it contains much that is interesting," replied the doctor. "You find all sorts of people here: there are Moors, Jews, Greeks, Portuguese, and Spaniards, besides the English. This is a free port, and vast quantities of goods are smuggled into Spain from this town."

They lunched at the Club-House; and it was a luxury to sit at the table with English people, who do not wear their hats, or smoke between the courses. After this important duty had been disposed of, the party walked to the *alameda*, as the Spaniards call it, or the parade and public garden as the English have it. It is an exceedingly pleasant retreat to an English-speaking traveller who has just come from Spain, for every thing is in the English fashion. It contains a monument to the Duke of Wellington, and another to General Lord Heathfield. The party enjoyed this garden so much that they remained there till it was time to go on board of the ship.

Three days were spent at the Rock, and many courtesies were exchanged between the sailors and the soldiers. The students saw a review of a brigade, and the officers were feasted at the mess-rooms of the garrison. The principal was sorely tried when he saw the wine passing around among the military men; but the students drank the toasts in water. In return for these civilities, the officers were invited on board of the vessels of the squadron; the yards were manned; the crews were exercised in the various evolutions of seamanship; and a bountiful collation was served in each vessel. Everybody was happy.

Dr. Winstock was a little more "gamy" than the principal; and, when he heard that there was to be a bull-fight at Seville on Easter Sunday, he declared that it would be a pity to take the students away from Spain without seeing the national spectacle. He suggested that the ceremonies of Holy Week would also be very interesting. The question was discussed for a long time. All the rest of their lives these young men would be obliged to say that they had been to Spain without seeing a bull-fight. The professors were consulted; and they were unanimously in favor of making a second visit to Seville. It was decided to adopt the doctor's suggestion.

"But it will be impossible to get into the hotels," added Dr. Winstock. "They all double their prices, and are filled to overflowing for several days before the ceremonies begin."

"Then, why did you suggest the idea of going?" laughed the principal. "The boys must have something to eat, and a place to sleep."

"I think we can do better than to go to the hotels, even if we could get into them," replied the doctor. "The Guadalquiver is very high at the present time, and the fleet will go up to Seville without quarrelling with the bottom. We can anchor off the *Toro del Oro*, and save all the hotel-bills."

This plan was adopted; and the order to coal the steamer for the voyage across the Atlantic was rescinded, so that she might go up the river as light as possible. Half a dozen officers of the garrison were taken as passengers, guests of the officers, for the excursion, as the steamer was to return to the Rock. On Tuesday morning the fleet sailed. While the schooners remained off Cadiz, the Prince ran in and obtained three pilots, — a father and his two sons, — and distributed them among the vessels. At the mouth of the river the Prince took her consorts in tow. They were lashed together, and a hawser extended to each of them. Off Bonanza the vessels anchored for the night; for the pilots would not take the risk of running in the darkness. In the morning the voyage was renewed. Portions of the country were flooded with water, for the ice and snows in the mountains were melting in the warm weather of spring. Indeed, there was so much water that it bothered the pilot of the steamer to keep in the channel, for the high water covered some of his landmarks. There were some sharp turns to be made; and the pilots in the Tritonia and Josephine had to be as active as their father in the steamer; for, in making these curves, the hawser of the outer vessel had to be slacked off; and, when the ropes were well run out, the steamer was stopped, and they were hauled in. But, before sunset, the fleet was at anchor off Seville.

The next day was Holy Thursday, and all hands were landed to see the sights. The city was crowded with people. All along the streets through which the procession was to pass, seats were arranged for the spectators, which were rented for the occasion, as in the large cities at home. The trip to Seville had been decided upon a week before the vessels arrived, and while they were at Malaga. Couriers had been sent ahead to engage places for the procession, and in the *Coliseo de Toros*. Lobo and Ramos were on the quay when the boats landed; and the students were conducted to the places assigned to them. They went early, and had to wait a long time; but the people were almost as interesting as the "*Gran Funcion*," as they call any spectacle, whether it be a bull-fight or a church occasion.

Not only was the street where they were seated full

of people, but all the houses were dressed in the gayest of colors; and no one would have suspected that the occasion was a religious ceremony. Printed programmes of all the details of the procession had been hawked about the streets for the last two days, and Lobo had procured a supply of them; but unfortunately, as they were in Spanish, hardly any of the students could make use of them, though the surgeon, the professors, and the couriers, translated the main items for them.

"I suppose you both understand the meaning of the procession we are about to see," said the doctor, while they waiting.

"I don't," replied Murray. "My father is a Scotchman, and I was brought up in the kirk."

"The week begins with Palm Sunday, which commemorates the entry of Christ into Jerusalem, when the people cast palm-branches before him; Holy Thursday celebrates the institution of the Lord's Supper; Good Friday, the crucifixion; Holy Saturday is when water used in baptism is blessed; and Easter Sunday, the greatest of all the holy days except Christmas, is in honor of the resurrection of the Saviour. On Holy Thursday, in Madrid, the late queen used to wash the feet of a dozen beggars, as Christ washed the feet of his disciples. I hear music, and I think the procession is coming."

It was not church music which the band at the head of the procession played, but lively airs from the operas. A line of soldiers formed in front of the spectators that filled the street, to keep them back; and the procession soon came in sight. To say that the boys were amused would be to express it mildly as the leading feature of the show came into view. It seemed to be a grand masquerade, or a tremendous burlesque. First came a number of persons dressed in long robes of white, black, or violet, gathered up at the waist by a leather belt. On their heads they wore enormous fools' caps, in the shape of so many sugar-loaves, but at least four feet high.

"You mustn't laugh so as to be observed," said the doctor to the first lieutenant. "These are the penitents."

"They ought to be penitent for coming out in such a rig," laughed Murray.

A pointed piece of cloth fell from the tall cap of the penitents over the face and down upon the breast, with round holes for the eyes. Some carried torches, and others banners with the arms of some religious order worked on them. These people were a considerable feature of the procession, and they were to be seen through the whole length of it.

After them came some men dressed as Roman soldiers, with helmet, cuirass, and yellow tunic, representing the soldiers that took part in the crucifixion. They were followed by a kind of car, which seemed to float along without the help of any bearers; but it was carried by men under it whose forms were concealed by the surrounding drapery that fell to the ground, forming a very effective piece of stage machinery. The car was richly ornamented with gold and velvet, and bore on its top rail several elegant and fancifully shaped lanterns in which candles were burning.

On the car was a variety of subjects represented by

a dozen figures, carved in wood and painted to the life. Above all the others rose Christ and the two thieves on the crosses. The Virgin Mary was the most noticeable figure. She was dressed in an elegant velvet robe, embroidered with gold, with a lace handkerchief in her hand. A velvet mantle reached from her shoulders over the rail of the car to the ground. Her train was in charge of an angel, who managed it according to her own taste and fancy. On the car were other angels, who seemed to be more ornamental than useful.

The rest of the procession was made up of similar materials, — holy men, women and children, crosses, images of saints, such as have often been seen and described. During the rest of the week, the students visited the cathedral, where they saw the blackened remains of King Ferdinand, and other relics that are exhibited at this time, as well as several other of the churches. Easter Sunday came, and the general joy was as extravagantly manifested as though the resurrection were an event of that day. Early in the afternoon crowds of gayly dressed people of all classes and ranks began to crowd towards the bull-ring. All over the city were posted placards announcing this *Gran Funcion*, with overdrawn pictures of the scenes expected to transpire in the arena. We have one of these bills before us as we write.

"As we are to take part in the *Funcion*, we will go to the *plaza*," said the doctor, as he and his friends left the cathedral.

"Take part!" exclaimed Murray. "I have no idea of fighting a bull. I would rather be on board of the ship."

"Perhaps I should have said 'assist in the *Funcion*,' which is the usual way of expressing it in Spain."

"Who is this?" said Sheridan, as a couple of young men wearing the uniform of the squadron approached the party. "Upon my word, it is Raimundo!"

The young men proved to be Raymond and Bark Lingall, just arrived from Gibraltar. The fugitive had resumed his uniform when he expected to join the Tritonia; and, if he had asked any officer of the garrison where the fleet had gone, he could have informed him. In the evening one of them spoke to Raymond at the hotel, asking him how it happened that he had not gone to Seville. This led to an explanation. Raymond and Bark had taken a steamer to Cadiz the next day, and had just arrived in a special train, in season for the bull-fight. The surgeon, who knew all about Raymond's history, gave him a cordial greeting; and so did his shipmates of the Tritonia.

"You are just in time to assist at the bull-fight," said Scott, who readily took up the Spanish style of expressing it, for it seemed like a huge joke to him.

"I don't care for the bull-fight, but I am glad to be with the fellows once more," replied Raymond, as he seated himself with the officers of the vessel.

Before the show began, he had reported himself to Mr. Lowington and Mr. Pelham; and some of the students who did not understand the matter thought he received a very warm greeting for a returned runaway. But all hands were thinking of the grand spectacle; and not much attention was given to Raymond and Bark, except by their intimate friends.

"If the people are so fond of these shows, I should

think they would have more of them," said Sheridan. "This is the first chance we have had to see one; and we have been in Spain four months."

"They cost too much money; and only the large places can afford to have them," replied the doctor. "It costs about two thousand dollars to get one up in good style. I will tell you all about the performers as they come in."

"But what are all those people doing in the ring?" asked Murray; for the arena was filled with spectators walking about, chatting and smoking.

"They are the men who will occupy the lower seats, which are not very comfortable; and they prefer to walk about till the performance begins. They are all deeply interested in the affair, and are talking it over."

"I don't see many ladies here," said Sheridan. "I was told that they all attend the bull-fights."

"I should think that one-third of the audience were ladies," replied the doctor, looking about the *plaza*. "At those I attended in Madrid, there were not five hundred ladies present."

The *Plaza de Toros* at Seville, which the people dignify by calling it the *Coliseum*, is about the same size as the one at Madrid, open at the top, and will seat ten or twelve thousand people. It is circular in form, and the walls may be twenty or twenty-five feet high. Standing in the ring, the lower part of the structure looks much like a country circus on a very large scale; the tiers of seats for the common people sloping down from half the height of the walls to the arena, which is enclosed by a strong fence about five feet high. Inside of the heavy fence enclosing the ring, is another, which separates the spectators from a kind of avenue all around the arena; and above this is stretched a rope, to prevent the bull, in case he should leap the inner fence, from going over among the spectators. This avenue between the two fences is for the use of the performers and various hangers-on at the *funcion*.

Above the sloping rows of seats, are balconies, or boxes as they would be called in a theatre. They are roofed over, and the front of them presents a continuous colonnade supporting arches, behind which are sloping rows of cushioned seats. In hot weather, awnings are placed in front of those exposed to the sun. Opposite the gates by which the bull is admitted is an elaborately ornamented box for the "*autoridad*" and the person who presides over the spectacle. The latter was often the late queen, in Madrid; and on the present occasion it was the *infanta*, the Marquesa de Montpensier. This box was dressed with flags and bright colors.

During the gathering of the vast audience, which some estimated at fifteen thousand, a band had been playing. Punctually at three o'clock came a flourish of trumpets, and two *alguacils*, dressed in sober black, rode into the ring; and the people there vacated it, leaping over the fences to their seats. When the arena was clear, another blast announced the first scene of the tragedy.

"Now we have a procession of the performers," said the doctor to his pupils. "The men on horseback are *picadores*, from *pica*, a lance; and you see that each rider carries one."

These men were dressed in full Spanish costume, and wore broad sombreros on their heads, something like a tarpaulin. They were mounted on old hacks of horses, worn out by service on the cabs or omnibuses. They are blindfolded during the fight, to keep them from dodging the bull. The legs of the men are cased in splints of wood and sole-leather to protect them from the horns of the bull. Each of them is paid a hundred dollars for each *corrida*, or performance.

"Those men with the red and yellow mantles, or cloaks, on their arms, are the *chulos*, whose part is to worry the bull, and to call him away from the *picador*, or other actor who is in danger," continued the surgeon. "Next to them are the *banderilleros;* and the dart adorned with many colored ribbons is called a *banderilla*. You will see what this is for when the time comes. The last are the *matadors*, or *espadas;* and each of them carries a Toledo blade. They are the heroes of the fight; and, when they are skilful, their reputation extends all over Spain. Montes, one of the most celebrated of them, was killed in a *corrida* in Madrid. Cuchares was another not less noted; and, when I saw him, he was received with a demonstration of applause that would have satisfied a king of Spain. I don't know what has become of him. I see that the names of four *espadas* are given on the bill, besides a supernumerary in case of accident. The *espadas* receive from two to three hundred dollars for a *corrida;* the *banderilleros*, from fifty to seventy-five; and the *chulos*, from fifteen to twenty."

An *alguacil* now entered the ring, and, walking over to the box of the authorities, asked permission to begin the fight. The key of the bull-pen was given to him. He returned, gave it to the keeper of the gate;

and made haste to save himself by jumping over the fence, to the great amusement of the vast audience.

Most of the students had been informed what all this meant by the interpreters and others; and they waited with no little emotion for the conflict to commence. The bull had been goaded to fury in the pen; and, when the gates were thrown open, he rushed with a bellowing snort into the ring. At first he seemed to be startled by the strange sight before him, and halted at the gate, which had been closed behind him. Two *picadores* had been stationed on opposite sides of the arena; and, as soon as the bull saw the nearest of these, he dashed towards him. The *picador* received him on the point of his lance, and turned him off. The animal then went for the other, who warded him off in the same way. The audience did not seem to be satisfied with this part of the performance, and yelled as if they had been cheated out of something. It was altogether too tame for them.

Then the first *picador*, at these signs of disapprobation, rode to the middle of the ring; and the bull made another onslaught upon him. This time he tumbled horse and rider in a heap on the ground. Then the *chulos* put in an appearance, and with their red and yellow cloaks attracted the attention of the bull, thus saving the *picador* from further harm. While the bull was chasing some of the *chulos*, more of them went to the assistance of the fallen rider, whose splinted legs did not permit him to rise alone. He was pulled out from beneath his nag; and the poor animal got up, goaded to do so by the kicks of the brutal performers. His stomach had been ripped open by the horns of the bull, and his entrails dragged upon the ground.

Some of the students turned pale, and were made sick by the cruel sight. A few of them were obliged to leave their places, which they did amidst the laughter of the Spaniards near them. But the audience applauded heartily, and appeared to be satisfied now that a horse had been gored so terribly. The *picador* was lifted upon the mangled steed, and he rode about the ring with the animal's entrails dragging under him. The *chulos* played with the bull for a time, till the people became impatient; and then he was permitted to attack the horses again. The one injured before dropped dead under the next assault, to the great relief of the American spectators. The audience became stormy again, and two more horses were killed without appeasing them.

"Now we shall have the *banderilleros*," said the doctor, as a flourish of trumpets came from the band-stand.

"I have got about enough of it," said Sheridan faintly.

"Brace yourself up, and you will soon become more accustomed to it. You ought to see one bull killed," added the surgeon.

Two men with *banderillas* in their hands now entered the ring. These weapons have barbs, so that, when the point is driven into the flesh of the bull, they stick fast, and are not shaken out by the motion of the animal. These men were received with applause; but it was evident that the temper of the assembled multitude required prompt and daring deeds of them. There was to be no unnecessary delay, no dodging or skulking. They were bold fellows, and seemed to be ready for business. One of them showed himself to the bull; and the beast made for him without an instant's hesitation.

The *banderillero* held his ground as though he had been tied to the spot; and it looked as if he was surely to be transfixed by the horns of the angry bull. Suddenly, as the animal dropped his head to use his horns, the man swung the *banderillas* over his shoulders, and planted both of the darts just behind the neck of the beast, and then dexterously slipped out of the way. This feat was applauded tremendously, and the yells seemed to shake the arena. Vainly the bull tried to shake off the darts, roaring with the pain they gave him.

Another flourish of trumpets announced the last scene of the tragedy, and one of the *espadas* bounded lightly into the ring. He was greeted with hearty applause; and, walking over to the front of the *marquesa's* box, he bent down on one knee, and made a grandiloquent speech, to the effect that for the honor of the city, in the name of the good people there assembled, and for the benefit of the hospital, he would kill the bull or be killed himself in the attempt, if her highness would graciously accord him the permission to do so. The *infanta* kindly consented; and the *espada* whirled his hat several times over his head, finally jerking it under his left arm over the fence. In his hand he carried a crimson banner, which he presented to the bull; and this was enough to rouse all his fury again.

For a time he played with the furious beast, which continually plunged at the red banner, the man skilfully stepping aside. At last he seemed to be pre-

pared for the final blow. Holding the banner in his left hand, he permitted the bull to make a dive at it; and, while his head was down, he reached over his horns with the sword, and plunged it in between the shoulder-blades. His aim was sure: he had pierced the heart, and the bull dropped dead. Again the applause shook the arena, and the audience in the lower part of the building hurled their hats and caps into the ring; and a shower of cigars, mingled with an occasional piece of silver, followed the head-gear. The victorious *espada* picked up the cigars and money, bowing his thanks all the time, while the *chulos* tossed back the hats and caps.

"'You can take my hat' is what they mean by that, I suppose," said Murray.

"That is one of the ways a Spanish audience has of expressing their approbation in strong terms," replied the doctor.

A team of half a dozen mules, tricked out in the gayest colors, galloped into the ring; and, when a sling had been passed over the horns of the dead bull, he was dragged out at a side gate. The doors had hardly closed upon the last scene before the main gates were thrown wide open again, and another bull bounded into the arena, where the *picadores* and the *chulos* were already in position for action. The second act was about like the first. Four horses were killed by the second bull, which was even more savage than the first. The *banderillero* was unfortunate in his first attempt, and was hooted by the audience; but in a second attempt he redeemed himself. The *espada* got his sword into the bull; but he did not hit the vital part, and he was unable to withdraw his weapon. The animal flew around the ring with the sword in his shoulders, while the audience yelled, and taunted the unlucky hero. It was not allowable for him to take another sword; and the bull was lured to the side of the ring, where the *espada* leaped upon a screen, and recovered his blade. In a second trial he did the business so handsomely that he regained the credit he had temporarily lost.

Many of the students did not stay to see the second bull slain; and not more than half of them staid till the conclusion of the *funcion*. One of the last of the bulls would not fight at all, and evidently belonged to the peace society; but neither the audience nor the *lidiadores* had any mercy for him.

"*Perros! Perros!*" shouted the audience, when it was found that the bull had no pluck.

"*Perros! Perros!*" screamed some of the wildest of the students, without having the least idea what the word meant.

"What does all that mean?" asked Murray.

"*Perros* means dogs. Not long ago, when a bull would not fight, they used to set dogs upon him to worry and excite him," answered the doctor.

"Well, will they set the dogs upon him?" inquired Murray.

"No, I suppose not; for here in the bill it says, 'No dogs will be used; but fire-*banderillas* will be substituted for bulls that will not fight at the call of the authorities.'"

This expedient was resorted to in the present case; the bull was frightened, and showed a little pluck.

After he had upset a *picador*, and charged on a *chulo*, he leaped over the fence into the avenue. The loafers gathered there sprang into the ring; but the animal was speedily driven back, and was finally killed without having done any great damage to the horses.

The last bull was the fiercest of them all; and he came into the arena roaring like a lion. He demolished two *picadores* in the twinkling of an eye, and made it lively for all the performers. "*Bravo, Toro!*" shouted the people, for they applaud the bull as well as the actors. The *espada* stabbed him three times before he killed him.

Six bulls and seventeen horses had been slain: the last one had killed five. Even the most insensible of the students had had enough of it; and most of them declared that it was the most barbarous spectacle they had ever seen. They pitied the poor horses, and some of them would not have been greatly distressed if the bull had tossed up a few of the performers. The doctor was disgusted, though he had done his best to have the students see this *cosa de España*. The principal refused to go farther than the gate of the *plaza*.

"I don't care to see another," said Dr. Winstock to his Spanish friend, who sat near him. "It is barbarous; and I hope the people of Spain will soon abolish these spectacles."

"Barbarous, is it?" laughed the Spanish gentleman. "Do you think it is any worse than the prize-fights you have in England and America?"

"Only a few low ruffians go to prize-fights in England and America," replied the doctor warmly. "They are forbidden by law, and those who engage in them are sent to the penitentiary. But bull-fights are managed by the authorities of the province, presided over by the queen or members of the royal family."

All hands returned to the vessels of the squadron; and early the next morning the fleet sailed for Gibraltar. The river was still very high; and, though the Prince stirred up the mud once or twice, she reached the mouth of the river in good time, and the squadron stood away for the Rock, where it arrived the next day.

Raymond was delighted to be on board of the Tritonia again, and at his duties. Enough of his story was told to the students to enable them to understand his case, and why he had been excused for running away. New rank had been assigned at the beginning of the month, and Raymond found on his return that he was second master, as before; the faculty voting that he was entitled to his old rank.

Bark Lingall had worked a full month since his reformation; and when he went on board the Tritonia, at Seville, he was delighted to find that he was third master, and entitled to a place in the cabin. On the voyage to Gibraltar, he wore the uniform of his rank, and made no complaint of the sneers of Ben Pardee and Lon Gibbs, who had not yet concluded to turn over a new leaf.

As soon as the Prince had coaled, and the vessels were watered and provisioned for the voyage, the fleet sailed; and what new climes the students visited, and what adventures they had, will be related in "Isles of the Sea; or, Young America Homeward Bound."

LEE & SHEPARD'S

LIST OF

JUVENILE PUBLICATIONS.

OLIVER OPTIC'S BOOKS.

Each Set in a neat Box with Illuminated Titles.

Army and Navy Stories. A Library for Young and
Old, in 6 volumes. 16mo. Illustrated. Per vol........$1 50

    The Soldier Boy.   The Yankee Middy.
    The Sailor Boy.   Fighting Joe.
    The Young Lieutenant.   Brave Old Salt.

Famous "Boat-Club" Series. A Library for Young
People. Handsomely Illustrated. Six volumes, in neat
box. Per vol.................................. 1 25

    The Boat Club; or, The Bunkers of Rippleton.
    All Aboard; or, Life on the Lake.
    Now or Never; or, The Adventures of Bobby Bright.
    Try Again; or, The Trials and Triumphs of Harry West.
    Poor and Proud; or, The Fortunes of Katy Redburn.
    Little by Little; or, The Cruise of the Flyaway.

Lake Shore Series, The. Six volumes. Illustrated.
In neat box. Per vol........................... 1 25

    Through by Daylight; or, The Young Engineer of the
      Lake Shore Railroad.
    Lightning Express; or, The Rival Academies.
    On Time, or, The Young Captain of the Ucayga Steamer.
    Switch Off, or, The War of the Students.
    Break Up; or, The Young Peacemakers.
    Bear and Forbear; or, The Young Skipper of Lake
      Ucayga.

LEE & SHEPARD'S JUVENILE PUBLICATIONS.

Soldier Boy Series, The. Three volumes, in neat box. Illustrated. Per vol........................... 1 50

    The Soldier Boy; or, Tom Somers in the Army.
    The Young Lieutenant; or, The Adventures of an Army Officer.
    Fighting Joe; or, The Fortunes of a Staff Officer.

Sailor Boy Series, The. Three volumes in neat box. Illustrated. Per vol................................ 1 50

    The Sailor Boy; or, Jack Somers in the Navy.
    The Yankee Middy; or, Adventures of a Naval Officer.
    Brave Old Salt; or, Life on the Quarter-Deck.

Starry Flag Series, The. Six volumes. Illustrated. Per vol... 1 25

    The Starry Flag; or, The Young Fisherman of Cape Ann.
    Breaking Away; or, The Fortunes of a Student.
    Seek and Find; or, The Adventures of a Smart Boy.
    Freaks of Fortune; or, Half Round the World.
    Make or Break; or, The Rich Man's Daughter.
    Down the River; or, Buck Bradford and the Tyrants.

The Household Library. 3 volumes. Illustrated. Per volume.. 1 50

    Living too Fast.   In Doors and Out.
        The Way of the World.

Way of the World, The. By William T. Adams (Oliver Optic)...12mo 1 50

Woodville Stories. Uniform with Library for Young People. Six volumes. Illustrated. Per vol.....16mo 1 25

    Rich and Humble; or, The Mission of Bertha Grant.
    In School and Out; or, The Conquest of Richard Grant.
    Watch and Wait; or, The Young Fugitives.
    Work and Win; or, Noddy Newman on a Cruise.
    Hope and Have; or, Fanny Grant among the Indians.
    Haste and Waste; or, The Young Pilot of Lake Champlain.

LEE & SHEPARD'S JUVENILE PUBLICATIONS.

Yacht Club Series. Uniform with the ever popular "Boat Club" Series. Completed in six vols. Illustrated. Per vol.................................16mo 1 50

Little Bobtail ; or, The Wreck of the Penobscot.
The Yacht Club ; or, The Young Boat Builders.
Money Maker ; or, The Victory of the Basilisk.
The Coming Wave ; or, The Treasure of High Rock.
The Dorcas Club ; or, Our Girls Afloat.
Ocean Born ; or, The Cruise of the Clubs.

Onward and Upward Series, The. Complete in six volumes. Illustrated. In neat box. Per vol.......... 1 25

Field and Forest ; or, The Fortunes of a Farmer.
Plane and Plank ; or, The Mishaps of a Mechanic.
Desk and Debit ; or, The Catastrophes of a Clerk.
Cringle and Cross-Tree ; or, The Sea Swashes of a Sailor.
Bivouac and Battle ; or, The Struggles of a Soldier.
Sea and Shore ; or, The Tramps of a Traveller.

Young America Abroad Series. A Library of Travel and Adventure in Foreign Lands. Illustrated by Nast, Stevens, Perkins, and others. Per vol. 16mo 1 50

First Series.

Outward Bound ; or, Young America Afloat.
Shamrock and Thistle ; or, Young America in Ireland and Scotland.
Red Cross ; or, Young America in England and Wales.
Dikes and Ditches, or, Young America in Holland and Belgium.
Palace and Cottage ; or, Young America in France and Switzerland.
Down the Rhine ; or, Young America in Germany.

Second Series.

Up the Baltic ; or, Young America in Norway, Sweden, and Denmark.
Northern Lands ; or, Young America in Russia and Prussia
Cross and Crescent ; or, Young America in Turkey and Greece.
Sunny Shores ; or, Young America in Italy and Austria.
Vine and Olive ; or, Young America in Spain and Portugal
Isles of the Sea ; or, Young America Homeward Bound.

LEE & SHEPARD'S JUVENILE PUBLICATIONS.

Riverdale Stories. Twelve volumes. A New Edition. Profusely Illustrated from new designs by Billings. In neat box. Per vol.................................

 Little Merchant.   Proud and Lazy.
 Young Voyagers.   Careless Kate.
 Robinson Crusoe, Jr.   Christmas Gift.
 Dolly and I.   The Picnic Party.
 Uncle Ben.   The Gold Thimble.
 Birthday Party.   The Do-Somethings.

Riverdale Story Books. Six volumes, in neat box. Cloth. Per vol.................................

 Little Merchant.   Proud and Lazy.
 Young Voyagers.   Careless Kate.
 Dolly and I.   Robinson Crusoe, Jr.

Flora Lee Story Books. Six volumes in neat box. Cloth. Per vol.................................

 Christmas Gift.   The Picnic Party.
 Uncle Ben.   The Gold Thimble.
 Birthday Party.   The Do-Somethings.

Great Western Series, The. Six volumes. Illustrated. Per vol... 1 50

Going West; or, The Perils of a Poor Boy.
Out West; or, Roughing it on the Great Lakes.
Lake Breezes.

Our Boys' and Girls' Offering. Containing Oliver Optic's popular Story, Ocean Born; or, The Cruise of the Clubs; Stories of the Seas, Tales of Wonder, Records of Travel, &c. Edited by Oliver Optic. Profusely Illustrated. Covers printed in Colors. 8vo........... 1 50

Our Boys' and Girls' Souvenir. Containing Oliver Optic's Popular Story, Going West; or, The Perils of a Poor Boy; Stories of the Sea, Tales of Wonder, Records of Travel, &c. Edited by Oliver Optic. With numerous full-page and letter-press Engravings. Covers printed in Colors. 8vo.................................... 1 50

www.ingramcontent.com/pod-product-compliance
Lightning Source LLC
Chambersburg PA
CBHW030550300426
44111CB00009B/927